POLICE AND POLICING IN INDIA

A Select Bibliography

Editor

Nehal Ashraf

Commonwealth

Police and Policing in India

ISBN : 81-7169-187-7

Edition : 2026

Published by :
COMMONWEALTH PUBLISHERS (P) LTD.
4831/24, Govind Lane,
Ansari Road, Darya Ganj,
New Delhi - 110002
Ph. : 23272541, 23242541
e-mail : commonwealthpublishers2016@gmail.com

Distributed by :
ARJUN PUBLISHING HOUSE
4831/24, Govind Lane,
Ansari Road, Darya Ganj,
New Delhi - 110002
Ph. : 23272541, 23242541
e-mail : arjunbooks2001@gmail.com

Laser Typesetting by :
Dimple Computers
Delhi

Printed at :
Divine Digital Press
Delhi

Foreword

People's interest in police and policing in India has increased considerably in recent decades. This is largely in the context of the governability of the country. Serious doubts have been raised about the competence of the police to maintain internal order. A large number of books have been published, committees and commissions have given their reports. Planners, administrators, and public men have expressed their opinion on these matters. The public has given vent to its feelings through dissent and protest. A large number of articles have appeared in the media and journals. Anybody wishing to pursue research in this field has to go through all this material.

Mr. Nehal Ashraf has in this volume brought together nearly 3800 titles of books, articles and reports published in recent years. He has classified the titles into 34 heads each dealing with different aspects of the general theme. The heads have been devised with a great deal of thought. It is hoped that the volume will be of great help to researchers and to generalist, who might like to know more about what is happening around us bearing on the problem.

Sachchidananda
UGC Emeritus Fellow

Preface

In the modern age, the role of police and policing are vital factors in building a healthy society. The police is expected to safeguard the interest of the general mass through the constitutional norms and legislation. However, the police system does not function as smoothly as expected by the constitution. Hence serious doubts have been raised about the competence of the police in every walk of the society. There seems sometimes, a complete loss of faith in police among the general mass. This reflects a dangerous trend for healthy growth of society. Police exercises a growing influence on all aspects of society's life. Thus, the study of police and policing requires a comprehensive approach involving many disciplines. In contemporary social science research the literature on police and policing is scattered in several monographs, journals, edited books, reports, proceedings etc. There is an urgent need to bring together a list of main publications of this area to provide a base for further research.

The main purpose of compiling this bibliography is, however, to assist the social scientists, administrator, the librarian etc. to have access to ready references. Moreover an individual researcher may easily select his own research theme from it. In fact I was tempted to do work on this subject because of the persistent demands of the contemporary researchers on different aspects of police and policing.

I am grateful to Professor Sachchidananda, UGC Emeritus Fellow, who has always been a source of inspiration and encouraged me to take up this work. He has been kind enough to write the foreword for this book as well. I express my gratitude to the Registrar of this Institute, Dr. M.P. Pandey who has always promoted my academic endeavours. I am thankful to Mr. R.C. Khan, I.P.S. and the colleagues from

A.N. Sinha Institute of Social Studies particularly, Dr. Arif Hassan, Dr. Nil Ratan, Dr. Sunita Singh Sengupta, and Mr. B.N. Patnaik who have helped me in one way or the other during the preparation of this manuscript. I must also express my thanks to Dr. S.F. Rab, Library-in-charge, A.N.S. Institute of Social Studies, Patna for his valuable suggestions. To my wife Kishwar and other family members I am grateful to their encouragement and support.

The book could not have seen the light of day if Mr. B.R. Verma of Commonwealth Publishers had not taken keen interest in seeing it through the press.

Patna
30th April, 1992

Nehal Ashraf

Contents

1

Police-in-General

Abraham, A.S. : Bombay's whiff of anarchy paradigm of a vulnerable order. *Times of India*, 27 August, 1982, 6.

Acharya, G.N. : Days of agony. *Mainstream*, V. 20 (52) 28 August, 1982, 9-10.

Allen, Mary Sophia : Lady in blue : An autobiography. London, Stanley Paul, 1963.

Alvares, X. : Bombay's suburbs have become unsafe. *Illustrated Weekly of India*, V. 99 (45) 26 November, 1978, 10-11.

Arcuri, Alam F., Gunn, Mary M. and Lester David : Moonlighting by police officers : A way of life. *Psychological Reports*, V. 60(1) February, 1987, 210.

Arthur, J.E. and Hood, J.A. : A bursary tour of America. *Police Journal*, June, 1966, 292-304.

Arthur, J.E. and Hood, J.A. : A bursary tour of America. *Poiice Journal*, July, 1966, 339-44.

Arthur, T.C. : Reminiscences of an Indian police official. London, Sampsonlow Marston and Co., 1894.

Babani, Anoop : A cops' life. *Economic Times*, 12 April, 1981, 5.

Banton, Michael : Sociology of the police—II. *Police Journal*, V. 46(4) October-December, 1973, 341-62.

Basu, P.K. : Thunder that failed. In S.K. Ghosh (ed.) : Police administrators : Reminiscences. New Delhi, Ashish Publishing House, 1989, 5-27.

Bayley, David H. : Comparative practices. *Seminar*, No. 252, August, 1980, 21-23.

Benyon, J. (ed.) : Policing issues. In Benyon, J. (ed.) : Scarman and After. Oxford, Pergamon Press, 1984.

Benyon, John : Police signs of the times. *Parliamentary Affairs*, V. 40(1) January, 1987, 130-33.

Bhattacharya, Birendra Kumar : Cultural scene in Poland, *Mankind*, V. 12(8) November, 1988, 23-27.

Bordua, David : Police. New York, John Wiley and Sons, 1967.

Bordua, David J. (ed.) : Police : Six sociological essays. New York, Wiley, 1967.

Brave policeman. (Editorial). *Times of India*, 17 September, 1986, 8.

Carlson, Lowrence D. and Lester, David : Thrill seeking in police officers. *Psychological Reports*, V. 47 (3, Part 2) December, 1980, 1102.

Carstairs, R. : Little world of an Indian district officer. London, Macmillan, 1912.

Case of defective—Sergeant challenor. *Link*, V. 6(47) 5 July, 1964, 39-40.

Central Police Training College : Talks before the Indian police in 1957. Abu, CPTC, 1958.

Chapman, Bnan : Police state. London, Pall Mall Press, 1970.

Chaudhuri, S.C. : Reminiscent. In S.K. Ghosh (ed.) : Police administrators : Reminiscences. New Delhi, Ashish Publishing House, 1989, 28-41.

Coatman, J. : Police. London, Oxford University Press, 1959.

Cox, Edmund : My thirty years in India. London, Mills & Boon Ltd., 1909.

Cramer, James : World police. London, Cassell, 1964.

Crawford : Reminiscences of an Indian police official. London, Roxburghe Press.

Cross, Stan : Turning points : An alternative view of becoming a policeman. *Journal of Police Science and Administration*, V. 5(2) June, 1977, 155-64.

Cumming, E. : Policeman as philosopher, guide and friend. *Social Problem*, V. 12(2) 1965.

Curry, J.C. : Indian police. London. Faber & Faber Limited.

Denyer, Tom (and others) : Policeman as alienated laborer. *Journal of Police Science and Administration*, V. 3(3) September, 1975, 251-58.

Desai, Morarji : Tasks before police. *Indian Police Journal*, V. 24(2) October-December, 1977, 3-4.

Dutt, G.C. : My experiences of police work. In S.K. Ghosh (ed.): Police administrators : Reminiscences. New Delhi, Ashish Publishing House, 1989, 60-74.

Elliott, J.F. : New police. Springfield (III), Charles C. Thomas, 1973.

Evans, Peter : Police revolution. *C.B.I. Bulletin*, May 1975, 13-15.

Fagan, M. Michael and Ayers, Kenneth : The life of a police officer : A developmental perspective. *Criminal Justice and Behaviour*, V. 9(3) Sept., 1982, 273-85.

Farah, S.A. : In defence of police. *Indian Nation*, 21 June, 1988.

Farah, S.A. : Page from policeman's diary. *Indian Nation, Sunday Magazine*, January 25, 1987, II.

Farah, S.A. : Policeman's wife. *Indian Nation*, 7 May, 1989.

Fowler, Rod (and others) : Analyzing police hostage negotiations : Verbal interactional analysis technique. *Emotional First Aid : A Journal of Crisis Intervention*. V. 2(2) Summer, 1985, 16-28.

Fried Lander, C.P. and Mitchell, E. Police : servants or masters? London, Hart-Davis, 1974.

Fry, J.E. : Police in fact and fiction. *Police Journal*, December, 1963, 602-11.

Galliera, M.A. : Police in India. *Social Welfare*, V. 34(12) March, 1988, 33-34.

Gandhi, Krishna : People, police and politicians. *Economic and Political Weekly*, V. 14(47) 24 November, 1939, 1913-14.

Ghosh, S.K. : Betrayal of the police. Delhi, Manas Publications, 1991.

Ghosh, S.K. : Challenge. Calcutta, Academic Publishers, 1967.

Ghosh, S.K. : Indian mafia. New Delhi, Ashish Publishing House, 1991.

Ghosh, S.K. : Indian police at crossroads. Calcutta, Eastern Law House, 1977.

Ghosh, S.K. : Law breakers and keepers of peace. Calcutta, Ghosal, 1951.

Ghosh, S.K. : Life of a policeman : The worst of both worlds. *Statesman*, 28 October, 1981, 6.

Gill, S.S. : Police : A vulnerable force. *Hindustan Times*, 10 August, 1988, 11.

Gouldsbury, C.E. : Life in the Indian police. New Delhi, Manu Publications, 1977.

Gouldsbury, Charles Elphistone : Life in the Indian police. London, Chapman & Hall, 1912.

Heble, Madhukar S. : National Police Academy. *Illustrated Weekly of India*, V. 101(35) 13 August, 1980, 13.

Hilton, Jennifer : Police, politics and young people. *Police Journal*, January-March, 1972, 10-12.

Hinz, Lieselotte : Police and Sociology in West Germany. *Police Journal*, April-June, 1974, 161-72.

Hollins, S.T. : No ten commandments : Life in the Indian police. London, Hutchinson, 1954.

India, Ministry of Home Affairs : Civil list of Indian police service. Delhi, Controller of Publications, 1988.

Irving, Barrie : Police foundation after the launch. *Police Journal*, V. 54(4) October-December, 1981, 363-69.

Jacob, Tan : Future of the police. *Police Journal*, July, 1967, 309-20.

Janmejaya, Prem : Police ! Police. Delhi, Parag Prakashan, 1986.

Knetkor, V.G. : A great injustice. In S.K. Ghosh (ed.) : Police administrators : Reminiscences. New Delhi, Ashish Publishing House, 1989, 107-116.

Kennedy, Dantel B. and Kennedy, Bruce : Applied Sociology for police. Springfield, Charles & Thomas, 1979.

Kirkham, George L. : From professor to patrolman : A fresh perspective on police. *C.B.I. Bulletin*, May, 1975, 1-8.

Kitson, S. : Philatelic policeman. *Indian Police Journal*, V. 28(2) October-December, 1981, 29-33.

Klockars, Carl B. : The idea of police. New Delhi, Sage Publications, 1985.

Kooken, Don L. : Ethics in police service. Springfield (III), Charles C. Thomas, 1957.

Kothari, Rajni : Police in the dock. *Hindustan Times (Mag)*, 29 March, 1987, 9.

Krishnamurthi, S. : Some problems of the constabulary. *Indian Police Journal*, April, 1964, 57-59.

Krishnamurti, N. : What is a policeman. *Tamil Nadu Police Journal*, January-March, 1972, 29.

Krohn, Marvin D. (and others) : Is chivalry dead ? An analysis of changes in police dispositions of males and females. *Criminology : An Interdisciplinary Journal*, V. 21 (3) August, 1983, 417-37.

Lahiri, B.N. : Dilemma of the police. *Indian Police Journal*, July-September, 1968, 15-17.

Lahiri, B.N. : Leaves from a policeman's diary. Meerut, Meenakshi, 1967.

Lakshminarayanan, V.R. : Appointments and disappointments : My life in the Indian police services. New Delhi, Vikas Publishing House, 1988.

Lawrence, Cristina (and others) : Women, stress and the police : A bibliography, 1959-1984. *Psycholagical Documents*, V. 15 (1) July, 1985.

Lewis, Roy : A force for the future. London, Maurice Temple Smith Ltd., 1976.

Lobo, John : Ethics and the police. *C.B.I. Bulletin*, V. 19(9) September, 1985, 1-3.

Lobo, John : In retrospect. In S.K. Ghosh (ed.) : Police administrators : Reminiscences. New Delhi, Ashish Publishing House, 1989, 117-128.

Macnamara, E.J. and Riedel, M. (ed.) : Police perspectives, problems, prospects. New York, Praeger, 1974.

Manickam, V. : Police ethics. *Tamil Nadu Police Journal*. July-September, 1972, 732.

McNee, David : Some thoughts for senior officers. *Police Journal*, July-September. 1974, 193-97.

Mehra, Ajay K. : What ails Indian police? *Indian Express*, 3 July, 1978, 4.

Mehtab, Harekrishna : Police responsibility. *Indian Police Journal*, April, 1957, 64-67.

Mishra, Sarat Chandra : Do we need police ? *Orissa Review*, January, 1978, 17-20.

Misra, A.P. : What is ailing the police ? Souvenir, 10th. Symposium of All-India Principals Police Training College dated 22-10-1981 to 24-10-1981, Patna, 4-6.

Misra, S.C. : Beyond rules. Ajmer, B.R. Trading, 1971.

Misra, S.C. : Police ethics and public relations. *National Police Academy Magazine*, November, 1967, 5-14.

Misra, Sharad Chandra : My police service in retrospect. *Prashasnika*, V. 4(1) January-March, 1975, 16-36.

Mitra, Dilip : Indian police today. *Sardar Vallabhbhai Patel National Police Academy Magazine*, November, 1977, 139-49.

Modak, S.C. : Our police. *Illustrated Weekly of India*, 12 December, 1971, 8-14.

Morris, Terence : Police force. *New Society*, V. 79 (1264) 30 March 1987, 12-14.

Morton, Geoffrey J. : Just the job : Some experiences of a colonial policeman. London. Hodder & Stoughton, 1957.

Mukherjee, A.P. : A new look at the police. *Sardar Vallabhbhai Patel National Police Academy Magazine*, July 1976, 82-86.

Mullick, B.N. : A philosophy for the police. Bombay, Allied Publishers, 1969.

Mullick, B.N. : Police ethics. *Indian Police Journal*, October, 1960, 1-10.

Mullick, B.N. : World's great policeman. New Delhi, Kalyani Publishers, 1978.

Murrell, Mary E. and Lester, David : Masculinity in police officers. *Psychological Reports*, V. 44(1) February, 1979, 1-4.

Murrell, Mary E. (and others) : Is the police personality unique to police officers ? *Psychological Reports*, V. 43(1) August, 1978, 298.

Narain, Govind : Talk to senior officers and probationers. *Sardar Vallabhbhai Patel National Police Academy Magazine*, November, 1977, 8-20.

Nath, Ravindra : Between the thugs and the police. *Indian Express*, 26 December, 1980.

Nath, Trilok : Forty years of Indian police. New Delhi, Gian Publishing House, 1990.

Nath, Trilok : Indian police. *Patriot* (*Mag*), 24 April, 1983, 1.

Nath, Trilok : Lessons for police : What India can learn from socialist countries. *Patriot*, 9 September, 1984, 1.

Nayar, Kuldip : On leaden feed to a fire. *Indian Express*, 6 June, 1979, 6.

Nehru, Jawaharlal : His talks to the police (Prime Minister's addresses and messages given to the police from time to time) *Indian Police Journal*, July, 1964.

Nehru, Jawaharlal : Nehru on police (ed.) by B.N. Mullik. Dehra Dun, Palit Dutta, 1970.

Nehru, Jawaharlal : Prime Minister's call to policemen (Speech delivered on 7.2.1960 at the closing ceremony of the 10th All India Police Athletics and Sports Meeting, Delhi). *Indian Police Journal*, April, 1960, 4-6.

Niederhoffer, Arthur and Blumber, Abraham S. : Ambivalent force : Perspective on the police. Waltham (Mass), Ginn, 1970.

Noorani, A.G. : People, their police and the policeman, *Janta*, 26 January, 1975, 35-36.

Padhi, S.S. : Religion, reality and police efficiency. *Orissa Review*, April, 1974, 26-29.

Padmanabhan, Chitra : All kinds of policemen. *Hindustan Times*, October 29, 1989, 13.

Panigrahi, B.K. : Till the memory lasts. In S.K. Ghosh (ed.) : Police administrators : Reminiscences. New Delhi, Ashish Publishing House, 1989, 129-135.

Pant, Govind Ballabh : A new look for the police. *Indian Police Journal*, July, 1956, 1-10.

Pant, P.M. : My moments to remember. In S.K. Ghosh (ed.) : Police administrators : Reminiscences. New Delhi, Ashish Publishing House. 1989, 136-145.

Parker, W.H. : Parker on police (ed.) by O.W. Wlson. Springfield (Ill), Charles, C. Thomas, 1957.

Pathak, B.N. : XXII All India police duty meet. *Indian Police Journal*, V. 26(1) July-September, 1979, 49-54.

Pathak, B.N. : XXIII All India police duty meet. *Indian Police Journal*, V. 26(4) April-June, 1980, 57-60.

Pathak, B.N. : XXIX All India police games, 1980. *Indian Police Journal*, V. 26(3) January-March, 1980, 67-76.

Police – Are they same everywhere : A case from Britain. *Radical Humanist*, V. 47(11) February, 1983, 13-14.

Police in hot water. *Link*, 14 (8) 3 October, 1971, 29.

Police or sena, which? *Swarajya*, V. 14(7) 16 August, 1969, 5.

Police, people and Prime Minister. *Mainsteam*, V. 19(17) 27 December, 1980, 1-3.

Policemen vs policemen. *Link*, V. 10(52) 4 August, 1968, 16-17.

Policemen wake up. *Link*, V. 11(48) 13 July, 1969, 15.

Prakash, Gyan : Police museum languishing in Patna. *Times of India*, June 3, 1991, 3.

Prasad, K.N. : Police : Some reflections. *Denouement*, V. 2 (6&7) January-February, 1991, 33-36.

Prime Minister and the police force. *People's Democracy*, V. 4(52) 28 December, 1980, 1.

Pulling, Christopher : Mr. Punch and the police. London, Butterworths, 1964.

Pulling, Christopher : Police. London, Robert Hale, 1962.

Raghavan, R.K. : An anatomy of the Indian police. *Indian Journal of Police Science*, V. 47(3) July-September, 1986, 399-412.

Rajagopal, P.R. : Dilemma of the police. *Hindustan Times*, 12 February, 1981, 9.

Rajagopal, P R. : Indian police I. *Hindustan Times*, 3 April, 1989, 11.

Rajagopal, P.R. : Indian police II. *Hindustan Times*, 4 April, 1989, 11.

Rajan, V.N. : Reminiscences. In S.K. Ghosh (ed.) : Police administrators : Reminiscences. New Delhi, Ashish Publishing House, 1989, 146-159.

Ramsingh : Advice to youth I.P.S. Probationers based on My police experience. *National Police Academy Magazine*, September, 1960, 11-24.

Ranganathananda, Swami : Swami Vivekanand and the police force. *Indian Police Journal*, January, 1963, 80-82.

Rajan, C.N. Chitta : Labour pains unlimited. *Mainstream*, V. 1 (38) 19 May, 1979, 1-3.

Rao, G.V. (ed.) : Thoughts on the Indian police. Bangalore, Government of Karnataka, 1982.

Raye, J.K. : Orissa police pigeon. *Indian Police Journal*, V. 29(3) January-March, 1983, 33-38.

Reiser, Martin : Police department psychologist. Springfield (III), Charles C. Thomas, 1973.

Restive police (Editorial). *Times of India*, 21 June, 1971, 6.

Roucek, Joseph S. : Sociology of the police control. *International Journal of Legal Research*, V. 7(1) June, 1972, 47-67.

Roy, B.K. : Police and homeopathy. *National Police Academy Magazine*, November, 1973, 70-74.

Roy, B.K. : What ails the Indian police today? *Decision*, V. 13(3) July, 1986, 221-25.

Ruchelman, Leonard : Police politics : A comparative study of three cities. Cambridge (Mass), Ballinger Publishing, 1974.

Rustamji, K.F. : Policemen : Villains or victims ? *Indian Express (Mag)*, 12 May, 1985, 5.

Rustamji, K.F. : To the rescue of the police. *Sunday Statesman*, 6 October, 1985, 3-4.

Saha, B.P. : Police in free India : Its faces and drawbacks. New Delhi. Konark Publications.

Scott, P.D. : A Psychiatrist's co-operation with the police: The Fifth James Smart Memorial Lecture. *Police Journal*, V. 50(1) January-March, 1977, 6-22.

Seares, Roberts : Police cadet. *Annals of the American Academy of Political and Social Science*. January, 1954.

Sen, Shankar : Police today. New Delhi, Ashish Publishing House, 1986.

Sharma, Prabhu Datta : Indian police and the dilemmas of development. In Suresh Kumar Sharma (ed.) : Dynamics of development : An international perspective, V. 1 General political and administrative. Delhi, Concept, 1977, 339-52.

Shastri, Lal Bahadur : Shastriji's advice to the police. *Indian Police Journal*, July, 1966, 10-17.

Singh, Harijai : A look at our police I. *Tribune*, July 21, 1977.

Singh, Harijai : A look at our police II. *Tribune*, July 22, 1977.

Singhvi, G.S. : When I look back. In S.K. Ghosh (ed.) : Police administrators : Reminiscences. New Delhi, Ashish Publishing House, 1989, 184-194.

Sinha, A.K.P. : Revolutionary in policeman's garb. *Indian Nation*, January 15, 1984.

Sinha, Alakh Kumar : Thirty-two years in the police and after. Patna, Sanjivan Press, 1952.

Sinha, M.K. : Philosophy of policing. *Indian Journal of Criminology and Criminalistics*, V. 1(2-3) June-September, 1981.

Sinha, M.K. : Police. In S.K. Ghosh (ed.) : Police administrators : Reminiscences. New Delhi, Ashish Publishing House, 1989, 195-201.

Sleeman, William Henry : Rambles and recollections of an Indian official. London, J. Hatchard and Sons, 1844.

Sociology of the police : Report to the nutfield foundation on a seminar on the sociology of the police. January 25-28, Bristol. *Police Journal*, July-September, 1971, 227-43.

Solmes, Alwyn : English policeman, 1871-1935. London, Allen & Unwin, 1935.

Steinberg, J. Leonard and McEvoy, Donald W. : Police and the behavioural sciences. Springfield, Charles C. Thomas, 1974.

Stracey, Eric : Odd man in : My years in the Indian police. New Delhi, Vikas Publishing House, 1981.

Streamlining the police : For what ? *People's Democracy*, V. 7(25) 20 June, 1971, 4.

Sullivan, John L. : Introduction to police science. New York, McGraw Hill, 1971.

Supercop is here. *Economic and Policing Weekly*, V. 12 (39) 24 September, 1977, 1961.

Taber, William R. : Police and academe : Some surprising similarities. *Police Journal*, V. 52 (4) October-December, 1979, 373-78.

Tripathy, B.K. : Towards a popular police (Paper) in 5th Police Science Congress, Nainital, 1966.

Tunisia President (Habib Bourguiba) : Police servant of the nation. Tunis, 1966.

Tyler, Mary : My years in an Indian prison. London, Victor Gollanez 1977.

Venugopal Rao, S. : Nehru and I. In S.K. Ghosh (ed.) : Police administrators : Reminiscences. New Delhi, Ashish Publishing House, 1989, 160-176.

Venugopal Rao, S. : Police service : Some compulsions and contradictions. *Indian Journal of Public Administration*, January-March, 1978, 11-20.

Whitaker Ben : Police. London, Eyreand Spotliswoode, 1964. Wilson, Patrick : Letter from Calcutta : Fire ball in the air. *Economic Weekly*, January 25, 1964, III.

Yadava, R.S. : In defence of Indian police. *Radical Humanist*, V. 47 (3) May, 1983, 16-19.

Zelig, Mark : Ethical dilemmas in police psychology. *Professional Psychology : Research and Practice*, V. 19 (3) June, 1988, 336-38.

2

Police System

Alderson, John C. : Police in 1980's. *Indian Police Journal*, V. 28 (3) January-March 1982.

Alienated police force : Many changes but there is big credibility gap. *Link*, V. 13 (40) 27 June, 1971, 15-16.

Allen, Gregory : New police : London and Dublin—The birth of the Dublin metropolitan police. *Police Journal*, V. 50 (4) October-December, 1977, 304-17.

Alvares, Claude : Tamil Nadu's police state. *Indian Express* (*Mag*), 10 January, 1982, 1.

Andhra Pradesh : Inspector general of police. The history of the Andhra Pradesh police (Centenary : 1861-1961). Hyderabad, 1961.

Arul, F.V. : International criminal police organisation : Interpol. *C.B.I. Bulletin*, V. 23 (8) August, 1989, 1-3.

Arul, F.V. : Obsolescence of dual control. *Indian Police Journal*, V. 25 (1) July-September, 1978, 15-20.

Arul, F.V. : Why a national police commissioner : The obsolescence of dual control. *Indian Police Journal*. V. 25 (1) July-September, 1978.

Auten, James H. : Police management in Illinois, 1983. *Journal of Police Science and Administration*, V. 13 (4) December, 1985, 325-37.

Autonomy to police opposed. *Times of India*, 29 May, 1979.

Badal, M. : What's wrong with our police. *Times of India*, 19 March, 1978, 8.

Banerjee, S. (and others) : Restructuring civil police. *Vikalpa*, V. 4 (4) October, 1979, 333-38.

Baratan, R.K. : What is wrong with the police : I—Distorted priorities. *Times of India*, 12 July, 1978, 8.

Baratan, R.K. : What is wrong with the police : II—Distorted priorities, *Times of India*, 13 July, 1978, 6.

Basu, Ranu : Colonial municipal policy and Indian response : Municipal government and police in Calcutta, 1850-1852. *Bengal Past & Present* V. 100 (2) January-June, 1981, 1-46.

Bayley, David H. : Police in India. *Economic and Political Weekly*, V. 5 (45) 6 November, 1971, 2287-91.

Becke, Shirley : First half-century. *Police Journal*, November 1969.

Becker, Harold K. : Police system of Europe : A survey of selected police organisations. Springfield, Charles C. Thomas, 1973.

Berkeley, George : European police : Challenge and change. *Public Administration Review*, September-October, 1968, 424-30.

Beveridge, Peter : Inside in C.I.D. London, Evans, 1957.

Bhadauria, Y.S. : Reactions of history sheeters towards police surveillance. *Indian Journal of Social Work*, V. 41 (1) April, 1980, 45-50.

Bhadauria, Y.S. : Sociology of police history sheeters. *Indian Journal of Social Research*, V. 23 (3) December, 1982, 265-68.

Bhattacharjee, Ajit : Failure of the system. *Indian Express*, 3 July, 1979, 6

Bhattacharya, Mohit : Organisation and system of policing of medium size cities. New Delhi, Institute of Public Administration, 1973.

Blumberg, Abraham S. and Niederhoffer, A. : Social and historical setting. In Arthur Niederhoffer and Abraham S. Blumberg (ed.) : Ambivalent force : Perspective on the police. U.S.A., Gunn and Company, 1970.

Bodily, Samuel E. : Police sector design incorporating preferences of interest groups for equality and efficiency. *Management Science*, August, 1978, 1301-13.

Bose, A.C. : What is wrong with our police forces? *Amrita Bazar Patrika*, 28 January, 1969, 6.

Breathnach, Seamus : Irish police from earliest times to the present day. Dublin, Anvil Books, 1976.

Broken arm of the law : The plight of the Indian police. *Indian Express (Mag)*, 12 July, 1981, 1.

Brown, Jonathan F. : Maud and the police service. *Police Journal*, August, 1969, 366-69.

Bunyan, T. : History and practice of the political police in Britain. London, Julian Friedman, 1976.

Bunyan, T. : Political police in Britain. London, Quartet Books, 1977.

Bunyard, R.S. : Police : Organisation and command. Eastover, Plymouth : Macdonal and Evans, 1978.

Buoh, M.N. : Case of reviewing magistracy's role. *Times of India*, 18 January, 1982, 7.

Buoh, M.N. : Modernising the police. *Hindustan Times*, 14 February, 1982, 9.

Buoh, M.N. : Need for police without arms. *Times of India*, 26 November, 1981, 8.

Buoh, M.N. : Police in India. *Indian Express*, 23 May, 1981, 8.

Canada. Department of External Affairs. Information Division : Royal Canadian mounted police. *Indian Police Journal*, October, 1965, 51-58.

Cashyap, S.K.S. : Bihar home guards. *Sunday Indian Nation*, December, 6, 1981, 1.

Chand, Hot : Power of police and magistracy in India. Allahabad, Law Books House, 1954.

Chapman, D.H. : Police of the U.S.S.R. *Police Journal*, March, 1965, 109-15.

Chatterjee, Sumit K. : Police in ancient India 1861-1961. *Indian Police Journal*, (Centenary Issue) 1961, 11-18.

Chatterji, Basudev : The Darogah and the Countryside—The imposition of police control in Bengal and its impact (1793-1837). *Indian Economic and Social History Review*, V. 11(1) January-March, 1981, 19-42.

Chattopadhyay, Basudev : Cornwillis and the emergence of colonial police. *Bengal Past and Present*, V. 102(2) July-December, 1983, 11.

Chauhan, B.S. : Policing system in major cities. *Indian Police Journal*, V. 25(3) January-March, 1979, 33-42.

Cohn, Alvin (ed.) : Future of policing. New Delhi, Sage Publications, 1978.

Conquest, Robert (ed.) : Soviet police system. London, Bodley Head, 1968.

Consensus on giving policemen a new deal. *Times of India*, 9 June, 1979, 11.

Cramer, James : World's police. London, Cassell, 1964.

Critchiley, T.A. : History of police in England and Wales, 1900-1966. London, Constable, 1973.

Curry, J.C. : Indian police. New Delhi, Manu Publications, 1976 (Reprinted).

Curry, John Court: Indian police. London, Faber & Faber, 1932.

Dasgupta, Uma : Crime, law and the police in India, 1870-80. *Indian Economic and Social History Review*, V. 10(4) December, 1973, 333-70.

Deb, R. : Conflicts due to contradictions in social, political and administrative system in India and their implications for internal security. *Indian Police Journal*, V. 30(1) July-September 1983, 16-25.

Dubhashi, P.R. : Police in independent India. *Indian Journal of Public Administration*, V. 24 (1) January-March, 1978, 55-58.

Farah, S.A.: Bihar police. *Indian Nation*, 17 January, 1987.

Farah, S.A. : Indian police. *Indian Nation*, 7 November, 1987.

Farah, S.A. : Police then and now. *Indian Nation*, August 11, 1987.

Farah, S.A. : 2001 A.D. policing. *Indian Nation*, February 29, 1988, 4.

Farilicq, Rene : French police from within. London, Cassell, 1933.

Foran, W. Robert : Kenya police, 1827-1960. London, Robert Hate, 1960.

Fosdick. Raymond B.: American police system. New York, Century, 1920.

Fosdick, Raymond B. : European police system, New York, Century, 1916.

Ganguli, Amulya : West Bengal police. *Statesman*, 24, January, 1974, 4.

Ganguli, Amulya : West Bengal police. *Statesman*, 25 January, 1974, 4.

Ganguli, Amulya : West Bengal police. *Statesman*, 26 January, 1974, 5.

Gautam, D.N. : Police itself stumbling block to change. Souvenir 10th Symposium of All India Principals Police Training College. Dated 22-10-1981 to 24-10-1981, Patna 25-28.

Gautam, D.N. : What is wrong with Indian police ? New Delhi, Ashish Publishing House, 1988.

Germann, A.C. : Changing the police : Impossible dream? *Police Journal*, July-September, 1971, 197-206.

Gillance, K. and Khan, A.N. : Constitutional independence of police constable. *Police Journal*, V. 48(1) January-March, 1975.

Glover, Eric Harraden : English police : Its origin and development. London, *Police Chronicle*, 1934.

Glueck, Sholdon : Continental police practice : In the formative years. Springfield (III), Charles C. Thomas, 1974.

Gonzalez, Alberto J. : Argentinian federal police. *Indian Police Journal*, January, 1965, 30-33.

Gopalaswami, R.A. : Suggestions to modernise Tamil Nadu police force. *Swarajya*, V. 16(16) 16 October, 1971, 2-4.

Grant, Douglas : Policing then and now. *Police Journal*, V. 53(1) January-March, 1980, 55-61.

Gregory, F.E.C. : Changes in American systems of policing since 1960. *Police Jaurnal*, October-December, 1978, 357-65.

Griffiths, P. : To guard my people. Bombay, Allied Publishrs, 1971.

Gupta, Anand Swarup : Police in British India (1861-1947). New Delhi, Concept Publishing Company, 1979.

Gupta, Jyotirindra Das : India in 1980 : Strong center, weak authority. *Asian Survey*, V. 21(2) February, 1981, 147-61.

Hardwick, E. Glyn : Who should control the police? *Police Journal*, October-December, 1978, 349-56.

Hart, J.M. : British police, London, Allen & Unwin, 1951.

Holdaway, S. : Inside the British police : A force at work. Oxford, Basil Blackwell, 1983.

Holdaway, S. (ed.) : British police. London, Edward Arnold, 1979.

Jain, M.L. : Characteristics and development of riot gun. *Police Research and Development, Quarter I*, January-March, 1980, 11-13.

Jain, R.B : Modernizing the police force : A plea for professionalization. *Journal of the Institute of Public Administration*, V. 7(1) April-June, 1980, 50-56.

Jammes, J.R. : Some aspects of the French police. *Police Journal*, V. 55(2) April-July, 1982, 113-24.

Jeyasingh, J. Visuvathas . Changing perspectives in police services. *Indian Police Journal*, January-March, 1978, 43-45.

Jha, S.K. : Management of change : Its relevance of police. *Indian Police Journal*, V. 28(4) 1982, 37-41.

Jongboer, C.A. : Netherlands police. *Police Journal*, October-December, 1971, 312-17.

Joshi, G.P. and Bedi, B.S. : Police fatalities in India. *Police Research and Development, Quarter IV*, 1989, 1-19.

Kaul, M.K. : New police set up changes nothing. *Patriot*, 27 October, 1979.

Kettle, Martin and Bunyan, Tony : Police force of the future is now here. *New Society*, V. 53 (927) 21 August, 1980, 351-55.

Knights, P.D. : A look at the United States police. *Police Journal*, May, 1969, 199-209.

Krishnaswamy, N. : Modernization of the police. *Indian Journal of Criminology and Criminalistics*, V. 1 (2-3) June-September, 1981.

Kuykendall, Jack and Robert, Roy R. : Mapping police organizational change, from a mechanistic towards an organic model. *Criminology : An Interdisciplinary Journal*, V. 20(2) August, 1982, 241-56.

Lee, W.L. Melville : History of police in England. New Jersey, Patterson Smith Montclair, 1971.

Loveday, Barry : Joint authorities for police. *Local Government Studies*, V. 11(4) July-August, 1985, 13-20.

Madhya Pradesh, Police Department : History of the Madhya Pradesh police. Bhopal, 1965.

Madjitey, E.R.T. : Police in Ghana. *Indian Police Journal*, January, 1960, 10-18,

Majumdar, D.N. : Justice and police in Bengal (1765-1793). Calcutta, K.L. Mukhopadhyay, 1960.

Malaviya, P.D. : Restructuring of civil police : A syndicate study. *Transactions*, V. 27, 1978, 1-35.

Malaviya, P.D. : Why do not police change ? *Goa Today*, V. 13(1) August, 1978, 10.

Mallick, Sidu : Need to review police systems. *Times of India*, 24 August, 1982, 6.

Marx, G.T. and Archer, D. : Community police patrols : An exploratory inquiry. Cambridge, Harvard and MIT joint Center for urban studies, 1972.

Marx, G.T. and Archer, D. : Community police patrols and vigilantism. In H.J. Rosenberg and P.C. Sederberg (eds): Vigilante politics. Philadelphia, University of Pennsylvania Press, 1976.

Maswood, M.A.H. : Review of the set up of the West Bengal police by...and his recommendations, 1958-59. Alipore, Superintendent, Government Printing Press, 1960.

Mathur, K.M. : Need for change in basic organisational pattern. *Indian Police Journal*, V. 25(1) July-September, 1978.

Mathur, S.N. : Re-appraisal of relations between police and magistracy (Paper). In Second All India Police Science Congress, Bombay, September 1961.

Mecauley, R. Paul : An American's view of the British police. *Police Journal*, December 1967, 567-70.

Mehra, Ajay K. : Revamping Indian police. *Administrative Change*, V. 8(1) July-December, 1980, 77-88.

Melville, W.L. : History of police in England. London, Methuen, 1901.

Menon, N.C. : Delhi needs a police commissioner. *Hindustan Times*, 27 January 1974, 1.

Menon, N.C. : Delhi needs a police commissioner. *Public Administration* (India) February, 1974, 13-16.

Misra, S.C. : Over-militarisation of police a danger. *Indian Express*, 10 August, 1979, 9.

Mistra, S.C. : State police organisation in India. New Delhi, Central Reserve Police Force, 1975.

Misra, S.C. : Structural change. *Seminar*, No. 218, October 1976, 18-21.

Modak, E.S. : Our police. *Illustrated Weekly of India*, V. 92(50) 12 December, 1971, 8-14.

Modernisation (Editorial). *Economic Times*, 6 December, 1980, 5.

More, Harry W. : History of police management thought. *Police Journal*, April-June, 1979, 181-96.

Mosse, George L. (ed.): Police forces in history. California, Sage Publications, 1975.

Moylan, Hohn : Police in Britain. London, Longmans Green, 1948.

Muir, A.A. : Police in Norway. *Police Journal*, September 1963, 424-27.

Mullik, B.N. : Police organisation in France. *Indian Police Journal*, April, 1956, 21-30

Mullick, B.N. : Police through ages. *Indian Police Journal* (Centenary Issue), 1961.

Nath, D.C. : Police in 2001 A.D. *Indian Police Journal*, V. 25(1) July-September, 1978, 115-123.

Nath, T. : For a stronger arm of law. *Patriot* (*Mag*), 26 July, 1981, 1.

Nath, T. : New look for police force. *INFA Feature*, 7 January, 1976.

Nath, T. : Reorganising the police. *Hindustan Times*, 31 January, 1979, 7.

Nath, Trilok : For a new look police. *Patriot* (*Mag*). 21 September, 1986, 1.

Nath, Trilok : Forty years of Indian police. New Delhi, Concept Publications, 1982.

National Police Academy, Hyderabad : Report on the desirability and feasibility of separation of 'Law', 'Police' and 'Order' Police, 1984.

National Police Academy : Need for change in the basic structure of police (Working paper and proceedings of a Seminar, November 1974). *Sardar Vallabhbhai Patel National Police Academy Magazine*, November, 1975, 56-83.

Nayyar, Gurbachan Singh : Civil and criminal justice under Maharaja Ranjit Singh. *Sikh Review*, V. 28 (320) August-September, 1980, 44-48.

Nigam, S.R. : Scotland yard and the Indian police. Allahabad, Kitab Mahal, 1963.

O'Brien, G.M. : Australian police force. Melbourne, Oxford University Press, 1960.

O'Connor, Dennis M : Soviet people's guards : An experiment with civic police. *New York University Law Review*, June, 1964, 579-614.

Offentiche Sicherheit, Viena ; Police in ancient Egypt. *Indian Police Journal*, October-December, 1973, 60-63.

Ostrom, Elinor and Whitaker, Gordon : Does local community control of police make a difference? *American Journal of Political Science*, February, 1973, 48-76.

Pandalai, K.M. : Case for cosmopolitan police force. *Hindu*, 12 March, 1980.

Pandey, Anil Kumar : Policing in ancient India. *Indian Police Journal*, V. 32 (2) April-June, 1985, 3-10.

Pandey, Anil Kumar : Policing in ancient India : An eyeless system. *Police Research and Development, Quarter I*, January-March, 1985, 1-5.

Pattabhiram, M. : Modernisation of police. *Hindu*, 17 November, 1975, 6.

Pattabhiram, M. : Modernisation of police. *Police Research and Development, Quarter I*, January-March, 1976, 15-16.

Petrick, Richard L. : Bureaucratic decentralisation and the distribution of urban services : The case of team policing. *Policy Studies Review*, V. 1 (3) February, 1982, 581-95.

Phillips, Alan : Living legend : The story of the Royal Canadian mounted police. London, Cassell, 1957.

Police of tomorrow. *Illustrated Weekly of India*, V. 104 (13) 27 March. 1983, 14-15.

Pravinsinhji : Greater Bombay police : Modus operandi bureau. *Indian Police Journal*, July, 1957, 13-19.

Puri, Kishen : Memoirs of the Marwar police. Jodhpur, Jodhpur State, 1936.

Rai, Haridwar : District Magistrate and Police Superintendent in India : The controversy of dual control. *Journal of Administration Overseas*, July, 1967, 122-29.

Rai, Haridwar : Dual control of law and order administration in India : A study in magistracy and police relationship. *Indian Journal of Public Administration*, V. 13 (1) January-March, 1967, 43-46.

Raina, Asoka : Inside row : The story of India's secret service. New Delhi, Vikas Publishing House, 1981.

Ramachandran, D. : Police service : An agenda for improvement. *Indian Journal of Public Administration*, V. 24 (1) January-March, 1978, 127-151.

Ramaswami, P.N. : Magisterial and police guide. Madras, Law Journal Office, 1959.

Rawlings, Front : Norwegian police. *Police Journal*, February, 1965, 55-59.

Reith, Charles : A new study of police history. London, Oliver and Boyd, 1956.

Reith, Charles : A short history of the British police. London, Oxford University Press.

Reith, Charles : Blind eye of history : A study of the origins of the present police era. London, Faber and Faber, 1962.

Reorganizing the police in M.P. *Link*, V. 18 (4) 7 September, 1975, 15.

Reynolds, Quentin : Police headquarters. London, Cassell, 1956.

Rolph, C.H. : Reorganising the police. *New Statesman*, 27 January, 1967, 105.

Rubin, F. : Policing system of Hungary. *Police Journal*, V. 53 (1) January-March, 1980, 20-29.

Rustamji, K.F. : Police in Japan. *Indian Police Journal*, April, 1962, 5-20.

Rustamji, K.F. : Politics of mob fury. *Indian Express (Magazine)*, 19 January, 1986, 3.

Rustamji, K.F. : The I.A.S.-I.P.S. feud. *Hindustan Times*, June 12, 1987, 6.

Rustamji, K.F. : What's wrong with Delhi police? *Hindustan Times*, 15 October 1978, 1.

Saha, Kalyani : Police and development : A case study of West Bengal 1951-1971. Delhi, Manas Publications, 1991.

Sahu, B.P. : Police in free India. Delhi, Konark, Publishers, 1989.

Sahu, Nabin Kumar : History of Orissa police. Cuttack, *Orissa Police Magazine*, 1961.

Saksena, N.S. : Police in France. *Indian Police Journal*, V. 27 (3) January-March, 1981, 9-11.

Saksena, N.S. : Why district set up is running down? *Times of India*, September 25, 1980, 6.

Seminar proceedings and recommendations. *Journal of Social Studies State Governments*, V. 5 (3-4) July-December, 1972, 336-42.

Senoren, Cleto B. : Philippine police system manual. *International Police Academy Review*, October, 1973, 6-9.

Shanti Prasad : Towards a new police. *Indian Police Journal*, July, 1964, 47-54.

Sharma, Prabhu Datta : Indian police : A development approach. New Delhi, Research Publications in the Social Sciences, 1977.

Shepherd, David : Republic of Vietnam's national police. *Military Review*, June, 69-74.

Sikkim police undergo sea change. *Times of India*, 23 April, 1977, 6.

Singh, Gyanoo : Changing contours of law and order problems. *Indian Nation*, (Sunday Magazine) December 18, 1983, 1.

Singh, Nityanand : Bihar police : Past and present. *Hindustan Times*, Feb. 10, 1991, 7.

Singh, Nityanand : Pre-independence police : Its dilemma. *Hindustan Times*, August 15, 1989, 15.

Singh, S.N. : Indigenous police in Chotanagpur in the 18th and early 19th century. *Journal of Historcial Research*, V. 18 (1) 15 August, 1975, 78-84.

Singhvi, G.C. : District Magistrate and District police constraints, dilemmas and imperatives. *Indian Journal of Public Administration*, V. 19 (4), October-December, 1973, 495-524.

Singhvi, G.C. : District Magistrates and police : Certain misconceptions. *Sardar Vallabhbhai Patel National Academy Magazine*, November, 1977, 103-108.

Singhvi, G.C. : Inspector-General of Police : Oldish debate, newish approach. *Journal of the National Academy of Administration*, V. 26 (4) October-December, 1971, 59-64.

Sinha, B.M.K. : Police today : A study. *Indian Nation*, 12 May, 1975.

Sinha, M.K. : In father's footstepts : A policeman's odyssey. New Delhi, Vanity Books, 1981.

Sinha, M.K. : Indian police. *Indian Nation*, 25 November, 1968, 4.

Sinha, M.K. : Indian police. *Indian Nation*, 26 November, 1968, 4.

Sinha, M.K. : Police problems : Why dual control is demoralising. *Statesman*, 2 July, 1977, 6.

Sinha, N.P. : Police then and now. *Hindustan Times*, January 1, 1989, 6.

Sinha, S.K. : Police in India. *U.S. I. Journal*, V. 100 (419) April-June, 1970, 141-47.

Sinha, Vraj Mohan : Indian police system : An overview. *Radical Humanist*, V. 47 (11) February, 1983, 37-40.

Smith, Bruce : Police systems in the United States. New York, Harber and Bros, 1949.

Something wrong with our police. (Editorial). *Janata*, V. 25 (12) 12 April, 1970, 1-2.

Stead, Philip John : Police of Paris. London, Staples Press, 1957.

Stunton, Bruce : Police in Australia : A critique. Australian Institute of Criminology, 1978.

Suntook, N.F. : Police in the Andamans. *Indian Police Journal*, October, 1954, 33-37.

Swank, Calvin J. : Police in 1980 : Hypotheses for the future. *Journal of Police Science and Administration*, V. 13 (3) September, 1975, 294-300.

Tendero, Avelino and Thomas, M. Ladd : Organisation of the Manila police department. Manila, Institute of Public Administration, University of Philippines, 1953.

Tobias, J.J. : Case against nationalizing the police. *Police Journal*, September, 1967, 399-404.

Tobias, John J. : British colonial police. In Philip John Stead (ed.) : Pioneers in policing. New Jersey, Patlerson Smith, Montclair, 1977.

Tripathi, B.K. : History of Orissa police. *Crapler*, 31 October, 1975, 13-16.

Tripathi, S.V.M. : Organisational analysis : Police. *National Police Academy Magazine*, November, 1972, 46-52.

Tuli, Vinod : Release of arrested persons on bail and misuse of the system. *Police Research and Development, Quarter II*, 1982, 1-12.

Vaidyanathan, S.S. : Wanted a new police manager. *Indian Journal of Public Administration*, V. 24 (1) January-March, 1978. 183-93.

Venugopal Rao, S. : Bihar police (A Systems Study) in India. Bureau of Police Research and Development. Study reports, 1975, New Delhi, 1976, 113-42.

Venugopal Rao, S. : Present status and organisational future of the police in India. In G. Ram Reddy and K. Seshadri (eds.) : Developing society and police. Hyderabad, Osmania University, 1972, 27-40.

Verghese, B.G. : System credibility. *Seminar* No. 218, October, 1977, 22-25.

Vohra, K.B. : Need for re-orientation of police. *C.B.I. Bulletin*, February, 1973, 8-9.

Wagoner, Carl P. : Police alienation : Some sources and implications. *Journal of Police Science and Administration*, V. 4 (4) December, 1976, 388-403.

What is wrong with our police? *Link*, V. 21 (41) 20 May, 1979, 8-10.

Wilson, O.W. : Police planning. Springfield (Ill), Charles C. Thomas, 1957.

Winant, T.T. : Police of Tokyo. *Police Journal*, April-June, 1971, 167-172.

3

Police—Rural

Bajwa, S.S. : Village chowkidar and rural policing. *Indian Journal of Police*, V. 25 (1) July-September, 1978.

Bambawale, P.A. : Policing in rural areas (Paper). In Second All India Police Science Congress, September 1961.

Basu, Asit Kumar : Reorganisation of rural police in West Bengal. *Indian Journal of Public Administration*. V. 24 (1) January-March, 1978, 173-182.

Bhanot, M.L. : Rural policing in India : The perspective and the prospective. *Police Research and Development*, *Quarter II*, July-September, 1977, 1-23.

Birge, J.R. and Pollock, S.M. : Modelling rural police patrol. *Journal of the Operational Research Society*, V. 40 (1) January, 1989, 41-54.

Central Police Training College : Rural policing : Background papers of the seminar held on 14 to 16th December, 1964, Abu, CPTC, 1965.

Chaturvedi, S.K. : Rural policing in India. Delhi, B.R. Publication, 1988.

Das Surangan and Chattopadhyay, Basudeb : Rural crime in police perception : A study of village crime note books. *Economic and Political Weekly*, V. 26 (3) January 19, 1991, 129-35.

Gupta, R.C. : Ideal communication system in rural police in India. *Indian Police Journal*, V. 25 (2) October-December, 1978, 25-28.

India. Police Commission : History of police organisation in India and Indian village police : Being select chapters of the report of the Indian Police Commission, 1902-03. Calcutta, University of Calcutta, 1913.

Johan, I.J. : Rural police : Origin and forms. *Indian Police Journal*, July, 1959, 47-51.

Kasture, G.K. : Towards a new order in rural policing (Paper). In 5th Police Science Congress, Nainital, 1966.

Kowalewski, David (and others) : Police environments and operational codes : A case study of rural setting. *Journal of Police Science and Administration*, V. 12 (4) December, 1984, 363-72.

Kumar, A. : Policing in rural areas (Paper). In Second All India Police Science Congress, Bombay, September, 1961.

Mishra, S.C. : Neglect of rural policing. *Administrative Change*, V. 7 (1) July-December, 1979, 67-78.

Mishra, S.C. : Rural development and village policing. *Sardar Vallabhbhai Patel National Academy Magazine*, November, 1977, 76-79.

Muguve, M.G. : Policing in rural areas (Paper). In Second All India Police Science Congress, Bombay, September 1967.

Nagarkar, V.V. : Policing in rural areas (Paper). In Second All India Police Science Congress, Bombay, September 1961.

Nath, Trilok : Policing the villages. *Hindustan Times*, 23 December, 1976, 9.

Nath, Trilok : Policing the villages. *Indian Police Journal*, V. 23(4) April-June, 1977, 57-60.

Pant, P.M. : Policing in rural areas (Paper). In Second All India Police Science Congress, Bombay, September 1961.

Ramanna, K.G. : Rural and urban police standards of constabulary (Paper). In 7th Police Science Congress, Jaipur, 1968.

Sahani, S.S. : Policing in rural areas (Paper). In Second All India Police Science Congress, Bombay, September 1961.

Saraf, V.K. : Optimum jurisdiction of a rural police station for efficient police administration (Paper). In 5th Police Science Congress, Nainital, 1966.

Singh, Nityanand : Policing panchayats. *Hindustan Times*, July 9, 1989, 6.

Sinha, B.N. : Rural policing : Implications of panchayati raj set-up (Paper). In 5th Police Science Congress, Nainital, 1966.

Trimbakro : Policing in rural areas (Paper). In Second All India Police Science Congress, Bombay, September, 1961.

Varma, A.P. : Panchayati raj and rural police (Paper). In 5th Police Science Congress, Nainital, 1966.

Vohra, K.B. : Rural policing in India : A comparative study. *Transactions*, V. 21, November, 1975, 1-31.

4

Police—Urban

Barocas, Harvey A. : Urban policemen : Crisis mediators or crisis creators ? *American Journal of Orthopsychiatry*, V. 43(4) July, 1973, 632-39.

Edwards, S.M. : Bombay city police : A historical sketch, 1972-1976. London, Oxford University Press, 1923.

Holdaway, Simon : Changes in urban policing. *British Journal of Sociology*, V. 28(2) June, 1977, 119-37.

Larson, Richards C. : Urban police patrol : Analysis. Cambridge, (Mass), MIT Press, 1972.

Mladenka, Kenneth R. and Hill, Kim Quaite : Distribution of urban police services. *Journal of Politics*, V. 40(1) February, 1978, 112-33.

Murphy, Patrick V. : Development of the urban police. *Current History*, June, 1976, 245-248.

Pachon, Harry P. and Lovrich, Nicholas P. : Consolidation of urban public services : A focus on the police. *Public Administration Review*, V. 37(1) January-February, 1977, 38-47.

Quareshy, Ahtestiam : Problems of urban policing : Crime in the city. *Hindustan Times*, 14 May, 1978, 1.

Reddy, S. Sudhakar : NTR's technical retreat in urban police bill. *New Age*, V. 34(3) January, 1986, 7.

Reid, Thomas A.: Training suburban police in the management of social interaction disturbances. *Crisis Intervention*, V. 6(3) 1975, 2-12.

Rios, Bob (and others) : Need for psychological services as perceived by urban police departments. *Psychological Reports*, V. 43(1) August, 1978, 126.

Rubinstein, J. : City police. New York, Farrer, Straus and Giroux, 1973.

Saksena, N.S. : Our city police systems : A few efficiency tests. *Indian Police Journal*, April-June, 1976, 7-9.

Snibbe, John R. and Snibbe, Homa M. : Urban policemen in transition : A psychological and sociological review. Springfield (III), Charles C. Thomas, 1973.

Van Maanen John : Police socialization : A longitudinal examination of job attitudes in an urban police department. *Administrative Science Quarterly*, V. 20(2) June, 1975, 207-28.

5

Police—Traffic

Asogwa, S.E. : The use of the police for limited road accident data collection in developing countries. *Accident Analysis and Prevention*, V. 14(3) June 1982, 203-08.

Bakhshi, Prem Iqbal : Electronic device in the aid of traffic police. *Science and Culture*, V. 51(2) February, 1975, 63-65.

Bawa, P.S. : Legal aspect of the traffic problem. *Police Research and Development, Quarter IV*, October-December, 1979, 11-15.

Bawa, P.S. : Traffic management : Scope for police community relation. *Indian Police Journal*, V. 26(4), April-June, 1980, 14-20.

Braslavsky, N. : Research notes on traffic policing. In Braddly, D. (ed.) : Police management workshop. Glasgow, University of Strathclyte, Centre for Police Studies, 1982.

Farah, S.A. : Patna traffic police. *Indian Nation*, March 10, 1988, 4.

Gangopadhyay, A. : Syndicate study on policing a major city : Administration of traffic enforcement. *Transactions*, V. 37, 1983, 1-141.

Gardiner, John A. : Traffic and the police : Variations in law enforcement policy. Cambridge (Mass), Harvard University Press, 1969.

Iyer, Shyamala Mani : Public aid in traffic control. *Indian Nation*, August 5, 1987, 4.

Khan, M.Z. : Traffic wardens : The Delhi experiment in police-public partnership. *Indian Journal of Criminology and Criminalistics*, V. 3(384) July-October, 1983, 130-34.

Lester, David and Arcuri, Alan F. : Personality correlates of police discretion to enforce traffic laws. *Psychological Reports*, V. 43 (3, Part 2) December, 1978, 1166.

Mohan, S. : Diagnosis and training for work culture change in Delhi traffic police. *Management Review* V. 17(1) 1990, 15-19.

Nath, Trilok : Police and city traffic. *Tribune*. 1 June, 1976.

Sarain, S.M. : Road users behaviour and awareness on road traffic safety. *Police Research and Development, Quarter IV*, October-December, 1985, 18-22.

Sinha, U.N. : Road safety week. *Indian Nation*, April 10, 1989, 4.

Villetorte, P. : Traffic police in major European cities. *Indian Police Journal*, October, 1967, 17-25.

6

Police Reform

Bharadvaja, Brahma : Police reform in India. *Modern Review*, November, 1973, 367-70.

Bhat, B.N. : Legal and judicial reforms for improved police effectiveness. *C.B.I. Bulletin*, V.24(2) February, 1990, 36.

Broeker, Gallen : Rural disorder and police reform in Ireland, 1812-36. London, Routledge & Kegan Paul, 1970.

Brown, Jorathon F. : Reform of local government and the police service. *Police Journal*, April, 1970, 167-70.

Brown, W.J. : Structural reform in municipal policing. *Canadian Police College Journal*, V. 10(2) 1986, 75-85.

Carte, E. and Carte, Eleine H. : Police reform in the United States, Berkeley, University of California Press, 1975.

Gupta, Anandswarup : Police reform in retrospect. *Indian Journal of Public Administration*, V. 24(1) January-March, 1978, 59-67.

Hans, Toch : Agents of change : A study in police reform. New York, John Wiley, 1975.

Kamte, N.M. : Reforming the police. *Indian Express*, 7 December, 1976, 6.

Kanetkar, V.G. : Our Police : Need for drastic reforms. *Indian Journal of Public Administration*, V. 24(1) January-March 1978, 1-9.

Malaviya, P.D. : In search of hot water : A quest for structural reforms in the police. *Indian Journal of Public Administration*, V. 31(3) July-September, 1985, 805-26.

Mandal, Archana : Police reform : Sir George Campbell's administration in Bengal 1871-1874. *Calcutta Review*, April-June, 1978, 98-107.

Menon, Maohava N.R. : Some thoughts on police reforms: Recruitment and training. *Journal of Social Studies State Governments*, V. 5(3-4) July-December, 1972, 270-74.

Mukherjee, A.P. : A new look of the police. *Sardar Vallabhbhai Patel National Police Academy Magazine*, July 1976, 82-86.

Mukhoty, Gobinda : Face-lift for police. *Economic and Political Weekly*, 21 October, 1978, 1770.

Narayana Rao, M.V. : Reforms in police administration since independence. *Indian Journal of Public Administration*, July-September, 1963, 203-72

Nath, T. : Piecemeal police reform. *Patriot*, 13 September, 1980, 2.

Police reform (Editorial). *Times of India*, 16 November, 1971, 8.

Police reform (Editorial). *Times of India*, 4 June, 1981, 8.

Police reforms. *Indian Journal of Public Administration*, V. 24(1) January-March, 1978, 260-67.

Rao, K.V. : Police administration : A reform proposal. *Journal of the Lal Bahadur Shastri National Academy of Administration*, Spring, 1973, 127-147.

Reforming the police (Editorial). *Times of India*, 17 September, 1971, 6.

Reforming the police (Editorial). *Times of India*, 22 March, 1980, 8.

Rustamji, K.F. : Police reform only a distant dream ? *Mainstream*, V. 16(21-22) 7 February, 1981, 51-53.

Savage, Stephen P. : Political control or community liason ? Two strategies in the reform of police accountability. *Political Quarterly*, V. 55(1) January-March, 1984, 48-59.

Shanti Prasad : Police reforms. *Hindustan Times*, 21 January, 1972, 7.

Sharma, Brahma Prakash : Let us remodel our police system. *Caravan*, June 1972, II, 13-17.

Sharma, Brahma Prakash : Police and its ways : Need for reform. *Indian Express*, 27 September, 1978, 6.

Sharma, P.D. : Dilemmas and dimensions of police reforms in India. *Indian Journal of Public Administration*, V. 31(3) July-September, 1985, 788.

Sharma, P.D. : Law and order : A perspective on police reform in India. *Indian Police Journal*, V. 25(4) April-June 1979, 18-20.

Sherman, Lawrence W. : Scandal and reform : Controlling police corruption. Berkeley, University of California Press, 1978.

Singhvi, G.C. : Some aspects of reforms in police administration. *Indian Journal of Police Administration*, V. 31(3) July-September, 791-804.

Sinha, M.K. : Reforms in police administration. *Indian Police Journal*, October, 1961, 42-44.

Spencer, Sarah : Weakness of police authorities and the case for reform. *Local Government Studies*, V. 11 (6) November-December, 1985, 31-34.

Terrlill, Richard J. : Politics, reform and the early nineteenth-century reports on the committees on the police of the metropolis. *Police Journal*, V. 53(3) July-September, 1980, 24-56.

Thoughts on police reforms. V. 8, 1966. Mt. Abu, Central Police Training College.

Toch, Hans (and others) : Agents of change : A study in police reform. New York, John Wiley, 1975.

Vohra, K.B. : A syndicate study on need for reforms in the existing system of police administration, disciplinary control and accountability. *Transactions*, V. 27, 1978, 36-106.

Will police be at all reformed (Editorial). *New Age*, V. 29(24) 14 June, 1981, 2.

7

Police Administration

Abraham, C.M. : Police discretion and judicial attitude. *Cochin University Law Review*, V. 5(1) March, 1981, 01-05.

Alderson, J. : Law and disorder. London, Haminsh Hamilton, 1984.

Alderson, J. : People, government and police. In Brown J. and House G. (eds.) : Police and the Community. Farnbarough, Saxon House, 1975.

Alexander, P.J. : Police administration in Kerala : A developmental approach. University of Kerala, 1980.

Alexander, P.J. : Should the police and public order be incorporated in the concurrent list (Paper). In 7th Police Science Congress, Jaipur, 1968.

Allen, David N. : Police supervision on the street : An analysis of supervisor/officer interaction during the shift. *Journal of Criminal Justice*, V. 10(2) 1982, 91-109.

Allen, R.J. : Effective supervision in the social service. London, McGraw-Hill, 1978.

Anand, Eshwar : Towards a new police culture. *Indian Express*, 8 April, 1988.

Anandan, A.D. : Value of environment in police station. *Indian Police Journal*, July 1958, 48-52.

Anandhachari, T. : Democracy and social defence. *Seminar*, No. 216, October, 1977, 26-29.

Anandhachari, T. : Participative management in the police. *Indian Police Journal*, V. 28(1) July-September, 1981, 4-9.

Anandhachari, T. : Police and criminal administration in India: Need for a systems approach. *Indian Journal of Public Administration*, V. 24(1), January-March, 1978, 169-72.

Anderson, Robert W. : Towards a cost-benefit analysis of police activity. *Public Finance*, V. 29(1) 1974, 1-18.

Archambeault, William G. and Weirman, Charles L. : Critically assessing the utility of police bureaucracies in the 1980 : Implications of management theory. *Journal of Police Science and Administration*, V. 11(4) December, 1983, 420-29.

Arcuri, Alan F., Gunn, Mary M. and Lester, David : Measuring police discretion. *Perceptual & Motor Skills*, V. 64(3), part 1, June, 1987, 774.

Aslan, Paul : Police licensing centres in chaos. *Civil Service Journal*, V. 69(1) 17 February, 1989, 1.

Bahuguna, H.N. : New perspectives in police administration. *Socialist India*, 23 March, 1973, 13-15.

Bailey, H.D. : Police and political development in India. New Jersey, Princeton Univ. Press, 1969.

Bajpai, K.D. : Departmental enquiries : Cause of delay and remedial measures. *Transactions*, V. 35, 1982, 1-44.

Balakrishna, Rao : Police administration (Paper). In 7th Police Science Congress, Jaipur, 1968.

Balakrishnan, Sheela : Study in law and order problem. *Administrator*, V. 23(3-4) July-December, 1978, 543-45.

Balasiddamuni, P. (and others) : A frontier police production function : Measurement of relative technical efficiency of police force. *Police Research and Development, Quarter II*, April-June, 1990, 1-10.

Baldivin, Robert and Kinsey, Richard : Police powers and politics. London, Quarlet Books, 1982.

Banerjee, A.N. : Co-ordination between the railway and the district police. *C.B.I. Bulletin*, V. 21(4) April, 1987, 5-6.

Bard, Morton : The unique potentials of the police in interpersonal conflict management. *International Journal of Group Tensions*, V. 3(3-4) 1973, 68-75.

Barse, Sheela : Police accountability. *Indian Police Journal*, V. 36(2) April-June, 1989, 2-5.

Bartle, R. : Policemen in court. *Police Journal*, V. 56(4) October-December, 1983, 334-38.

Bawa, P.S. : Manpower planning in relation to law and order. *Indian Police Journal*, V. 24(1) July-September, 1977, 21-26.

Bawa, P.S. : Need for a scientific outlook in police working. *Indian Police Journal*, V. 28(2) October-December, 1981, 7-11.

Bayley, D.H. : Police and political development in India. Princeton, Princeton University Press, 1969.

Bayley, David B. : Police and political change in comparative perspective. *Law and Society Review*, August, 1971, 91-112.

Bayley, David H. : Police and political order in India. *Asian Survey*, V. 23(4) April, 1983, 484-96.

Bell, John : Police and accountability. *Local Government Studies*, V. 15(1) January-February, 1989, 57-69.

Bennett, Peter : Structuring police functional sections and units. *Police Journal*, V. 61(4) January-March, 1988, 25-40.

Bhambhri, C.P. : Making police force more effective. *Times of India*, 28 January, 1982, 8.

Bhardwaj, R.K. : Indian police administration. New Delhi, National Publishing House, 1978.

Bhargava, S.P.: Police panchayat collaboration in Rajasthan. *Indian Police Journal*, January, 1962, 20-26.

Bhattacharjee, Ajit : Police and politicians. *Indian Express*, 12 June, 1979.

Bhattacharya, Mohit : City police management. *Indian Journal of Public Administration*, V. 24(1) January-March, 152-168.

Bhattacharya, Mohit : Organisation and system of policing of medium size cities : Condensation by A. Gupta. *Police Research and Development*, January-June, 1974, 1-12.

Bopp, William J. : Police administration : Selected readings. Boston, Holbrook Press, 1973.

Bordua, David J. and Reisa, Albert J. : Command, control and charisma : Reflections on police bureaucracy. *American Journal of Sociology*, July, 1966, 68-75.

Bouza, Anthony V. : Police administration, organization and performance. New York, Pergamon Press, 1978.

Bowley, A.S. : Police and the planners. *Police Journal*, V. 46(4) October-December, 1973, 308-14.

Bradley, D. (ed.) : Police management workshop. Glasgow, University of Strathcylyde, Centre for Police Studies, 1982.

Braithwaite, Wanda : Police officers as decision makers. *Dissertation Abstracts International*, V. 34(4-B-) October, 1973, 1767-68.

Brief, Arthur P, (and others) : Correlates of supervisory style among policemen. *Criminal Justice and Behaviour*. V. 3(3) September, 1976, 263-71.

Bristow, A.P. : Police supervision. Illinois, U.S.A., Charles C. Thomas, 1971.

Brogden, M. : A police authority : The denial of conflict. *Sociological Review*. V. 25(1) 1977.

Brogden, M. : Police : Autonomy and consent. London, Academic Press, 1982.

Brown, Jonathan F. : Police and local government : A comment. *Police Journal*, V. 47(4) October-December, 1974, 301-03.

Brown, W.J. : Organization assessment, determining the state of a police organization. *Journal of Police Science and Administration*, V. 14(4) December, 1986, 267-284.

Bunyan, Tony : Political police in Britain. London, Julian Fiedmann Publishers, 1976.

Bunyard, R.S. : Police and the law. *Police Journal*, V. 56(1) January-March, 1983, 7-14.

Bunyard, R.S. : Police management handbook. London, McGraw Hill, 1979.

Butler, A.J.P. : Police management. Farnborough, Gower, 1984.

Cacioppe, Ron L. and Mock, Philip : Developing the police officer at work. *Leadership and Organization Development Journal*, V. 6(5) 1985, 48.

Card, R. : Police accountability and the control of the police. *Bramshill Journal*, V. 1(1) 1979.

Causes of failure of police cases in courts : The remedies. Hyderabad, National Police Academy, 1976.

Central Police Training College, Abu, Second Advance Course, 1961. Handicaps of police work in India : Their remedies.

Chambliss, William J. and Seidman, Robert B. : Law, order and power. London, Addison-Wesley Publishing Co., 1971.

Chatterjee, Basudeb : Study in the police administration of West Bengal. Calcutta, Apurba, 1973.

Chaturvedi, A.C. : A syndicate study on policing in major cities : Organisational structure, administration and welfare. *Transactions*, V. 37, 1973, 259-306.

Chaturvedi, Anil : District administration : Dynamics of discord. New Delhi, Sage Publications, 1988.

Chaturvedi, S.K. : Developing cities and police administration. *Indian Police Journal*, V.29(2) October-December 1982, 29-33.

Chaturvedi, S.K. : Maintenance of order under police commissionarate system in Delhi : An empirical evaluation. *Indian Police Journal*, V. 30(2) October-December, 1983, 22-29.

Chaturvedi, S.K. : Metropolitan police administration in India. New Delhi, B.R. Publishing House, 1985.

Chaturvedi, S.K. : Thana punargathan. *Police Vigyan Patrika*, B.P.R.D., January-March, 1986.

Chaturvedi, T.N. : Emerging perspectives in law and order : A facet of administrative change. In Ramesh K. Arora (ed.) : Administrative change in India. Jaipur, Aalekh, 1975, 314-56.

Chaturvedi, T.N. : Police administration. New Delhi, Indian Institute of Public Administration, 1982.

Chavan : Ban on cops made it worse. *Times of India*, 25 April, 1985, 1.

Cizankas, Victor I. and Hanna, Donald G. : Modern police management and organization. Englewcod Cliffs (N J.), Prentice Hall, 1977.

Clutterbuck, David : Putting order into the law. *Indian Police Journal*, V. 23(2) October-December, 1976, 27-32.

Conlin, J. : Local and central government police administration. London, Cassell, 1967.

Crawshaw, R.W. : Police and the political system : A system analysis approach. *Police Journal*, V. 60(1) January-March, 1987, 72-84.

Criag, David W. : Police administration in Northern Europe. *Local Government Newsletter*, February, 1969, 1-2.

Dang, Satyapal : Police and politicians. *Mainstream*, V. 25 (39) 13 June, 1987, 5.

Dang, Satyapal : Punjab police : Why ineffective? *Mainstream*, V. 24(48) August, 1986, 5.

Dass, K.K. : More complex problem. *Seminar*, No. 218, October, 1977, 33-34.

Dass, K.K. : Union-State relations : Administration of law and order. *Indian Journal of Public Administration*, July-Sept., 1970, 330-340 ; Comments by G.C. Singhvi and authors rejoinder. *Indian Journal of Public Administration*, April-June, 1971, 280-81.

Datta Ray, Sunanta K. : Police and politicians : Paying the price of dependence. *Statesman*, 29 August, 1982, 6.

Davis, Edward M. : Staff one : A perspective on effective police management. Englewood Cliffs (N.J.). Prentice-Hall, 1978.

Dayal, John : Police, people and the state. *Link*, V. 25(35) 10 April, 1983, 7-10.

Deb, R. : Duty to be fair. *Indian Police Journal*, V 28(2) October-December, 1980, 46-49.

Deb, R. : Police and the law. In S.K. Ghosh (ed.) : Police administrators : Reminiscences. New Delhi, Ashish Publishing House, 1989, 42-59.

Desai, A.R. : Growing government lawlessness. *Economic and Political Weekly*, V. 21(23) 7 June, 1986, 1002-03.

Devlin, Daniel : Police procedure, administration and organization. London, Butterworth, 1966.

Dhanoa, S.S. : Police administration : Its challenges and prospects. *Indian Journal of Public Administration*, V. 24(1) January-March, 1978, 49-54.

Diaz, S.M. : Concept of police accountability. *Sardar Vallabhbhai Patel National Police Academy Magazine*, November, 1977, 61-69.

Drummond, Douglas S. : Police culture. London, Sage Publications, 1976.

Dubhashi, P.R. : Police in independent India. *Indian Journal of Public Administration*, V. 24(1) January-March, 1978, 55-58.

Dutta, Subodh Chandra : How Jyoti Basu and D.I.G.-IB brought politics into police? *Organiser*, V. 23(44) 13 June, 1970, 10.

Dutta, Vijay Ranjan : Panchayats and the police. *Kurukshetra*, December, 1969, 13-14.

Eastman, George D. (ed.) : Municipal police administration. Washington, International City Management Association, 1969.

Englert, Don : Police chief as a management team builder. *Indian Police Journal*, V. 28(1(July-September, 1981, 31-36.

Ericson, Richard V. : Police bureaucracy and decision making : The function of discretion in maintaining the police system. *Police Journal*, June, 1972, 59-65.

Farah, S.A. : Law and order situation. *Indian Nation*, January, 14, 1989, 4.

Farah, S.A. : Myth of police budget. *Indian Nation*, 12 May, 1987.

Farah, S.A. : Patna : Law and order problem. *Indian Nation*, May 24, 1988, 4.

Farah, S.A. : Police decay I. *Indian Nation*, February 3, 1988, 4.

Farah, S.A. : Police decay II. *Indian Nation*, 12 March, 1988, 4.

Farah, S.A. : Police decay III. *Indian Nation*, 13 March, 1988, 4.

Farah, S.A. : Road blockade in Patna. *Indian Nation*, 18 February, 1989.

Farah, S.A. : Saga of famous spies. *Indian Nation*, 26 June, 1986.

Farah, S.A. : System of police administration. *Indian Nation*, April 23, 1988, 4.

Farah, S.A. : Top blaming the bottom. *Times of India*, 22 April, 1987.

Farah, S.A. What ails police? *Indian Nation*, 29 May, 1987.

Farah, S.A. : With malice towards none. *Indian Nation*, (*Sunday Magazine*), August 14, 1988, 1.

Favreau, Donald F. and Gillespie, Joseph E. : Modern police administration. Englewood Cliffs (N.J.), Prentice-Hall, 1978.

Feiner, Robert : Fuzy thoughts : The police and law-and-order politics. *Sociological Review*, V. 28(2) May 1980, 377-413.

Finnimore, Peter : What should be the relationship between policing and politics in contemporary society? *Police Journal*, V. 57(1) January-March, 1984, 8-18.

Fogelson, Robert M. : Big city police. Cambridge, Harvard University Press, 1977.

Fox, Vernon : Sociological and political aspects of police administration. *Sociology and Social Research*, October, 1965, 39-48.

Fuld, Leonhard Felix : Police administration : A critical study of police organisations in the United States and abroad. New York, G.P. Putnams, 1910.

Gains, Larry K. and Ricks, Trustt A. : Managing the police organization : Selected readings. New York, West Publishing Co., 1978.

Gangopadhyay, Abhijit : Impact of frequent transfers on police officers. *Transactions*, V. 36, 1982, 88-151.

Garudachar, B.N. : Police job of the station level is of interesting and challenging. Proceedings of seminar, Mt. Abu, National Police Academy, 1972, 32, 38.

Genz, John L. and Lester, David : Authoritarianism in policemen as a function of experience. *Journal of Police Science and Administration*, V. 4(1) March 1976, 9-13.

Ghosh, S.K. : District administration: Institutional failures (Threat of administrative collapse). In S.K. Ghosh (ed.) : Police administrators : Reminiscences. New Delhi, Ashish Publishing House, 1989, 75-80.

Ghosh, S.K. : Keeping the peace : For whom the bell tolls. New Delhi, Ashish Publishing House, 1991.

Ghosh, S.K. : Lawbreakers and keepers of peace. Calcutta, Eastern Law House, 1969.

Ghosh, S.K. : Magisterial and police guide. Calcutta, Satchidananda Prakashani, 1977.

Ghosh, S.K. : Police administration : Organization and procedure. Calcutta, Eastern Law House, 1973.

Ghosh, S.K. : Police administration : Reminiscences. New Delhi, Ashish Publishing House, 1989.

Ghosh, S.K. : Politicians and police. *Hindustan Times*, November 2, 1989, 7.

Ghosh, Sadhan Kumar : Politicisation of police in West Bengal. *Swarajya*, V. 16(4) 24 July, 1971, 13-14.

Goodall, Robert : Management by objectives : A conceptual application for police. *Police Journal*, April-June, 1974, 178-86.

Goodall, Robert : Management by objectives : A conceptual application for police. *Police Journal*, July-September, 1974, 251-61.

Gopalaswami, R.A. : Suggestions to modernise Tamil Nadu police force. *Swarajya*, 16 October, 1971, 2-4.

Gore, M.S. : Long arm of the law. *Indian Express* (*Magazine*) 17 June, 1979, I.

Greenberg, David F. (and others) : Effect of police employment on crime. *Criminology : An Interdisciplinary Journal*, V. 21(3) August, 1983, 375-94.

Greene, Jack R. (ed.) : Managing police work. California, Sage Publications, 1982.

Gupta, A. : Accountability of police. *Sardar Vallabhbhai Patel National Police Academy Magazine*, November, 1977, 21-26.

Gupta, R.G. : Modern city control room. *Police Research and Develoment, Quarter-IV*, October, 1982, 1-5.

Gupta, Ranjit : 100 years of India's police administration. *Civic Affairs*, September, 1961, 21-23.

Hale, Charles, D. : Fundamentals of police administration. Boston, Holbrook Press, 1977.

Handcuffing the police. *Times of India*, 11 May, 1975, 6.

Hardwicks, Slyn : Why should control the police ? *Police Journal*, V. 51(4) October-December, 1978, 349-56.

Heble, Madhukar S. : Police, politics and politicians. *Indian Express*, 10 July, 1980, 6.

Hendrickson, Thomas A. : Police legal adviser and his changing role. *C.B.I. Bulletin*, April, 1977, 6-7.

Hennessy, James J. : PPBS and police management. *Police Chief*, July, 1972, 62-67.

Hernandez, Armand P. : Motivation and municipal police departments : Models and an empirical analysis. *Journal of Police Science and Administration*, V. 10(3) September, 1982, 284-88.

Hewitt, William H. : British police administration, Springfield, Ill, Charles C. Thomas, 1965.

Hillgren, James S. (and others) : Primary stressors in police administration and law enforcement. *Journal of Police Science and Administration*, V. 4 (4) December, 1976, 445-49.

Holdaway, Simon : Police accountability : A current issue. *Public Administration*, V. 60 (1) Spring, 1982, 84-91.

Hooda, R.K. : Constitutional and legal position of the police in India. *National Police Academy Magazine*, November, 1967, 40-56.

Hooja, G.B.K. : Crisis of Indian police. *Prashasnika*. V. 9 (1-2) January-June, 1980, 17-20.

Hudson, R.C. : A matter of confidence : Police, government and society in France since 1981. *Police Journal*, V. 41 (2) April-June, 1988, 169-74.

Hudson, Robert : Democracy and the Spanish police forces since 1975. *Police Journal*, V. 61 (1) January-March, 1988, 53-62.

Iannone, N.F. : Supervision of police personnel. Englewood Cliffs, N.J., Prentice-Hall, 1975.

Igbionovia A. Patrick Edobor : Police in trouble : Administrative and organisational problems in the Nigeria police force. *Indian Journal of Public Administration*, V. 28 (2) April-June, 1982, 334-72.

Imberi, Peter : Management-planning, performance and finance. *Police Journal*, V. 62 (3) July-September, 1989, 184-93.

Institute for Training in Municipal Administration : Municipal police administration. Chicago, ICMA, 1961.

International City Managers Association : Municipal police administration. Chicago, International City Managers Association, 1954.

Jacobs, James and Sanders, Andrew : Should police be armed? *New Society*, V. 77 (1228) 11 July, 1986, 12-13.

Jain, Girilal : Popularity versus legitimacy : The backlog of distrust. *Times of India*, 6 February, 1980.

Jatav, H.C. : Man management in police organisation. *Indian Police Journal*, V. 28 (4) April-June, 1982, 2-6.

Jayawardene, C.H.S. : Contexual constraints on police administration. *Indian Journal of Criminology*, July, 1982.

Jayawardene, C.H.S. : Internal organizational constraints on police efficiency. *Indian Police Journal*, V. 31 (3) July-September, 1984, 10-16.

Jerath, Aroti R. : Police case diaries are fiction. *Indian Express*, 21 December, 1980.

Jha, Sudhir Kumar : Management of change : Its relevance to policy. *Indian Police Journal*, V. 28 (4) April-June, 1982, 37-41.

Jones, Sandra and Levi, Michael : Law and order and the causes of crime : Some police and public perspectives. *Howard Journal of Criminal Justice*, V. 26 (1) February, 1987, 1-14.

Joshi, G.P. : Managerial philosophy of the police organisation in India. *Indian Police Journal*, V. 26 (4) April-June, 1980, 21-25.

Joshi, G.P. : System of crime records in the police stations. *Police Research and Development, Quarter III*, 1976, 1-3.

Juliani, T.J. (and others) : Municipal policing in Canada : A developmental perspective. *Canadian Police College Journal*, V. 8 (4) 1984, 315-85.

Jungle law rule by Punjab police. *New Age*, V. 19 (39) 14 November, 1971, 9.

Kak, H.N. : Decentralisation of police administration. *Indian Journal of Public Administration*, January-March, 1962, 40-51.

Kakkar, P.C. : Integrated crime records system. *Indian Police Journal*, V. 26 (3) January-March, 1980, 4-11.

Kakkar, P.C. : Intergrated national law enforcement records. *Indian Journal of Public Administration*, V. 24 (1), January-March, 1978, 217-21.

Kalhan, D.N. : Making of policemen. *Times of India*, 26 July, 1970, 6.

Kannupillai, V. : How to measure police productivity. *Police Research and Development, Quarter I*, January-March, 1983, 1-2.

Kansas University. Government Research Centre : Police administration and management school : A report. Lawrence (Kansas), Government Research Center, 1969.

Kant, H.E. Shri Krishan : Criminalisation of politics and its impact on electoral process. *Police Research and Development, Quarter I*, January-March, 1990, 1-4.

Kanth, Amod : Metropolitan police department of Tokyo : Acomparison with Delhi police. *Indian Police Journal*. V. 36 (1) January-March, 1989, 11-17.

Kanth, D. Ravi : Has Andhra become a 'police desam'? *Hindustan Times* (*Mag*). 30 November, 1986, 5-6.

Karve, D.G. : Police administration in India. *Indian Journal of Public Administration*, V. 11 (4) October-December, 1965, 307.

Katyal, K.K. : Policemen and politicians, *Hindu*, 9 November, 1981, 8.

Kenney, J.P. : Police administration. Springfield. Illinois, Charles C. Thomas, 1959.

Kenney, John P : Police administration, Springfield, (III), Charles C. Thomas, 1975.

Kenney, John P. : Police and human relations in management. *Journal of Criminal Law, Criminology and Police Science*, July-August 1954.

Kenney, John P. : Police management planning. Springfield (III), Charles C. Thomas, 1959.

Keney, John P. : Team policing organisation : A theoretical model. *Police Journal*, August, 1972, 10-22.

Kettle, Martin : Police and the left. *New Society*, V. 70 (1146), 6 December, 1984, 366-67.

Kettle, Martin : Police take a political road. *New Society*, V. 51 (908), 28 February. 1980, 444-45.

Khanna, K.C. : Decemation of the police : Politics takes its toll. *Times of India*, 20 December, 1983, 6.

Khera, S.S. : District administration in India. Bombay, Asia Publishing, House, 1961.

Khera, S.S. : Policy making in Government. *Management in Government*, V. 11 (4) January-March, 1980, 199.

Kilory-Silk, Robert : Who polices the police? *Local Government Chronicle*, 26 September, 1978, 1045-46.

Knetkar, V.G. : Police and political interference. *Free Press Journal*, 2 August, 1979.

Krishankant, H.E. Shri : Criminalisation of politics and its impact on electoral process. *Police Research and Development, Quarter I*, January-March, 1990, 1-4.

Krishnaswamy, Aiyyangar : Police administration in India. In G. Ram Reddy and K. Seshadri (eds.) : Developing society and police. Hyderabad, Osmania University, 1972, 21-26.

Krishnaswamy, N. : Management by objectives in the police. *Indian Police Journal*, January-March, 1976, 34-48.

Kulkarni, V.B. : Police and the politician. *Indian Police Journal*, January, 1971, 11-14.

Kumar, Santh : A syndicate study on restructuring of civil police for efficient public service, operational effectiveness and employee's satisfaction. *Transactions*, V. 31, 1980. 1-55.

Kumar, Swadesh : A micro-analysis of the work schedule of S.H.Os. *Police Research and Development, Quarter III*, July-September, 1979, 6-12.

Lafargue, Paul : Police and the anarchists. *People's Democracy*, V. 6 (49) 6 December, 1970, 3.

Lahari, S.K. : Police power. Calcutta, Law Book Society (n.d.).

Lall, John : Undue dependence on army : Result of demoralisation of police. *Times of India*, 1 September, 1980, 6.

Langworthy, Robert H. : Police department size and agency structure. *Journal of Criminal Justice*, V. 13 (1) 1985, 15-27.

Lannone, N.F. : Supervision of police personnel. Englewood Cliffs, N.J., Prentice-Hall, 1975.

Law and order (Editorial). *Times of India*, 21 January, 1978, 6.

Law and order : No need for alarm. *Times of India*, 24 September, 1978, 1.

Lele, Vijay : Polic and politics. *Sunday Standard*, 18 November, 1979.

Leonard, V.A. : Police organisation and management. Brooklyn, Foundation Press, 1964.

Leonard, V.A. : Police patrol organisation. Springfield (Ill), Charles C. Thomas, 1970.

Loveday, Barry : Recent developments in police complaints procedure : British and North America. *Local Government Studies*, V. 15(3) May-June, 1989, 25-58.

Loveday, Barry : Role of the police committee. *Local Government Studies*, V. 9(1) January-February, 1983, 39-52.

Lowe, Richard : Management consultant and the police. *Police Journal*, July-September, 1971, 207-11.

Luthra, B.R. : A syndicate study on police as a plan subject : Pros and cons. *Transactions*, V. 34, 1-29.

Macnamara, Donal E.J. : American police administration in mid century. *Public Administration Review*, Summer, 1950, 181-89.

Madan, J.C. : Police administration in medieval India. Shodhak, 1974, 305-15.

Mahajan, Krishan : Police and legal information, *Hindustan Times*, July 31, 1990, 7.

Mahanta, J. and Kathpalia, V.K. : Does police set-up create a mind reversal environment? *Indian Police Journal*, V. 36(2) April-June, 1989, 35-38.

Manning, Peter K. : Modern police administration : The rise of crime focused policing and critical incident analysis. In Rita Donelau (ed.) : Maintenance of order in society. Canada, Canadian Police College, 1982.

Manning, Peter K. and Butler, A.J.P. : Perceptions of police authority. *Police Journal*, V. 55(4) October-December, 1982, 333-44.

Mark, Robert : Metropolitan police and political demonstrations. *Police Journal*, V. 48(3) July-September, 1975, 191-203.

Marshall, Geoffrey : Police and government : The state and accountability of the English constable, London, Methuen, 1965.

Marwah, Ved : Sub-culture. *Seminar*, No. 218, October, 1977, 14-17.

Marxist plot to paralyse police force in West Bengal. *Organiser*, V. 23(21) 3 January, 1970, 5.

Mathur, B.S. : Police administration in Mewar during the 19th century. *Journal of Rajasthan Institute of Historical Research*, January-March, 1971, 20-27.

Mathur, K.M. : Problem of police accountability in a democratic society. *Indian Police Journal*, V. 25(4) April-June, 1979, 30-42.

Mathur, K.M. : What causes disorders : Some theories. *C.R.P.F. Samachar*, July 31, 1987, 11-5.

Mathur, Krishna Mohan : Confrontation management. *SVP National Police Academy Magazine*, V. 34, November, 1975, 93-98.

Mathur, Krishna Mohan : Law and order administration with special reference to terrorism. *Indian Journal of Public Administration*, V. 35(2) April-June, 1989, 233-260.

Mathur, Krishna Mohan : Police accountability to the law and the people. *Administrator*, V. 23(2) April-June, 1979, 439-48.

Mathur, Krishna Mohan : Police accountability to the law and the people. *Police Research and Development, Quarter-I,* January-March, 1980, 1-7.

Mathur, Krishna Mohan : Police culture : Need for a closer scrutiny. *Indian Journal of Public Administration,* V. 36(3) July-September, 1990, 589-602.

Mathur, Y.B. : Police administration in the Punjab : 1949-1975. *Journal of Indian History,* V. 42(1) April, 1964, 195-217.

Mclaughlin, Pat : Police management of public drunkenness in Scotland. *British Journal of Criminology,* V. 25(4) October, 1985, 334-64.

Meagher, M. Steven : Organizational integrity : Role of the police executive in the management process. *Journal of the Police Science and Administration,* V. 13(3) September, 1985, 236-43.

Mehra, Ajay K. : Police in changing India. New Delhi, Usha Publications, 1985.

Mehra, Ajay K. : Revamping Indian police. *Administrative Change,* V. 8(1) July-December, 1980, 77-88.

Melnicoe, W.B. and Melnicoe, J. : Element of police supervision. London, Glencoe Press, 1969.

Mishra, K.K. : Police administration in ancient India. Delhi, Mittal Publications, 1987.

Mishra, S.N. : Democratic politics and police performance : a case study in police-panchayati raj relationship. *Indian Journal of Politics,* V. 12(1-2) April-August, 1978, 77-83.

Mishra, S.N. : Panchyat level. *Seminar,* No. 255, November, 1980, 21-24.

Mishra, S.N. : Police-panchayati raj relation : An experience of gram panchayat level. *Indian Journal of Political Science,* V. 39(2) April-June, 1978, 228-39.

Mishra, S.S. : Police and politics. Central Police Training College, Abu. 10th Advanced Course, Jan-June 1965.

Misra, S.C. : Control of police. *Sardar Vallabhhhai Patel National Police Academy Magazine,* November, 1978, 40-47.

Misra, S.C. : Police administration in India. Mt. Abu, National Police Academy, 1970.

Misra, S.C. : Rule of law. *Seminar* No. 252, August, 1980, 17-20.

Misra, Sharad Chandra : Police administration in India. Hyderabad, National Police Academy, 1972.

Misra, Surat and Arora, J.C. : A survey of public complaints in selected urban police stations of Delhi. *Police Research and Development, Quarter III*, July-September 1980, 1-10.

More, Harry, W. : History of police management thought. *Police Journal*, V. 52(2) April-June, 1979, 181-96.

More on Left Front and the police. *Economic and Political Weekly*, V. 14(46) 17 November, 1979, 1873-74.

More powers for police raj. *Economic and Political Weekly*, V. 14(44) 3 November, 1979, 1778.

Morgan, Rod : Police consultative groups : The implications for the governance of the police. *Political Quarterly*, V. 57(1) January-March, 1986, 83-88.

Moriarty, C.C.H. : Police procedure and administration. London, Butterworth, 1955.

Mukerjee, Dilip : Police and politicians : Need for new relationship. *Times of India*, 7 August, 1969, 6.

Mukerjee, I. : Better utilisation of manpower in the police. *Indian Police Journal*, V. 31(4) October-December, 1984, 27-31.

Murray, Joseph A. : Police administration and criminal investigation. New York, Arco, 1968.

Mylonas, Anastrassios D. : Perception of police power : A study in four cities. *Criminal Law Education and Research Centre, Management Series*, V. 8, 1973, 131.

Namboodiripad, E.M.S. : Right Communist : Kerala Congress govt's police policy (editorial). *People's Democracy*, V. 5(47) 23 November, 1969, 8.

Nandy, Raj : Police: A management failure. *Indian Express*, 11 July, 1979, 11.

Narasimhan, C.V. : Accountability. *Seminar*, No. 218, October, 1977, 30-32.

Narsimha, C.B. : Police and elections. *Police Research and Development, Quarter I*, January-March 1990, 5-7.

Narayan, S. : Movements development : Police and judiciary in tribal world. New Delhi, Inter-India Publications, 1988.

Narayana, M.K. : Problems of the police under conflicting systems of government. Central Police Training College, Abu, Fifth Advanced Course, June-December 1962.

Nath, T. : Law and order : A fresh look. *Hindustan Times*, 2 March, 1980.

Nath, T. : Orders for police to obey : The test or legality. *Hindustan Times*, 14 May, 1978, 1.

Nath, T. : Police administration and emergency. *INFA Feature*, 24 December, 1975.

Nath, T. : Police and panchayats (Paper). In 5th Police Science Congress, Nainital, 1966.

Nath, Trilok : Indian police administration : Guide for public officers. New Delhi, Sterling Publishers, 1984.

National Police Academy : Police : Strength and cost (A syndicate study, 16th Advanced Course, January-July 1968). *Transactions of the National Police Academy*, November 1969, 76-98.

National Police Academy : Role of supervisory officers in police administration (Report of syndicate). *Transactions of the Central Police Training College*, November, 1964, 21-52.

Nayar, Kuldip : Existing police culture under attack. *Indian Nation*, August 1983, 4.

Noorani, A.G. : Centre and law and order. *Indian Express*, December 26, 1986.

Noorani, A.G. : Governmennt, police and citizen. *Indian Express*, 14 February, 1974, 4.

Noorani, A.G. : Government, police and citizen. *Public Administration*, January 1974, 15.

Noorani, A.G. : People, their police and the politician. *Janata*, V. 30(1) 26 January, 1975, 35-36.

Noorani, A.G. : Police accountability. *Indian Express*, 12 March, 1981, 6.

Noorani, A.G. : Police and government. *Indian Express*, 29 July, 1977, 4.

Noorani, A.G. : Police and its legal accountability. *Economic and Political Weekly*, V. 18(51) 17 December, 1983, 2155.

Noorani, A.G. : Policemen obeying their superiors. *Economics and Political Weekly*, V. 17(3) 16 January, 1982, 59-60.

Not for lack of powers. *Economic and Political Weekly*, V. 13(35) 2 September, 1978, 1487.

Orissa: Demoralisation in police. *Link*, V. 23(25) 1 February 1981, 23.

Osterloh, William J. : Police supervisory practice. New York, John Wiley, 1975.

Pal, Bulbul : We have destroyed our police. *Indian Express* (*Mag.*) 5 September, 1982, 5.

Palkhivala, A. : Maintenance of law and order. *Decision*, V. 13(3) July, 1986, 198.

Pandey, A.K. : Development administration and the local police. Delhi, Mittal Publications, 1987.

Panel for politicians keeping off police. *Times of India*, 25 August, 1979, 1.

Panzarella, Robert : Management versus policing by objectives. *Police Journal*, V. 57(2) April-June, 1984, 110-28.

Parker, K.A.L. : Constitutional structure of the metropolitan police. *Police Journal*, V. 53(4) October-December, 1980, 324-339.

Parker, K.A.L. : Constitutional structure of the metropolitan police. *Police Journal*, V. 54(1) January-March, 1981, 8-21.

Plehwe, R. : Some aspects of the constitutional status of Australian police force. *Public Administration* (*Australia*), Septembr 1973, 268-85.

Police : A law unto themselves. *Economic and Political Weekly*, V. 17(22) 29 May, 1982, 900.

Police : A symposium on the problems of law and order in a democracy. *Seminar*, No. 218, October, 1977, 10-47.

Police chief. *Link*, V. 20(10) 16 October, 1977, 20-21.

Police finance administration. *Indian Journal of Public Administration*, V. 24(1) January-March, 1978, 268-73.

Police record. *Link*, V. 13(20) 27 December, 1970, 20-21.

Police told : Get ready to liquidate opposition parties at election time. *New Age*, V. 14(43) 23 October, 1966, 5.

Police under Left Front government. *Economic and Political Weekly*, V. 17(50) 11 December, 1982, 1985.

Police urged to act as guardian of poor. *Times of India*, 18 November, 1975, 4.

Policed democracy (Editorial). *Economic and Political Weekly*, V. 28(12) 24 March, 1973, 573.

Politicisation is good for the top. *Economic and Political Weekly*, V. 16(47) 21 November, 1981, 1879-80.

Police lapses. *Link*, V. 12(19) 21 December, 1969, 17.

Prasadrao, V.G. : Police and politics in Tamil Nadu. *Times of India*, 9 June, 1984, 8.

Prasad, Surat : New prosecution set-up. *Indian Police Journal*, V. 26(2) October-December, 1979, 56-65.

Prasher, Rajender : Police administration : Organization and structure, recruitment and training, unionism and public relations. New Delhi, Deep and Deep Publications, 1986.

Priyadarshi, Ashok : Of handcuffs and fetters. *Hindustan Times*, July 21, 1991, 7.

Program budgeting for police departments. *Yale Law Journal*, March, 1967, 822-38.

Qaudri, S.M. Afzal and Wani, Abdul Latif : Police, politics and discretion with special reference to Jammu and Kashmir State. *Indian Journal of Criminology*, V. 16(1) January, 1988, 15-20.

Rajgopal, P.R. : Indian police-I : Rot has set in. *Hindustan Times*, April 5, 1989, 7.

Rajgopal, P.R. : Indian police-II : Rot has set in. *Hindustan Times*, April 6, 1989.

Rajgopal, P.R. : Perils of politicising the police. *Indian Express*, 15 February, 1989, 8.

Ramachandran, D. : Case for a functional rearrangement of police sub-units district police administration (Paper). In 5th Police Science Congress, Nainital, 1966.

Ramakant : District police administration. Unpublished M. Phil. Dissertation, Meerut University, 1984.

Ramana Reddy, K.V. : Politician and policeman. *Frontier*, 7th January, 1978, 12-14.

Ramanna, K.G. : Police forces of India and their cost: A preliminary note. *Transactions of the Central Police Training College*, October, 1962, 1-7.

Rao, K.V. : (A) Note on managerial approach to police administration. *Journal of the Society for the Study of State Governments*, July-December, 1972, 260-65.

Rao, K.V. : Police administration. *Journal of the Lal Bahadur Shastri Academy of Administration*, Spring, 1973—127-47.

Rao, S.V. : Police administration. New Delhi, Indian Institute of Public Administration, 1982.

Rao, V.G. Prasad : Police and politics in Tamil Nadu. *Times of India*, 9 June, 1984, 8.

Rath, R. : Police and socio-political order. *Decision*, V. 13(3) July, 1986, 165-68.

Ravindra, Kumar : Police raj. Why not? *Statesman*, 17 July, 1981, 1.

Ray, Amal : Police administration and Centre-state relations in India. *Indian Journal of Public Administration*, V. 24(1) January-March, 1978, 38-44.

Reddy, G. Sreenivas and Reddy, M. Gopinath : Some legislation and police. *Mainstream*, V. 22(21) 21 January, 1984, 12-14.

Reed, Bill : Issues and trends in police discretion. *C.B.I. Bulletin*, V. 15(7) July, 1981, 7-9.

Regan, D.E. : Financing the role of police committees. *Public Administration*, V. 61(1) Spring, 1983, 97-109.

Regan, D.E. : Police service : An extreme example of central control over local authority staff. *Public Law*, Spring, 1966, 13-24.

Reiner, R. : Politics of the police. Brighton, Wheatsheat, 1985.

Reiner, Robert : Police rules, O.K. *Contemporary Review*, V. 231 (1338) July, 1977, 17-21.

Report of the working group on police administration. Administrative reforms commission, Nasik, Government of India Press, 1970.

Reporter, G.T. : Goa police : Inefficient or inexperienced? *Goa Today*, V 11(3) October, 1976, 9.

Riccio, Lucius C. : Future of policing. London, Sage Publications, 1978.

Roberg, Ray R. : Improving the quality of police work environments, *C.B.I. Bulletin*, V. 15(12) December, 1981, 6-8.

Roberg, Ray R. and Kirchoff, Judith Johnson : Management trauma in a small city police department : A case study. *Journal of Police Science and Administration*, V. 9(3) September, 1981, 85-95.

Ruchelman, L. (ed.) : Who rules the police? New York, University Press, 1973.

Rustamji, K.F. : Law and order and political uncertainty. *Mainstream*, V. 18(1 6) (Annual Number), 1979, 49.

Rustamji, K F. : Law without justice, order without method. *Indian Express* (*Mag.*), 1 July, 1984, 1.

Rustamji, K.F. : Police collapse in the capital. *Indian Express*, 15 November, 1984, 6.

Rustamji, K.F. : (The) Problem. *Seminar*, No. 218, October 1977, 10-13.

Rustamji, K.F. : What's behind police inefficiency : Excessive political pressures. *Decan Herald*, 4 August, 1989, 6.

Saha, B,P. : Interferences and police administration. *Indian Police Journal*, V. 32(2) April-June, 1985, 15-18.

Saha, B.P. : Who is to blame for the growing violence : Power hungry politician and a plaint police. *Telegraph*, 24 Aug., 1990, 6.

Saha, Sisir Ranjan : Calcutta city police administration : Some problems. *Indian Police Journal*, April-June, 1973, 23-26.

Saksena, N.S. : Enfeeblement of Punjab police. *Times of India*, 21 June, 1983, 6.

Saksena, N.S. : Indian police impartial : No evidence to question credenlials, *Times of India*, 9 October, 1980, 6.

Saksena, N.S. : Law and order in India. New Delhi, Abhinav Publications, 1987.

Saksena, N.S. : Need to boost low police morale. *Times of India*, October 1, 1991, 6.

Saksena, N.S. : Neglect of police stations. *C.B.I. Bulletin*, June, 1976, 1-4.

Saksena, N.S. : Police budgets grow by leaps and bounds. *Times of India*, 13 March, 1987, 6.

Saksena, N.S. : Politicians and police. *Statesman*, July 21, 1981, 8.

Saksena, N.S. : Politicians and the police, *Times of India*, 31 October, 1979, 8.

Saksena, N.S. : Politicians and police. Lessons of the Karnataka controversy. *Statesman*, 21 July, 1981, 6.

Saksena, N.S. : Politics of lawlessness. *Times of India*, 7 June, 1984.

Saksena, N.S. : Refusal of police to register and investigate cognizable crimes. *Decision*, V. 13(3) July, 1981, 209-16.

Saksena, N.S. : Some contradictions in the administrative system in India. *Indian Police Journal*, V. 30(1) July-September, 1983, 12-15.

Saksena, R.N. : Commentaries on U.P. police regulations as amended up-to-date. Allahabad, Central Law Agency, 1962.

Salvi, R.G. : Co-ordination of the work of correctional judicial and police officers. *Metcalf House Journal*, January 1958, 67.

Sastry, B.S. : Planning for law and order. *Sardar Vallabhbhai Patel National Police Academy Magazine*, July 1976, 93-101.

Sattrav : Law, order and inflation. *Free Press Journal*, 28 January, 1980.

Schubert, Frank A. : Police policy and rule making : The need for definition. *Journal af Police Science and Administration*, V. 9(3) September, 1981, 261-71.

Sebastian, P.A. : State and the police. *Economic and Political Weekly*, V. 23(43) 22 October, 1988, 2210-11.

Selke, William L. and Pepinsky, Harold E. : Politics of police reporting in Indianapolis, 1948-1978. *Law and Human Behaviour*, V. 6(3-4) 1982, 327-42.

Sen, Gouri : Working conditions. *Seminar*, No. 252, August, 1980, 28-31.

Sen, Sankar : Police forced to be bullies. *Amrita Bazar Patrika*, 20 July, 1982, 6.

Sen, Sankar : Role of the police supervisors. *Amrita Bazar Patrika*, 30 April, 1982, 6.

Sen, Sankar : Role of the police supervisors. *Indian Police Journal*, V. 29(1) July-September, 1982, 2-5.

Sengupta, Sunita Singh : Police work culture : A pilot survey. *Denouement*, V. 2(6 & 7) January-February, 1991, 37-42.

Sethi, N K. and Kakkar, Jagdish C. (eds.) : Administration of law and order. Jaipur, Rajasthan Regional Branch, Indian Institute of Public Administration, 1976.

Shah, Goni Raj : Indian police. New Delhi, Cosmo Publications, 1989.

Sharma, Jyoti : Police between centre and states in India. *Political Science Review*, V. 29(1-2) January-June, 1989, 142-152.

Sharma, P.D. : Ideas and issues in police administration in India. *Journal of Political Studies*, V. ?(2) January 1980, 157-177.

Sharma, P.D. : Law and order administration in India. Administrative challenges of the 1970s. *Indian Journal of Public Administration*, V. 18(4) 1971, 754-85.

Sharma, P.D. : Police administration in the states. *Indian Journal of Public Administration*, V. 22(3) July-September, 1976, 495-514.

Sharma, P.D. : Police and political order in India. New Delhi, Research Publications, 1984.

Sharma, P.D. : Secrecy needs in police administration. *Indian Journal of Public Administration*, V. 25(4) October-December.

Sharma, Prabhu Datta : Law and order administration: Some basic issues. *Prashashika*, April-June, 1974, 7-27.

Sharma, Prabhu Datta : Police administration, democracy and federalism in India, *Political Science Review*, V. 11(1) January-March, 1972, 43-67.

Sharma, Prabhu Datta : Police-panchayati raj relations : A case study in Rajasthan. *Political Science Review*, V. 13(1-4) January-December, 1974, 209-39.

Sharma, Surendra: Indian police: A developmental approach: A review article (on P.D. Sharma's Book "Indian police : A developmental approach"). *Administrator*, V. 22(2-3) Summer-Autumn, 1977, 1009-11.

Shatrugna, M. : Police rule continues. *Economic and Political Weekly*, V. 18(29) 16 July, 1983, 1262.

Singh, Balwant : Perspective on police, crime, law and order—2000. *Police Research and Development, Quarter III*, 1985, 1-8.

Singh, Balwant : Police and rural development. *Indian Police Journal*, V. 29(3) January-March, 1983, 28-29.

Singh, C.P. : A syndicate study on determination of yardsticks for measuring police efficiency. *Transactions*, V. 33, 1988, 192-227.

Singh, C.P. : A syndicate study on the cause of imbalance in the growth of civil and armed police wings, if any, since independence—restriction on remedial measures. *Transactions*, V. 32, 1981, 1-64.

Singh, K.K. and Arun Kumar : Police admit failure n nabbing criminal. *Times of India*, June 1, 1991, 1.

Singh, N.K. : Central police organisation : Whether separate cadre of I.P.S. necessary? *Indian Police Journal*, V. 32(2) January-March, 1985, 39-44.

Singh, P.N. : Possibility of immediate enhancement of the mobility of policemen within the current financial resources. *Police Research and Development, Quarter III*, July-September, 1983, 5-14.

Singh, Pratap : A syndicate study on policing in tribal areas. *Transactions*, V. 27, 1978, 167-224.

Singh, Sunita : Pressure on police administration : A conceptual framework. *Indian Police Journal*, V. 36(2) April-June, 1989, 12-17.

Singh, Ujjal : Custodians of law and order. *Madras Information*, V. 23(1) January, 1969, 3-4.

Singhvi, G.C. : Control police organisations and the Indian police service cadres. *Journal of Lal Bahadur Shastri Nat. Acad. Adm.*, V. 20(4) Winter, 1975, 1235-43.

Singhvi, G.C. : Credibility gaps in crime record convictions and releases. *Police Research and Development, Quarter II*, April-June, 1976, 1-4.

Singhvi, G.C. : Evasion of cognisable crime and its impact on police administration : A reflective analysis. *Management in Government*, V. 2(3) October-December, 1970, 215-29.

Singhvi, G.C. : Examination of the role of the Union government in policing. *C.B.I. Bulletin*, V. 12(3) March 1978, 5-7.

Singhvi, G.C. : India's contemporarypolice culture. *Indian Journal of Public Administration*, V. 36(3) July-September, 1990, 580-588.

Singhvi, G.C. : National planning and police. *Indian Journal of Public Administration*, V. 17(4) October-December, 1971, 745-53.

Singhvi, G.C. : Non-registration of cognizable cases at police stations. *Police Research and Development, Quarter I*, January-March, 1984, 1-7.

Singhvi, G.C. : Police administration : A divisional dimension. *Indian Police Journal*, V. 27(4) April-June, 1981, 14-19.

Singhvi, G.C. : Police administration vis-a-vis the police Act of 1961 : An overview. *Police Research and Development, Quarter IV*, 1975, 13-16.

Singhvi, G.C. : Prosecutors in magisterial courts. *Management in Government*, V. 17 (1) April-June, 1985, 61-73.

Singhvi, G.C. : Two way flow of police officers between line jobs and staff jobs. *Indian Police Journal*, V. 30 (1) July-September, 1983, 8-11.

Singhvi, G.C. : Recent trends and developments in police administration in India. *Indian Journal of Public Administration*, V. 17 (3) July-September, 1971, 495-511.

Sinha, Arun : Police, politicians and handlums. *Economic and Political Weekly*, V. 12 (40) 1 October, 1977, 1695.

Sinha, M.K. : Administration : Then and now. *Hindustan Times*, May 12, 1991, 7.

Sinha, M.K. : Maharashtra police ordinance : A step in the wrong direction. *Indian Nation*, April 15, 1988.

Som, Nirupom : Calcutta police down the years. *Statesman*, August 24, 1980, 10.

Stevens, William K. : Punjab police are given broad powers. *New York Times*, October 8, 1983, 13.

Stollar, Hylan B. : Need for achievement in work output among policemen. *Dissertation Abstracts Internatianal*, V. 38(98) March, 1978, 4521.

Symonds, Martin : Policemen and policework : A psycho-dynamic understanding. *American Journal of Psychoanalysis*, V. 32 (2) 1972, 163-69.

Tarkende, V.M. : Police raj : The reality. *Radical Humanist*, V. 47(11) February, 1983, 3-5.

Terrill, Richard J. : Politics, government and the eighteenth century committees of inquiry into the police of metropolitan London. *Police Journal*, April-June, 1980, 110-23.

Texas University. Institute of Public Afairs : Municipal police administration in Texas : A survey. Austin, Institute of Public Affairs, 1960.

Thomas, J.L : Police administration. London, Police Review, 1953.

Toch, Hans : Police, prisons and the problem of violence. Maryland, National Institute of Mental Health, 1977.

Tripathi, K.P. Police and law and order. *Searchlight*, 1 June, 1983, 4.

Tripathi, Srinivas : Politicians and police patronise goondas in U.P. *New Age*, V. 20(12) 23 March, 1980, 5-6.

Tripathy, A B. : Effective automation of records system. *Police Research and Development, Quarter III*, July-September, 1982, 1-5.

Trivedi, Harshad R. : Socio-cultural dimensions of police administration. *Indian Journal of Public Administration*, V. 24(1) January-March, 1978, 21-30.

Trivedi, J.P. : City police administration. *Indian Police Journal*, April 1973, 41-44.

Tuli, Vinod : Compensation to victims of crime : A condensation. *Police Reasearch and Development, Quarter III*, July-September 1979, 1-5.

Tuli, Vinod : Functional division of work in police station. *Police Research and Development, Quarter I*, January-March. 1982, 11.

Turner, David R. : Police administrative aide. New York, Arco, 1974.

Upadhyay, B.B. : Police process, concept, structure and function. *C.B.I. Bulletin*, V. 12(2) February, 1978, 4-6.

Vanagunas, Stanley : Police budget crunch : Problem or opportunity. *International Journal of Public Administration*, V. 3(3) 1981, 331-54.

Varghese, A. : Constables : Our weakest link. *National Police Academy Magazine*, November, 1972, 27-36.

Veerabhadriah, H. : An insight into police administration. In G.S. Halappa (ed.) : Studies in State Administration. Dharwar, Karnatak University, 1970, 229-42.

Venkatarangaiya, M. : Impact of politics on the rule of law. In G. Ram Reddy and K. Seshadri (eds.) : Developing society and police, Hyderabad, Osmania University, 1972, 13-20.

Venugopal Rao, S. : Police accountability : Need for reform. *Indian Express*, 26 August 1978.

Verma, K.R.P. : Statistically assigning weights to the factors worth considering for determining allocation of man-power in patrolling (Paper). In Second All India Police Science Congress, Bombay, September 1961.

Verma, Kapil : U.P. steps to improve working of police. *Hindustan Times*, 11 February, 1976.

Verma, Nalin : Wanted : A modern police force. *Hindustan Times*, September 15, 1991, 4.

Vogel, Jostua H. : Police station's planning and specifications. Washington (D.C.), University of Washington Press, 1964.

Vohra, K.B. : A syndicate study on the problems of policing and administering the tribals. *Transactions*, V. 22, April 1976, 35-86.

Vohra, V.K. : Decision making in police. *Transactions*, V. 26, 1978, 126-159.

Wagh, M.H. : Police administration in a welfare state (Paper). In Second All India Police Science Congress, Bombay, September, 1961.

Wagoner, Cart P. : Organizational structure and police alienation Unpublished Ph. D. dissertation, Deptt. of Sociology, Indiana University, 1971.

Wagoner, Corl R. : Police alienation : Some sources and implications. *Journal of Police Science and Administration*, V. 4(4) 1976, 389-403.

Watts, K.L. : Policeman's predicament : Oath or allegiance to the constitution (Paper). In 7th Police Science Congress, 1968, Jaipur.

Welsh, Laurance : Management in police : Can it be more human and more efficient? *Police Journal*, July-September, 1971, 58-60.

West Bengal government move to ensure safety of policemen. *Times of India*, 15 September, 1970, 9.

Wheatley, Lord : Police and the law. *Police Journal*, July-September, 1975, 179-90.

Whisenand, Paul M. : Police supervisions : Theory and practice. Englewood Cliffs (N.J.), Prentice Hall, 1976.

Whisenand, Paul M. and Ferguson, R. Fred : Managing of police organisations. Englewood Cliffs, N.J., Prentice Hall, 1978.

Whitrod, R.W. : Police administration : The response to change. *Australian Journal of Public Administration*, V. 37(3) Sep tember, 1978, 235-99.

Whitrod, R.W. : Thoughts on the introduction of a police administration grade. *Public Administration* (*Australia*), June, 1960, 121-33.

Who is demoralising police (Editorial). *Mainstream*, V. 18 (48) 26 July, 1980, 1-2.

Whose law, whose order (Editorial). *Janata*, V. 36 (36) 8 November, 1981, 1-2.

Why the force is restive. *Illustrated Weekly of India*, V. 104(13) 2 March, 1983, 11-12.

Wilcox, A.F. : Nationalising the police. *Local Government Chronicle*, 5684, 5 March, 1976, 218-19.

Wilson, James Q. : Dilemmas of police administration. *Public Administration Review*, September-October, 1968, 407-17.

Wilson, James Q. : Emerging patterns in American police administration. *Police Journal*, April-June, 1973, 1955-66.

Wilson, O.W. : Police administration. New York, McGraw Hill Book Company, 1963.

Wilson, O.W. : Police records : Their installation and use. Chicago, Public Administration Service, 1942.

Wilson, O.W. and Mc Laren, Roy Clinton : Police administration. New York, McGraw Hill, 1963.

Wilson, Roy A. : Police administration in Australia. *Police Magazine*, May-June 1971, 44-50.

Yadava, R.S. : In defence of Indian police. *Radical Humanist*, V. 48(2) May, 1983, 16-19.

8

Police Uniform

Blakeslee, Fred Gilbert : Police uniforms of the world. Hollywood (Calif), The Author, 1934.

Cramer, Games : Uniforms of the world police with brief data on organisation, system and weapons. Springfield (Ill), Charles. C. Thomas, 1968.

Mauro, Robert : Constables new clothes : Effects of uniforms on perceptions and problems of police officers. *Journal of Applied Social Psychology*, V. 14(1) January-February, 1984, 42-56.

Mishra, Ashutosh : Discrimination in uniforms. *Times of India*, August 12, 1989, 8.

Tanzel, James H. and Cizanckas, Victor : The uniforms experiment. *Journal of Police Science and Administration*, V. 1(4) December, 1973, 421-24.

Webb, J. : Badge. Englewook Cliffs (N.J.), Prentice-Hall, 1958.

9

Police Personnel

Adlam, K. Robert : Police personality : Psychological consequences of being a police officer. *Journal of Police Science and Administration*, V. 10(3) September 1982, 344-49.

Akbar, M.J. : Year of the policeman. *Sunday*, January, 1978, 15.

Alexander, P.J. : Electoral process and police behaviour : A case of study of bye-elections in a state. *Indian Journal of Public Administration*, V. 26(2) April-June, 1980, 278-302.

Ananthachari, T. : Conduct of the police personnel in the society. *Indian Police Journal*, V. 29(1) July-September, 1982, 34-40.

Anstey, Edgar : Staff development in the police service. *Police Journal*, July, 1964, 308-13.

Applegate, James L. (and others) : Interpersonal constructs and communicative ability in a police environment : A preliminary investigation. *International Journal of Personal Conduct Psychology*, V. 2(4) Fall, 2989, 185-99.

Arcaya, Jose M. : Police and the emotionally disturbed : A psychoanalytic theory of intervention. *International Journal of Offender Therapy and Comparative Criminology*, V. 33(1) April, 1984, 37-48.

Arcuri, Alan F. : Police pride and self-esteem : Indications of future occupational changes. *Journal of Police Science and Administration*, V. 4(4) December, 1976, 436-44.

Arul, F.V. : Musings of a retired police officer. In S.K. Ghosh (ed.) : Police Administration : Reminiscences. New Delhi, Ashish Publishing House, 1989, 1-4.

Ashton, Nancy L. and Lester, David : Helping behaviour in police officers and reasons for choice of career. *Psychological Reports*, V. 51(3, part 2) December, 1982, 1126.

Austin, Thomas L., Hale, Donna C. and Ramsey, Lola J. : Effect of layoff on police authoritarianism. *Criminal Justice and Behaviour*, V.14(2) June, 1987, 194-210.

Bahn, Charles : Police socialization in the eighties : Strains in the forging of an occupational identity. *Journal of Police Science and Administration*, V. 12(4) December, 1984, 390-94.

Balch, David E. : Performance rating systems : Suggestions for the police. *Journal of Police Science and Administration*, V. 2(1) March, 1974, 40-49.

Banerjee, Sumanta : Rights of policemen in a democracy. *Decision*, V. 13(3) July , 1986, 179-82.

Banerji, B.B. : Popular police officer. *National Police Academy Magazine*, November, 1968, 9-12.

Banton, Michael : Labour-management relations in an American police department. *Police Journal*, October-December 1972, 302-11.

Barocas, Marvey A. : Latrogenic and preventive intervention in police family crisis situations. *International Journal of Social Psychology*, V. 20(1-2) Spring-Summer, 1974, 113-21.

Batrol, Curt R. : Psychological characteristics of small town police officers. *Journal of Police Science and Administration*, V. 10(1) March, 1982, 58-63.

Bayley, David H. : Forces of order : Police behaviour in Japan and the United States. Barkeley (Calif), University of California Press, 1976.

Bayley, David H. : Tactical choices of police patrol officers. *Journal of Criminal Justice*, V. 14(4) 1986, 329-348.

Bennett, Richard R. : Becoming blue : A longitudinal study of police recruit occupational socialization. *Journal of Police Science and Administration*, V. 12(1) March, 1984, 47-58.

Bertram, Francis D. : Prediction of police academy performance and on the job performance from police recruit screening measures. *Dissertation Abstracts International*, V. 36(10-A) April, 1976, 65-43.

Bhan, Kiran Sumbali and Puri, Kiran : A study of values of new entrants to police force. *Police Research and Development, Quarter II*, April-June, 1985, 5-7.

Bhanot, M.L. : Economisation of manpower through modernisations : Case study of the Delhi police. *Police Research and Development Journal, Quarter* II, April-June, 1977, 1-22.

Black, Donald : Manners and customs of the police. New York, Academic Press, 1980.

Bloom, Joseph D. (and others) : Lifetime police contracts of discharged psychiatric security review board clients. *International Journal of Law and Psychiatry*, V. 8(2) 1986, 189-202.

Brief, Arthur P. (and others) : Correlates of supervisory style among policemen. *Criminal Justice and Behaviour*, V. 3(3) 1976, 263-271.

Brief, Arthur P. (and others) : Leader behaviour in a police organisation revisited. *Human Relations*, V. 34(12) December, 1981, 1037-51.

Broderick, John : Law, order and the police : A study of factors that influence police attitudes. *Dissertation Abstract International*, V. 34 (1-A) July, 1973, 421-22.

Burgin, Asbury L. : Organizational socialization in the induction of new police officers. *Dissertation Abstracts International*, V. 35(11-B) May, 1975, 5691-92.

Burke, Ronald J. : Career orientations and type A behaviour in police officers. *Psychological Reports*, V. 57 (3 part 2) December, 1985, 1239-1246.

Burke, Ronald J. : Career stages, satisfaction and well-being among police officers. *Psychological Reports*, V. 62(1) August, 1989, 3-12.

Burke, Ronald J. and Deszca, Eugene : Changes in career orientations in police officers : An exploratory study. *Psychological Reports*, V. 61(2) October, 1987, 515-26.

Burke, Ronald J. and Deszca, Eugene : Correlates of psychological burnout phases among police officers. *Human Relations*, V. 39(6) June, 1986, 487-501.

Burke, Ronald J. (and others) : Correlates of burnout phases among police officers. *Group & Organization Studies*, V. 9(4) December, 1984, 451-66.

Buzawa, Evas : Determining patrol officer job satisfaction : Role of selected demographic and job specific attitudes. *Criminology : An Interdisciplinary Journal*, V. 22(1) February, 1984, 61-81.

Carlson, Helena M. and Sutton, Markleys : Some factors in community evaluation of police street performance. *American Journal of Community Psychology*, V. 7(6) December, 1979, 583-91.

Carlson, Helena M. : Psychological and situational factors involved in the evaluation of police performance. *Dissertation Abstracts International*, V. 36(12-B, Part 1) June, 1976, 6440.

Chary, S. Saminath : Some problems of police constables : An empirical study. *Journal of State Police and Administration*, V. 1(1) January-June, 1978, 74-80.

Chaturvedi, J.N. : Humanizing the police. *Statesman*, 23 October, 1979.

Check, James V. and Klein, John, F. : The personality of the American police : A review of the literature. *Crime & Justice*, V. 5(1) May, 1977, 33-46.

Cherry, Thelma M. and Lester David : An exploratory study of police officers' satisfaction in marriage. *Psychological Reports*, V. 45(3) December, 1979, 794.

Chusmir, Leonard H. : Motivational need pattern for police officers. *Journal of Police Science and Administration*, V. 12(2) June, 1984, 141-45.

Cochran, Nancy : Dogmastism and social control : Some personality characteristics of police officers. *Personality and Social Psychology Bulletin*, V. 1(1) 1974, 213-15.

Cohen, Bernard and Chaiken, Jan M. : Police background characteristics and performance. Lexington (Ma), Lexington Books, 1973.

Colman, A. : Attitudes of British police officers : A rejoinder. *Sociology*, V. 17(3) 1983.

Colman, A. and Gorman, P. : Conservatism, dogmatism and authoritarianism in British police officers. *Sociology*, V. 16(1), 1982.

Consul, S C. : Law relating to police personnel in India. Delhi, Metropolitan, 1965.

Cooper, Cary L. and Bradshaw, Keith : An assessment of the social skills of police officers. *Journal of Management Studies*, October, 1975, 523-27.

Cooper, Cary L. (and others) : A psychometric profile of British police officers authorized to carry firearms : A pilot study. *International Review of Applied Psychology,* V. 35(4) October, 1986, 539-546.

Coppolino, Joseph S. : An investigation of the value systems of police and non-police and their relationship to the perception of values and events in one episode of a television series about the police. *Dissertation Abstracts International,* V. 37(2-A) August, 1975, 672.

Corrigan, Roberts S. (and others) : Superstition in police officers. *Psychological Reports,* V. 46(3 part 1) June, 1980, 830.

Cutter, A.H. : Metropolitan police cadet force. *Police Journal,* November, 1966, 554-61.

Dhillon, K.S. : Attitudinal change in police. *Indian Police Journal,* V. 28(1) July-September, 1981, 26-30.

Diaz, S.M. : Man management (Paper). In 5th Police Science Congress, Nainital, 1966.

Diaz, S.M. : Police expectations, perceptions and attitude to public in India. *Indian Journal of Criminology,* V. 17(1) January, 1989, 42-52.

Dietrich, Joseph F. and Janette, Smith : Nonmedical use of drug including alcohol among police personnel : A critical literature review. *Journal of Police Science and Administration* V. 14(4) December, 1986, 300-306.

Drucker, Marvin and Goldstein, George : A mental health consultation programme to the police. *Psychiatric Hospital,* V. 14(4) Fall, 1983, 225-28.

Eisenberg, Terry (and others) : Police personnel practices in State and local governments. Philadelphia, Free Police Foundation, 1973.

Ellis, Duke E. : A study of police attitudes. *Dissertation Abstract International,* V. 33(9-B) March, 1973, 4502-03.

Elmes, Frank : Police as a career, London, Batsford, 1962.

Epstein, C. : Intergroup relations for police officers. Baltimore, Williams. 1962.

Fabricatore, Joseph M. and Dash, Jerry : Suicide, divorce and psychological health among police officers. *Essence,* V. 1(4), 1977, 225-31.

Fagan, Ronald W. : Police attitudes toward capital punishment. *Journal of Police Service and Administration*, V. 14(3) September, 1986, 193-201.

Farah, S.A. : Agony of police in Bihar, Patna. A.T.S., C.I.D.

Farah, S.A. : Agony of policing : My years in the C.I.D. *Indian Nation*, June 27, 1988, 4.

Farah, S.A. : Bonded labour in uniform. *Indian Nation*, 8 May, 1988.

Fatima, Biloees and Qureshi, Afzal : Power motive, hope of power and fear of power among male and female police personnel. *Indian Journal of Criminology*, V. 12(1) January, 1984, 55-57.

Fenster, C. Abraham and Locke, Bernard : Neuroticism among policemen : An examination of police personality. *Journal of Applied Psychology*, V. 57 (3) June, 1973, 358-59.

Fenster, C. Abraham and Locke, Bernard : The "dump cop" : Myth or reality ? An examination of police intelligence. *Journal of Personality Assessment*, V. 37(3) June, 1973, 276-81.

Fernandes, Allwyn : Bombay police motivation. *Times of India*, 11 August, 1980.

Fielding, Nigel : Police socialization and police competence. *British Journal of Sociology*, V. 35(4) December, 1984, 568-90.

Forcese, Dennis and Copper, Joseph : Police retirement : career succession or obsolescence ? *Candian Police College Journal*, V. 9(4) 1985, 413-24.

Frees, Lewis E. : Police behaviour as a function of individual, organizational and community structures. *Dissertation Abstracts International*, V. 36(4-B) October, 1975, 1965-66.

Gangopadhyay, Abhijit : A syndicate study on group morale and job involvement of the subordinate ranks of police. *Transactions*, V. 32, 1981, 124-280.

Gangopadhyay, Abhijit : A syndicate study on ranking of jobs factors and level of jobs satisfactions among subordinate ranks of police. *Transactions*, V. 31, 1988, 117-231.

Gangopadhyay, Abhijit : A syndicate study on value system in the subordinate ranks of police. *Transactions*, V. 34, 1981, 57-127.

Germann, A.C. : Police personnel management. Springfield (III), Charles C. Thomas, 1958.

Ghosh, S.K. : Police in ferment. New Delhi, Light and Life Publications, 1981.

Gibbons, Thomas J. Policemen awards. *Police Chief*. 27 April, 1960.

Gocke, B.W. : Morale in a police department. *Journal of Criminal Law and Criminology*, September-October, 1945.

Goldstein, Harman : Guidelines of effective use of police manpower, *Public Management*, October 1963, 218-22.

Gourley, G. Douglas : Recognition and status for rank in fire policemen. *Journal of Criminal Law and Criminolagy*, May-June, 1949.

Grant, Michael G. : Relationship of moonlighting to job dissatisfaction in police officers. *Journal of Police Science and Administration*, V. 5(2) June, 1977, 193-96.

Gudjonsson, Gisti H. and Adlam, K.R. : Personality patterns of British police officers. *Personality and Individual Differences*, V. 4(5) 1983, 507-12.

Gupta, Smita and Subramanian, Vidya : A raw deal for the policemen. *Indian Express*, 1 July, 1984, 1.

Hadar, Ilana : Occupational socialization of policemen. *Dissertation Abstracts International*, V. 37(1-B) July, 1976, 438.

Hall, M.F. : Man management theories and the police. *Police Journal*, August, 1968, 387-92.

Hallett, Hugh V. : Police service of England and Wales. *International Police Academy Review*, October 1974, 15-20.

Henewig, Wayne B. : Police personality : A Jungian perspective. *Crime and Delinquency*, V. 74(2) April, 1978, 152-72.

Hanna, D.G. and Gentel, W.E. : Guide to primary police management concepts. Springfield, Illinois, Charles C. Thomas, 1971.

Harihar, M.S. : Humanizing the police. *Hindustan Times*, December 26, 1980, 9.

Hawkins, H.J. : Police career in France. *Police Journal*, May, 1970, 214-21.

Hayes, Colin : Police personnel evaluation : A tool of police management. *Police Journal*, V. 53(3) July-September, 1980, 266-71.

Hazer, John T. and Alvares, Kenneth M. : Police work values during organizational entry and assimilation. *Journal of Applied Psychology*, V. 66(1) February, 1981, 12-18.

Heiman, Michael F. : Police suicide. *Journal of Police Science and Administration*, V. 3(3) September, 1975, 267-73.

Hendricks, Jem : Transactional analysis and the police : Family disputes. *Journal of Police Science and Administration*, V. 5(4) December, 1977, 416-20.

Herlitz, Claes and Brorsson, Bengt : Facing aids : Reactions among police officers, nurses and the general public in Sweden. *Social Science and Medicine*, V. 30(8) 1990, 913-918.

Hewitt, William H. : New directions in police personnel administration : Lateral entry and transferability of retirement credits. Lexington, Lexington Books, 1975.

Hilber, Susan B. : Social isolation among police officers. *Dissertation Abstracts International*, V. 39(11-A) May 1979, 6976.

Hogan, Robert : Personality characteristics of highly rated policemen. *Personal Psychology*, V. 21(4) Winter, 1971, 679-86.

Huang, Ming S. (and others) : Type A behaviour in the police and general population. *Journal of Psychology*, V. 115(2) November, 1983, 171-75.

Iannone, N.F. : Supervision of police personnel. Englewood Cliffs (N.J.), Prentice-Hall, 1975.

India : Central Police Training College : Centre's role in the police functions. Background papers and proceedings of the seminar held on 19th to 21st November, 1965.

India, National Police Academy, Abu : "Need for motivational techniques in police service". Background papers and proceedings of the seminar held on 15th and 16th November, 1972.

Inn, Andres and Wheeler, Alan C. : Individual differences, situational constraints, and police shooting incidents. *Journal of Applied Social Psychology,* V. 7(1) January-March, 1977, 19-26.

Iyer, T.G.L. : Personnel management in the police. *Indian Journal of Public Administration,* V. 24(1) January-March, 1978, 87-95.

Jackson, R.L. : Canadian police labour relations in the 80's : New environmental concerns. *Canadian Police College Journal,* V. 10(2) 1986, 86-138.

Jermier, John M. and Berkes, Leshe J. : Leader behaviour in a police command bureaucracy : A closer look of the quasi-military model. *Administrative Science Quarterly,* V. 24(1) March, 1979, 1-23.

Johansson, Charles B. and Elint, Robert T. : Vocational preference of policemen. *Vocational Guidance Quarterly,* V. 22(1) 1973, 40-42.

Johnson, Edward E. : Problems in assessing police and fire fighter candidates. *Journal of Police Science and Administration,* V. 12(4) December, 1984, 404-06.

Johnson, John A. and Hogan, Robert : Vocational interests, personality and effective police performance. *Personnel Psychology,* V. 34(1) Spring, 1981, 49-53.

Jones, J. Mervyn : Organizational aspects of police behaviour. Mants, Gower Publishing Company, 1980.

Joshi, G.P.: Performance appraisal in the police. *Police Research and Development, Quarter II,* April-June, 1978, 1-20.

Joshi, G.P. (and others) : Promotion prospects of constabulary in the police. *Police Research and Development, Quarter IV,* October-December, 1990, 1-36.

Just, Clifford E. : Police organisation and the police family. *C.B.I. Bulletin,* V. 18(12) December, 1984, 8-9.

Khoury, Robert M. and Khoury, Deanna C. : Job satisfaction and work performance of police. *Psychological Reports,* V. 51(1) August, 1982, 282.

Khoury. Robert M. and Khoury, Deanna C. : Professionalization of police : A question of altruism. *Psychological Reports*, V. 49(3) December, 1981, 896-98.

Kirkham, George L. : Criminologist as a policeman : A participant observation study. In Donal E.S. Macnamara and Mare Ridel (eds.) Police : Perceptives, problems, prospects. New York, Praeger Publishers, 1964, 35-52.

Kirmeyer, Sandra L. : Observing the work of police dispatchers : work overload in service organizations. *Applied Social Psychology Annual*, V. 5, 1984, 45-66.

Kleiman, Lawrence S. and Gordon, Michael E. : An examination of the relationship between police training academy performance and job performance. *Journal of Police Science and Administration*, V. 14(4) December, 1986, 293-299.

Klockars, Carl B. : Blue lies and police placebos : The moralities of police lying. *American Behavioural Scientist*, V. 27(4) March-April, 1984, 529-44.

Knauth, P. (and others) : Time budget studies of policemen in weekly or swiftly rotating shift systems. *Applied Ergonomics*, V. 14(4) December, 1983, 247-52.

Knowles, Patrick and Paterson Rolf : Measurement of flexibility in state police officers. *Journal of Police Science and Administration*, V. 1(2) June, 1973, 219-23.

Krishnamurti, N. : Manpower utilization and performance in the police. *Sardar Vallabhbhai Patel National Police Academy Magazine*, June, 1977, 21-28.

Krishnamurti, N. : What is a policeman. *Tamil Nadu Police Journal*, January-March 1972, 29.

Krishnaswamy, N. : Performance appraisal in the police. *Indian Police Journal*, V. 25(1) July-September, 1978, 48-50.

Langer, John H. : Guidelines for school—police cooperation in drug abuse policy department. *Journal of School Health*, V. 46(4) April, 1976, 197-99.

Lanier, David D. : Personality and attitudes of Kentucky police officers. *Dissertation Abstracts International*, V. 56(3-B) September, 1975, 1441.

Lavoie, F. (and others) : Police attitudes in assigning responsibility for wife abuse. *Journal of Family Violence*, V. 4(4) December, 1989, 369-388.

Leeson, G.W. : Expected length of service in the Danish state police compared with a representative group of English forces. *Police Journal*, January-March, 1980, 113-51.

Lefkowitz, Joel : Psychological attributes of policemen : A review of research and opinion. *Journal of Social Issues*, V. 31(1) 1975.

Leitner, Dennis W. and Sedlacek, William E. : Characteristics of successful campus police officers. *Journal of College Student Personnel*, V. 17(4) July, 1976, 304-08.

Lekhi, P.N. : Time for central action to solve police problem. *Indian Express*, 11 June, 1979, 9.

Leonard, V.A. : Police personnel administration. Springfield (III), Charles C. Thomas, 1970.

Lester, David : Attitudes of police officers to rotating shifts. *Psychological Reports*, V. 59(3) December, 1986, 1090.

Lester, David : Correlates of job satisfaction in police officers. *Psychological Reports*, V. 60(2) April, 1987, 550.

Lester, David : Relationship between subscale scores of police officers on the Kuder occupational interest survey. *Psychological Reports*, V. 46(3, part 2) June, 1980, 1276.

Lester, David : Type A personality in police officers. *Psychological Reports*, V. 52(3) June, 1983, 730.

Lester, David and Genz, John L. : Internal-external locus of control experience : A police officer and job satisfaction in municipal police officers. *Journal of Police Science and Administration*, V. 6(4) December, 1978, 479-8.

Lester, David and Guerin, Thomas W. : Further explorations of police officers satisfaction with their marriages. *Psychological Reports*, V. 50(2) April, 1982, 608.

Lester, David and Nagiewicz Carol A. : Low status of campus police : A preliminary study. *Psychological Reports*, V. 47(3, part 1) December. 1980, 738.

Lester, David (and others) : Personalities of English and American police. *Journal of Social Psychology*, V. III(I), June, 1980, 153-54.

Lester, David and Sheehan, Donald : Attitude of supervisors towards short police officers. *Psychological Reports*, V. 47(2) October, 1980, 462.

Love, Kevin G. : Empirical recommendations for the use of peer ranking in the evaluation of police officer performance. *Public Personel Management*, V. 12(1) Spril, 1983, 25-32.

Loveday, Barry : Joint boards for police in the metropolitan areas : A preliminary assessment. *Local Government Studies*, V. 13(3) May-June, 1987, 85-101.

Low, Pauline, C. : Career patterns in the police service. *Police Journal*, July-September, 1974, 2-3.

Luden, Walter A. : Mobility of officers in the constabularies of Great Britain. *Police Journal*, April-June, 1977, 95-115.

Lundman, Richard J. : Police behaviour : A sociological perspective. New York, Oxford University Press, 1980.

Machell, David F. : Recovering alcoholic police officer and the danger of professional emotional suppression. *Alcoholism Treatment Quarterly*, V. 6(2) 1989, 85-95.

Macnamara, E.J. and Riedel, M. (eds.) : Police : Perspectives, problems and prospects. New York, Praeger, 1974.

Mahanta, J. and Kathpalia, V.K. : Police hierarchy and personality. *Police Research and Development, Quarter IV*, October-December, 1984, 1-2.

Malaviya, P.D. : Attitudinal changes among subordinate ranks. Souvenir. 10th Symposium of All India Principals Police Training College. Dated 22.10.1981 to 24.10.1981, Patna, 68-72.

Malaviya, P.D. : Manpower planning career development of constables in state police forces. *Transactions*, V. 24, April, 1977, 1-30.

Maniha, John K. : Structural supports for the development of professionalism among police administrators. *Pacific Sociological Review*, July, 1973, 315-43.

Marmo, Michael : Off-duty behaviour by police : Arbitrators determine. If on the job discipline is appropriate. *Journal of Police Science and Administration*, V. 14(2) June, 1986, 102-11.

Martin, J.P. and Wilson, Gil : Police : A study in manpower. London, Heinemann, 1969.

Mastrofski, Stephen : Surveying clients to assess police performance : Focusing on the police citizen encounter. *Evaluation Review*. V. 5(3) June, 1981, 397-408.

Mathur, Krishna Mohan : Erosion of police morale : Its causes, its implications for public and its cure. *Indian Police Journal*, V. 29(2) October-December, 1982, 39-44.

Mathur, Krishna Mohan : Police behaviour and the need for attitudinal changes. *Administrator*, V. 25(2) Spring, 1980, 123-42.

McCall, Padrick : A two-tier police service. *Indian Police Journal*, V. 20(4) April-June, 1974, 30-33.

Mcginnis, James H. : Career development in municipal policing, II. *Canadian Police College Journal*, V. 9(3) 1985, 254-94.

Meagher, M. Steven and Yentes, Nancy A. : Choosing a career in policing. A comparison of male and female perceptions. *Journal of Police Science and Administration*, V. 14(4) December, 1986, 320-27.

Meynell, Lourence : Policeman in the family. London, Oxford University Press, 1953.

Mills, Carol J. and Bohannon, Wayne E. : Personality characteristics of effective state police officers. *Journal of Applied Psychology*, V. 65(6), December, 1980, 680-84.

Mingle, George : Police personnel evaluation and development. *Journal of Criminal Law and Criminology*, November-December, 1945.

Moriarty, Anthony and Field, Mark W. : Proactive interventions : A new approach to police EAP programs. *Public Personnel Management*, V. 19(2) Summer, 1990, 155-161.

Mukherjee, Dilip : Cause and consequences of low morale of police. *Statesman*, 10 November, 1967, 6.

Munoz, Mona : Job satisfaction in policemen and its relation to locus to control, ego, strength and performance. *Dissertation Abstracts International*, V. 34(6-B) December, 1973, 2946-47.

Nandy, Raj : Humanizing the police : Lessons of Delhi athi charge. *Hindustan Times*, 4 April, 1980, 1.

Nandy, Raj. : Humanizing the police : Lessons of Delhi lathi charge : *Hindustan Times*, 6 April, 1980, 1.

Narasimhan, C.V. : Evaluation of police performance. *Indian Journal of Criminology*, V. 17(2) July, 1989, 85-88.

Nath, Surendra : Role of motivation in police management. *Indian Police Journal*, January-March, 1975, 5-15.

Nath, Trilok : Lesson for police : What Indian can learn from socialist countries. *Patriot* (Magazine) 9 September, 1984, I.

Nath, Trilok : Recent police rebellion : Some root question. *Patriot*, 14 July, 1979.

National Police Academy : Need for motivational techniques in police service. Working paper and proceedings of a seminar November, 1972. *National Police Academy Magazine*, November, 1973, 110-29.

Nayar, Kuldip : Humanising the police. *Indian Express*, 17 December, 1980.

Orpen, Christopher : Effect of job involvement on the work-leisure relationship : Correlational study among bank clerks and police officers. *Psychological Reports*, V. 50(2) April, 1982, 335-64.

Ostrom, Elinor : Institutional arrangements and the measurement of police consequences : Applications to evaluating police performance. *Urban Affairs Quarterly*, June, 1971, 447-75.

Ottamakn, W. (and others) : Subjective health status of day and night working policemen. *Ergonomics*, V. 32(7) July, 1989, 847-54.

Peacock, Brain : Police officer's responses to 8 and 12 hour shift schedules. *Ergonomics*. V. 26(5) May, 1983, 479-93.

Peace, K.I. : Police negotiation : A new role for the community psychiatrist. *Canadian Psychiatric Association Journal*, V. 22(4) June, 1977, 171-75.

Pillai, V. Kamnu : How to measure police productivity. *Police Research and Development, Quarter I*, January, 1983, 1-2.

Poister, Theodore H. and McDavid, James C. : Victims—evaluations of police performance. *Journal of Criminal Justice*, V. 6(2) Summer, 1978, 133-49.

Police in India : An appraisal of their performance and problem (Editorial). *Indian Journal of Criminology*, V. 7(2) July, 1979, 81-84.

Police medal for meritorious service. *Times of India*, 26 January, 1969, 14.

Powell, Dennis D. : Race, rank and police discretion. *Journal of Police Science and Administraiion*, V. 9(4) December, 1981, 383-89.

Price, Barbara Raffel : Police professionalism. Lexington, D.C. Health and Co., 1977.

Promotion policies and the concept of meritocracy. Papers presented of a seminar. Mt. Abu, National Police Academy, 1970.

Regoli, Robert M. and Poole, Eric D, : Police professionalism and role conflict : A comparison of rural and urban departments. *Human Relations*, V. 33(4) April, 1980, 241-52.

Reming, George C. : Personality characteristics of supercops and habitual criminals. *Journal of Police Science and Administratian*, V. 16(3) September, 1988, 163-67.

Reporter, G.T. : Goa police going bankrupt. *Goa Today*, V. 12(10) May, 1978, 9.

Richard, J. (ed.): Police behaviour : A sociological perspective. London. OUP, 1980.

Romies, Wayne M. : C.B.I. condensation : Morale in a small police department. *C.B.I. Bulletin*, V. 14(2) December, 1980, 8-12.

Ronan, W.W. (and others): Prediction of job performance dimensions : Police officers. *Public Personnel Management*, V. 6(3) May-June, 1977, 173-80.

Roy, B.K. : Problems of retired police officer. *National Police Academy, Magazine*, November, 1972, 9-16.

Rustamji, K.F. : Police morale : Rationale for snap transfers. *Hindustan Times*, May 7, .988.

Saathoff, Gregory B. and John, Buckman : Diagnostic results of psychiatric evaluations of state police officers. *Hospital and Community Psychiatry*, V. 41(4) April 1990, 429-432.

Saha, B.P. : Ego and policemen. *Indian Police Journal*, V. 31(4) October, 1984, 10-13.

Saha, B.P. : Indifferent performance and high expectations. *Amrita Bazar Patrika*, 3 December, 1982, 6.

Saksena, N.S. : Charges against policemen : Inquiry obligatory for government. *Times of India*, 12 June 1985, 8.

Saunders, Daniel and Size, Patricia B. : Attitude about women abuse among police officers : Victims and victim advocates. *Journal of Interpersonal Violence*, V. 1(1) 1986, 25-42.

Schnitzius, John T. and Lester, David : Police professionals and job satisfaction. *Psychological Reports*, V. 46(2) April, 1980, 402.

Seckler, Donald A. : Length of service community social relationship and perceptions of community figures : A study of police personnel. *Dissertation Abstracts International*, V. 38(12-8) June, 1978, 6170-74.

Shah, Giriraj : Police and its problem. *Indian Express*, 29 November, 1977, 6.

Shah, Jyotsna : Studies in criminology : Probation services in India. *Police Research and Development, Quarter I*, January-March, 1976, 27-28.

Sheedy, Jame E. : Contact lenses for police officers. *Journal of the American Opdometric Association*, V. 57(9) September, 1986, 658-60.

Sheehan, Donald and Lester, David : Attitudes of short versus tall police officers. *Perceptual & Motor Skills*, V. 51(3, parts 1) December 1980, 878.

Shernock, Stank : Differential significance of sworn status and organizational position in the civilization of the police communications division. *Journal of Public Science and Administration*, V. 16(4) December, 1988, 288-302.

Sherrid, Samuel D. and Beech, Robert P. : Self-dissatisfaction as a determinant of change in the police values. *Journal of Applied Psychology*, V. 61(3) June, 1976, 273-78.

Shusman, Elizabeth J., Inwald, Robin E. and Knatz, Hilary F. : A cross-validation study of police's recruit performance as predicted by the IPI and MMPI. *Journal of Police Science and Administration*, V. 15(2) June, 1987, 162-69.

Sinde, Pradeep : Will the policemen survive ? *Decision*, V. 13(3) July, 1986. 217-20.

Singh, M.P. : Police problems and dilemmas in India. New Delhi, Mittal Publications, 1989.

Singh, Pratap : A syndicate study on 'the methods of bringing on' about proper motivation in the ranks of constables and head constables. *Transactions*, V. 30, 1980, 70-125.

Singhvi, G.C. : Central police organisations and the Indian police service cadres. *Journal of the Lal Bahadur Shastri National Academy of Administration*, V. 20(4) Winter, 1975, 1235-52.

Singhvi, G.C. : Evaluation of personnel performance in police perspectives. *Indian Police Journal*, V. 31(4) October-December, 1984, 2-9.

Singhvi, G.S. : Let us have Indian police service cadres for central police organizations also. *Indian Police Journal*, V. 31(1) January-March, 1984, 3-8.

Singhvi, G.C. : Some aspects of administrative reforms in police personnel system in India (Paper). In 7th Police Science Congress, Jaipur, 1968.

Skolnick, Jerome : Police : The new professionals. *New Society*, V. 77(1236) 5 September, 1986, 9-11.

Slaane, Charles F. : Police professionalization, *Journal of Criminal Law, Criminology and Police Science*, May-June, 1954.

Slovak, Jeffry S. : Work satisfaction and municipal police officers, *Journal of Police Science and Administration*, V. 6(4) December, 1978, 462-70.

Smith, Dennis : Dangers of police professionalization : An empirical anlysis. *Journal of Criminal Justice*, V. 6(3) Fall, 1978, 199-216.

Sreenivasan, K.N. : How policemen's hardships can be mitigated. *Hindu*, 31 August, 1982, 17.

Stahl, O. Glenn and Staugen Burger (eds.) : Police personnel administration. Washington (D.C.), Police Foundation, 1975.

Steinmann, Michael : Managing and evaluating police behaviour. *Journal of Police Science and Administration*, V. 14(4) December, 1986, 285-292.

Stenmark, David E. (and others) : Wives of police officers : Issues related to family job-satisfaction and job longevity.

Journal of Police Science and Administration, V. 10(2) June, 1982, 229-34.

Sterling, Bruce S. and Osen, John W. : Perceptions of demanding versus reasoning male and female police officers. *Personality and Social Psychology Bulletin*, V. 8 (2) June, 1982, 336-40.

Sullivan, Peggys, Dunham, Roger G. and Albert, Geoffrey P. : Attitude structures of different ethnic and age groups concerning police. *Journal of Criminal Law and Criminology*, V. 78(1) Spring, 1987, 177-196.

Sundeen, Richard A. : Police professionalization and community attachment and diversion of juveniles. *Criminology : Interdisciplinary Journal*, V. 11(4) February, 1974, 570-80.

Surendra Nath : Role of motivation in police management. *Indian Police Journal*, V. 21(3) January-March, 1975, 5-15.

Symonds, Martin : Emotional hazards of police work. In A. Nieder Holler and Abraham S. Blumberg (eds.) The ambivalent force : Perspectives on the police. U.S.A., Ginn and Co., 1970, 58-64.

Taggart, Martin : Police federation. *Police Journal*, V. 51 (1) January-March, 1978, 5-17.

Thapar, Romesh : Police problems. *Economic and Political Weekly*, V. 13(36) 9 September, 1978. 1535-36.

Thomas, M.V. : Need for motivational techniques in police service. Proceedings of seminar, Mt. Abu, National Police Academy, 1972, 22-31.

Tifft, Larry L. : The cop personality reconsidered. *Journal of Police Science and Administration*, V. 2(3) September, 1974, 266-78.

Tobias, J.J. : Future challenge of police manpower. *Police Journal*, July-September, 1971, 245-56.

Topp, Bruce W. and Kardash, Carel A. : Personality achievement and attrition : Validation in a multiple-jurisdiction police academy. *Journal of Police Science and Administration*, V. 14(3) September, 1986, 234-41.

Tripathi, B.K. : Police equipment : A step towards self-reliance. *Indian Journal of Criminology and Criminalistics*, V. 1 (2-3) June-September, 1981.

Varghese, A. : Attitudes of subordinate policemen : Two syndicate studies. *Transactions*, V. 17(2) 1-38.

Venugopal Rao, S. : Lighter side of policeman's lot. *Indian Police Journal*, January-March, 1974, 32-36.

Vikas, Ranjan and Kishore, Mukesh : Job satisfaction and occupational status of police personnel. *Asian Journal of Psychology and Education*, V. 17(2) March, 1986, 18-21.

Violanti, John M. (and others) : Disease risk and mortality among police officers : New evidence and contributing factors. *Journal of Police Science and Administration*. V. 14 (1) March, 1986, 17-23.

Vogel, Ronald and Adams, Reed : Police professionalism : A longitudinal cohort study. *Journal of Police Science and Administration*, V. 11(4) December, 1983, 1174-84.

Vuchinich, Samuel : Forced retirement due to psychiatric reasons overturned. *Mental and Physical Disability Law Reporter*, V. 10(6) November-December, 1986, 556.

Vulcano, Brent A. (and others) : Prevalence of psychosomatric disorders among a sample of police officers. *Social Psychology*, V. 19(4) 1984, 181-86.

Wagle, S.N. : Tough Lot of Maharashtra policemen. *Business Standard*, 10 June, 1979, 4.

Waitrowski, Michael D. : Issues in police performance evaluation. *Police Journal*, V. 58(1) January, 1985, 49-59.

Wattier, Philippe and Frydman, Marcel : Professional issues : Liability and licensure, liability of the police. *Mental and Physical Disability Law Reporter*, V. 9(3) May-June, 1985, 207-09.

West Bengal Police : More money less morale. *Eastern Economist*, V. 74 (213) 28 March, 1980, 652.

Weston, Paul B. and Fraley, Philip K. : Police personnel administration. Englewood Cliffs (N.J.) Prentice-Hall, 1980.

Whitaker, Ben : Police quality. *New Society*, 8 July, 1965, 14-16.

Whiteside, Horold D. (and others) : Differences in attribution of responsibility by police recruits and their wives. *Psychological Reports*, V. 41 (3, pt. I) December, 1977, 950.

Who cares for police rewards ? *Indian Express*, 22 September, 1991, 5.

Wilson, George P. (and others) : State intervention and victimless crimes : A study of police attitudes. *Journal of Police Science and Administration*, V. 13(1) March, 1985, 22-29.

Wilson, James Q. : Police and their problem : A theory. In A. Niederhofter and Abraham S. Blumberg (eds.) Ambivalent Force. Perspectives on the Police. U.S.A., Ginn and Co., 1970, 1970.

Wilson, James, Q : Varieties of police behaviour. Cambridge (Mass) Harvard University Press, 1968.

Wilson, O.W. : Problems in police personnel administration. *Journal of Criminal Law, Criminology and Police Science*. March-April, 1953.

Wing, Hilde : Estimation of the adverse impact of a police promotion examination. *Personnel Psychology*, V. 34(3) Fall, 1981, 503-10.

Zekkowitz, Phyllis : Liability of police and public. *Mental and Physical Disability, Law Reporter*, V. 11(3) May-June, 1987, 202-03.

10

Police Recruitment and Training

Acharya, M.R. : Present training programmes of the police in India : A review. *Journal of Social Studies State Government*, V. 5(3-4) July-December, 1972, 223-42.

Acharya, M.R. : Recruitment and promotion : Policies of the police personnel in India. (Paper, Seminar on Recruitment and Training Police Officer, August, 1972).

Adleman, Concetta S. : Teaching police crisis intervention techniques. *Victimology*, V. 2(1) Spring, 1977, 123-26.

Aleem, M.A. : Recruitment and promotion policy for police personnel in Andhra Pradesh. *Journal of Social Studies State Government*, V.5 (2) April-June, 1972, 146-54.

Ali, A.A. : Role and range of training. *National Police Academy Magazine*, November, 1973, 88-97.

Allem, M.A. : Recruitment and promotion policy for police personnel in Andhra Pradesh. In G. Ram Reddy and K.K. Seshadri (eds.) Developing society and police. Hyderabad, Osmania University, 1972.

Arul, F.V. : Police training. *Indian Police Journal*, July, 1958, 39-42.

Aussant, Gilles : Applied psychology in police training, police operations and human relations. *Indian Police Journal*, V. 27(2) October-December, 1986, 61-68.

Aylward, Jack : Psychological testing and police selection. *Journal of Police Science and Administration*, V. 13(3) September, 1985, 201-10.

Badalaments, Richard V. (and others) : Training police for their social role. *Journal of Police Science and Administration*, V. 1(4) December, 1973, 440-53.

Balch, David E. : Personality trait difference between successful and non-successful police recruits of a typical police academy and veteran police officers. *Dissertation Abstracts International*, V. 39(11-A) May, 6172.

Banerjee, A.K. : Recruitment and training of gazetted police officers. *Journal of Social Studies State Government*, V. 5(3-4) July-December, 1972, 324-28.

Bard, Moston : Training police as specialist in family crisis interventions. Washington (DC), Law Enforcement Administration, 1970.

Barocas, Harvey A. : Psychodrama techniques in training police in family crisis intervention. *Group Psychotherapy Psychodrama*, V. 25(1-20) 1972, 30-31.

Beasley, Kennethe : A study of police employment and training in Kansas. Lawrence (Kansas), Government Research Centre, 1953.

Bimstein, Donald : Sensitivity training and the police. *Police Journal*, May-June, 1989, 75-79.

Blankenship, Ralph L. and Crammer, James A. : Effects of education and training on police perceptions of mentally disordered juvenile behaviours. *Journal of Police Science and Administration*, V. 4(4) December 1976, 426-35.

Blum, Richard H. : Police selection. Springfield (III), Charles C. Thomas, 1964.

Bohigian, Haig : Higher education for police officers. *Police Journal*, April-June, 1979, 140-53.

Bremnan, James J. and Olmsted, Donald : Police work with delinquents : Analysis of a training programme. East Iansing, Social Science Research Bureau, Michigan State University, 1965.

Brewster, Richard : Australian police adopt new training methods. *Social Welfare*, V. 21(6) September, 1974, 25-26.

Brown, Louise and Willis, Andrew : Authoritarianism in British police recruits : Importation, socialization or myth? *Journal of Occupational Psychology*, V. 58(2) June, 1985, 97-108.

Brubeck, Elizabeth and Furnham, Adrian : Police officer selection : A critical review of the literature. *Journal of Police Science and Administration*, V. 13 (1) March 1985, 58-69.

Buchanan, Dale R. and Perry, Patrica A. : Attitudes of police recruits towards domestic disturbances : An evaluation of family crisis intervention. *Journal of Criminal Justice*, V. 13(6) 1985, 561-72.

Burkhart, Barry R. : Conceptual issues in the development of police selection procedures. *Professional Psychology*, V. 11(1) February 1980, 121-29.

Butler, A.J. and Cochrane, Raymond : An examination of some elements of the personality of police officers and their implications. *Journal of Police Science and Administration*, V. 5(4) December, 1977, 441-50.

Calahane, Cornelius F. : Policeman's guide : A manual of study and instruction. New York, Harper, 1952.

Carpenter, Bruce N. and Raza, Susan M. : Personality characteristics of police applicants, comparisons across subgroups and with other populations. *Journal of Police Science and Administration*, V. 15(1) March 1987, 10-17.

Casio. Wayne F. : Formal education and police officer performance. *Journal of Police Science and Administration*, V. 5(1) March, 1977, 89-96.

Central Police Training College, Abu. 5th Advanced Course June-December 1952 : Need for specification in the police.

Charote, M.L. and Ganguly, S.K. : Assessment of yoga training to police. *Indian Police Journal*, July-September, 1976, 34-43.

Chaturvedi, S.K. : Police training. *Police Vigyan Patrika*, October-December, 1985.

Cizon, Francis A. and Smith, William H.T. : Some guidelines for successful police-community training programme.

Washington (P.C.) : Office of Law Enforcement Assistance, U.S. Department of Justice, 1970.

Conser James A. : A case of state mandated minimum selection standards or police officers. *Public Personnel Management*, V. 7(2) March-April, 1978, 135-43.

Constabulary, Cheshire : Recruit selection and the problem of wastage. *Police Journal*, V. 56(4) October-December, 1983, 319-23.

Coppock, Robert W. and Coppock, Barbara Brattin : A step by step method for recruiting policemen and firemen. *Public Personnel Review*, April 1958, 97-103.

Crockett, Thompsons : Law enforcement education, 1968 : A survey and discussion of law enforcement education in the U.S. Washington (D.C), Professional Standards Division, International Association of Chiefs of Police, 1968.

Das, Dilip K. : Should we include criminology in police recruitment training. *Police Journal*, V. 41(2) April-June, 1988, 137-51.

Das, Dilip K. : State mandated training in police community relations : An evaluation. *Police Journal*, V. 63(3) July-December, 1987, 232-48.

Deo, K. : Police Training College, Hazaribagh, Bihar. Souvenir, 10th Symposium of All India Principals Police Training of College Dated 22.10.1981 to 24.10.1981, Patna, 61-07.

Dessureau, J.P : Reorganization problems and selection of personnel : Quebec provincial police. *Canadian Public Administration*, June, 1962, 180-85.

Dethe, V.K. : Police training college. *Illustrated Weekly of India*, V. 91(49) 6 December, 1970, 40-43.

Dhillon, K.S. : Attitudinal change in police (An effort to utilize the medium of sensitivity training to evolve a proper response to rapid social change). *Sardar Vallabhbhai Patel National Academy Magazine*, November, 1987, 97-102.

Diaz, S.M. : Police training for modernization. *Indian Journal of Criminology and Criminalistics*, V. 1(2-3) June-September 1981.

Diaz, S.M. : Professional education for the police service of India. *Indian Education, Planning and Development*, August, 1977, 53-60.

Diaz, S.M. : Reorientation of the training of middle-level managers in the police. *Indian Police Journal*, V. 28(1) July-September, 1981, 10-20.

Diener, Edward, Whitmore, James and Munn, James : Role of playing in police training. *Police Journal*, October-December, 1976, 261-69.

Dillman, Everett G. : Role of playing as a technique in police selection. *Public Personnel Review*, April, 1963, 116-18.

Donahue, Michael J. : Peer counselling for police officers, A programme for skill development and personal growth. *Dissertation Abstracts International*, V. 38(4-A) October, 1977, 1992-93.

Dralle, Penclope W. and Baybrook, Rebecca M. : Screening of police applicants. A replication of a 5 item MMPI research index validity study. *Psychological Reports*, V. 57(3, Part 2) December, 1985, 1031-34.

Driscoll, James M. (and others) : Training police in family crisis intervention. *Journal of Applied Behavioural Science*, V. 9(1) 1937, 62-82.

Dudycha, George J. : Psychology for law enforcement officers. Springfield, 1953.

Eastman, George D. and Mccain, James A. : Police managers and their perceptions of higher education. *Journal of Criminal Justice*, V. 1(2) Summer, 1973, 113-24.

Eighth symposium of heads of police training institutions. *Indian Police Journal*, V. 23(3) January-March, 1977, 6-8.

Ellison, Katherine W. : Community involvement in police selection. *Social Action and the Law*, V. 11(3) 1985, 77-78.

Ellison, Katherine W. : Police selection : An overview. *Social Action and the Law*, V. 11(3) 1985, 68.

Ellison, Katherine W. (and others) : Job preview in police selection. *Social Action and the Law*, V. 11(3) 1985, 75-76.

Ellison, Katherine W. (and others) : Montclair police selection procedure : A summary. *Social Action and the Law*, V. 11(3) 1985, 69-71.

Elmes, Frank : Education and training. *Police Journal*, February, 1970, 55-63.

Elmes, Frank : Personality and recruitment. *Police Journal* March, 1969, 113-17.

English, J. and Houghton, R. : Police training manual. London: McGraw Hill. 1975.

Fagan, M. Michael : How police officers perceive their field training appear. *Journal of Police Science and Administration*, V. 13(2) June 1985, 138-52.

Farah, S.A. : Training the policemen. *Indian Nation*, August 3, 1988, 4.

Fenn, G.E. : Training for police promotion examinations. *Police Journal*, December, 1964.

Fielding, N.G. and Fielding, J.L. : A study of resignation during British police training. *Journal af Police Science and Administration*, V. 15(1) March, 1987, 24-36.

Fielding, Nigel G. : Evaluating the role of training in police socialization : A British example. *Journal of Community Psychology*, V.14(3) July 1986, 319-30.

Fisher, Roy : Police recruitment and future police management. *Police Journal*, October-December 1972, 287-90.

Flynn, J.T. and Peterson, M. : Use of regression analysis in police patrolman selection. *Journal of Criminal Law, Criminology and Police Science*, V. 63(4) December, 1972, 564-69.

Fraunces, John P. : Teaching strategies for influencing police officers' perceptions of the degree of anxiety on inner city children. *Dissertation Abstracts International*, V. 38(1-A) July 1977, 170.

Fromkin, Howard L. (and others) : An evaluation of human relations training for police. *Catalog of selected Documents in Psychology*, V. 5, Winter 1975, 206-07.

Frost, Thomas M. : A forward look in police education. Springfield (Ill), Charles C. Thomas, 1959.

Frost, Thomas M. : Selection methods for police recruits. *Journal of Criminal Law, Criminology and Police Science*, May-June, 1955.

Gmmage, Allen Z. : Police training in the United States. Spring-field (Ill), Charles C. Thomas, 1963.

Garfitt, Alan : Book for police. London, Caxton, 1958.

Garratt, Gail A. (and others) : Training University police in black-American nonverbal behaviour. *Journal of Social Psychology*, V. 113(2) April, 1981, 217-29.

Gavin, James F. and Hamilton, John W. : Selecting police using assessment center methodology. *Journal of Police Science and Administration*, V. 3(2) June, 1975, 166-76.

Glauberman, Lloyd A. : Training the police in crisis intervention techniques. *Dissertation Abstracts International*, V. 38(5-8) November, 1977, 2428.

Good, Gregory W. Augsburger, Arol R. : Uncorrected visual acuity standards for police applicants. *Journal of Police Science and Administration*, V. 15(1) March, 1987, 18-23.

Gopalaswami, R.A. : Recruitment to police service in Tamilnadu. *Swarajya*, V. 16(20) 13 November, 1971, 2-3.

Gokhale, S.C. : Police-attitudes, training institute, organisational climate. *National Police Academy Magazine*, November, 1973, 43-60.

Gourley, G. Douglas : An experiment in the use of the conference method for training of police supervisors. *Journal of Criminal Law and Criminology*, September-October, 1948.

Gourley, G. Douglas : In-service training of policemen by universities and colleges. *Journal of Criminal Law, Criminology and Police Science*, July-August, 1953.

Gruber, Gerald : Police applicant test : A productive validity study. *Journal of Police Science and Administration*, V. 14(2) June, 1986, 121-29.

Gupta, Ranjit : Police and public order : The importance of training. *Times of India*, 14 April, 1980, 6.

Halawa, El-Sadik F. : Higher studies for police in U.A.R. *Indian Police Journal*, July 1975, 28-30.

Hancock, Barry W. and McClung, Curtis E. : Abstract-cognitive abilities in police selection and organisation. *Journal of Police Science and Administration*, V. 12(1) March, 1984, 99-104.

Hargrave, George E. and Hiatt, Deirdre : Use of the California psychological inventory in law enforcement officer selection. *Journal of Personality Assessment*, V. 53(2) Summer, 1989, 267-77.

Harris, Richard N. : Police academy : An inside view. New York, John Wiley, 1973.

Hazlett, Suzanne O. : Results of the selection procedure. *Social Action and the Law*, V. 11(3) 1985, 78-80.

Hess, Leer : Police entry tests and their predictability of score in police academy and subsequent job performance. *Dissertation Abstracts International*, V. 33(10 A) April, 1973, 5552.

Hicks, Randolph D. (and others) : Police perceptions of interpersonal communication training needs. *Journal of Crimimal Justice*, V. 13(6) 1985, 513-24.

Hilton, Jennifer : Instructions to the new police. *Police Journal*, V. 50(1) January-March, 1977, 23-28.

Holcomb, Richard : Selection of police officers. Iowacity, Iowa, University of Iowa Press, 1946.

Holmes, Benjamen : Selection of patrolmen. *Journal of Criminal Law, Criminology and Police Science*, January-February, 1942.

Igvinovia, Patrick Edobor : Recruitment problems of the Nigerian police. *Indian Police Journal*, V. 28(4) April-June, 1982, 42-50.

Ingleton, R. : French police training. *Police Journal*, October, 1970, 313-20.

International Association of Chiefs of Police : Current approaches : Police training and community relations—Survey Supplement. Washington (D.C.), IACP, 1965.

Jamadar, S.M. : Police training. *Times of India*, 31 January, 1976, 6.

James, Stephen P. (and others) : Personality differentiation in a police selection : Interview. *Journal of Applied Psychology*, V. 69(1) February, 1984, 129-34.

Janu, Samuel S. (and others) : Training police officers to distinguish mental illness. *American Journal of Psychology*, V. 137(2) February, 1980, 228-29.

John, K.C. : Kerala plan to train police as a service-oriented force. *Times of India*, 17 November, 1975, 6.

Johnson, Edward E. : Psychological tests used in assessing and sample of police and fire fighter candidates. *Journal of Police Science and Administration*, V. 11(4) December, 1983, 430-33.

Joshi, G.P. and Arora, J.C. : Recruitment in the police : A sample survey of policies and procedures. *Police Research and Development*, *Quarter III*, July-September, 1988, 1-24.

Kalia, V.K. : Need for ethical training in police. *Sardar Vallabhbhai Patel National Police Academy Magazine*, Nov., 1977, 125-30.

Kegan, Daniel L. : Perceived effects of sensitivity training : Samples of police officers, college students and a group of dynamics class. *Small Group Behaviour*, V. 7(2) May, 1976, 131-46.

Keller, Peter A. : Situational set and need for approval as variables in police recruits : Perceptions of Ghetto residents. *Dissertation Abstracts International*, V. 33 (3-B) September, 1972, 1289.

Knights, P.D. : Management training in the police service. *Police Journal*, September, 1969, 408-23.

Kramer, Howard C. and Barr, Donald J. : In-service training for campus police community. *Mental Health Journal*, V. 10(2) Summer, 1974, 180-84.

Kunce, Joseph T. and Anderson, Wayne P. : Assessment of nonpathological personality styles of policemen. *Journal of Clinical Psychology*, V. 44(2) March, 1988, 115-22.

Kuykendall, Jack L. Matthews, Donald E. and Usinger, Peter E. : An evaluation of police management training. *Police Journal*, October-December, 1977, 367-77.

Landy, Frank J. : The validity of the interview in police officer selection. *Journal of Applied Psychology*, V. 61(2) April 1976, 193-98.

Longer, John H. : Guidelines for school—police co-operation in drug abuse policy department. *Journal of School Health*, V. 46(4) April, 1976, 197-99.

Lawrence, S. : Pattern of police training. *Municipal Review*, September, 1966, 506.

Lawther, Wendell C. : Successful training for police performance : Evaluation systems. *Journal of Police Science and Administration*, V. 12(1) March, 1984, 41-46.

Lefkowitz, Joel : Evaluation of a supervisory training programme for police. *Personnel Psychology*, Spring, 1972, 95-106.

Lester, David : Graduation from a police training academy : Demographic correlates, *Psychological Reports*, V. 57(2) Oct., 1985, 542.

Lester, David : Predictors of graduation from a police training academy. *Psychological Reports*, V. 44(2) April, 1979, 362.

Lester, David : Selection of police officers: An argument of simplicity. *Police Journal*, V. 56(1) January-March, 1983, 53-55.

Lester, David and Purgavie, Charles : Predicting graduation from a police academy with the Kuder occupational interest survey. *Psychological Reports*, V. 47(1) August, 1980, 78.

Luthara, B.R. : 7th symposium of heads of police training. *Indian Police Journal*. October-December, 1975, 4-12.

Mahar, Patrick T. : Police physical ability tests : Can they ever be valid ? *Public Personnel Management*, V. 13(2) Summer, 1984, 173-83.

Mahurkar, P.P. : Recruitment and training of police officers. *Police Research and Development, Quarter III and IV*, July-December, 1972, 59-67.

Malouff, John M. and Schittee, Nicola S.: Using biographical information to hire the best new police officers : Research findings. *Journal of Police Science and Administration*, V. 14(3) September, 1986, 175-77.

Malviya, P.D. : Training of senior police officers: Some basic issues. *Indian Journal of Public Administration*, V. 34(3) July-September, 1988, 616-21.

Mathur, K.M. : Administration of police training in India. Delhi, Gian Publishing House, 1987.

Mathur, Krishna Mohan : Administration of police training in India. *Police Research and Development, Quarter II*, April-June, 1984, 25-31.

Matice, Kathryn L. : Effect of source, class, dogmatism and time on attitude change on police academy recruits. *Dissertation Abstracts International*, V. 39(11-B) May, 1979, 5568-69.

Matthews, Janet R. (and others) : Evolution of psychology course for police officers. *Teaching of Psychology*, V. 9(4) December, 1982, 235.

McAllister, W.J. : A degree for the police. *Police Journal*, July-September, 1972, 228-37.

Mcintosh, M.C. : Educational opportunities for the Scottish police. *Police Journal*, May, 1968, 205-08.

Mckenzie, Ian K. : Psychology and police education. A reply to Taylor. *Bulletin of the British Psychological Society*. May, 1984, 145-47.

Mcmanus. George : Human relations training for police. *Journal of Criminal Law, Criminology and Police Science*, May-June, 1955.

Meadows, Robert J. : Beliefs of law enforcement administrators and criminal justice educators toward the needed skill, competencies in entry level police training curriculum. *Journal of Police Science and Administration*, V. 15(1) March, 1987, 1-9.

Meadows, Robert J. : Police training strategies and the role perceptions of police recruits. *Journal of Police Science and Administration*, V. 13(3) September, 1985, 195-200.

Meier, Robert D. Farmer, Richard E. and Maxwell, David : Psychological screening of police candidates : Current perspectives. *Journal of Police Science and Administration*, V. 15(3) September, 1987, 210-15.

Mirdha, A.S. : Police Training School, Punjab, Phillauj. *Indian Police Journal*, October, 1954, 60-66.

Mirdha, Ram Niwas : Valedictory address (Seminar on recruitment and training of police officers, August 1972). *Journal of the Society for the Study of State Government*, V. 5(3-4) July-September-October-December, 1972, 329-35.

Mishra, D.M. : Recruitment and training of constables. *Journal of Social Studies State Governments* V. 5(3-4). July-December, 1972, 3 9-35.

Mishra, S.C. : Constabulary training in India (Paper) In 7th Police Science Congress, Jaipur, 1968.

Mitra, Abhijit : Recruitment and training of I P.S. officers. *Journal of the Society for Study of State Government*, V. 5(3-4) July-September-October-December, 1972, 312-23.

Moore, Tony : Police training for crisis : The use of simulation. *Police Journal*, V. 41(2) April-June, 1988, 119-36.

Moran, T. Kenneth : Pathways towards a non-discriminatory recruitment policy. *Journal of Police Science and Administration*, V. 16(4) December, 1988, 274-87.

Mullick, B.N. : Moral training for policemen. *Indian Police Journal*, V. 15(4) 1969, 15-25.

Mullick, B.N. : New scheme for police training. New Delhi, *Indian Police Journal*, V. 16(4) April-June, 1970, 2-17.

Mullineax, Jewel A. : Evaluation of the predictors used to select patrolmen. *Public Personnel Review*, April, 1955.

Mulvey, Edward P. and Reppucci, N. Dickon : Police crisis intervention training : An empirical investigation. *American Journal of Community Psychology*, V. 9(5) October, 1981, 527-46,

Murphy, Joseph J. : Current practices in the use of psychological testing by police agencies. *Journal of Criminal Law, Criminology and Police Science*, V. 63(4) December, 1972, 570-76.

Naik, V.V. : Meaning of training. *National Police Academy Magazine*, November, 1973, 24-30.

Naik, V.V. : Police training : A world symposium. *Integrated Management*, August, 1973, 24-30.

Narain, Govind : Training the police for better performance. *Indian Police Journal*, V. 27(1) July-September, 1980, 5-11.

Nash, Peggy W. : A trait study of police officers by educational level. *Dissertation Abstracts International*, V. 39 (4-A) October, 1978, 2153.

National Police Academy : Specialised training in law and order duties for police officers and Magistrates. Abu, NPA, 1971.

Newfield, Norbert L. and Reish, Joseph : Crisis intervention training for police : An innovative program. *Crisis Intervention*, V. 6(4) 1975, 28-35.

Oglesby, Thomas W. : Use of emotional screening in the selection of police applicants. *Public Personnel Review*, October, 1957, 228-31.

O'Hara, Kirk and Love, Kevin G. : Accurate selection of police officials within small municipalities : Ettu assessment center? *Public Personnel Management*, V. 16(1) Spring, 1987, 9-14.

Panakal, J.J. : Special training of police for prevention of juvenile delinquency (Paper) Second All India Police Science Congress, Bombay, September 1961.

Parker, Glenn M. : Human relations training : Improving police/community relations. *Training and Development Journal*, October, 1974, 7-12.

Parker, Menneth A.L. : Educational background of the police. *Police Journal*, V. 55(4) October-December, 1982, 320-24.

Perkins, Rollin M. : Police examinations. Brooklyn, Foundation Press, 1947.

Pfister, Gordon : Outcomes of laboratory training for police officers. *Journal of Social Issues*, V. 31(1) 1975, 115-21.

Poland, James M. : Police selection methods and the prediction of police performance. *Journal of Police Science and Administration*, V. 6(4) December, 1978, 384-93.

Police training. *Indian Journal of Police Administration*, V. 24(1) January-March, 1978, 281-304.

Pollack, Normanc : Use of written tests for police officer selection. *Public Personnel Review*, April, 1964, 124-8.

Pomrenke, Norman E. : Dilemma in police recruiting. *Popular Government*, November, 1965, 7-8.

Pomrenke, Norman E. : Minimum standards for police training. *Popular Government*, December, 1965, 20-21.

Pope, William R. (and others) : Philosophies of human nature and policemen : Study of differences between recruits and veterans. *Psychological Reports*, V. 42(3, part 2) June, 1978, 1335-38.

Prag, Yehuda : Training in the Israel police. *Public Administration in Israel and Abroad*, 1968, 85-90.

Prasad, D. Ravindra and Haragopal, G. : Recruitment of police personnel. In G. Ram Reddy and K. Seshadri (eds.) Developing society and police. Hyderabad, Osmania University, 1972.

Prasad, R.N. : Administration of police training in India. New Delhi, Gian Publishing House, 1987.

Price, Barbara R. and Adelbera, Sheldon : An evaluation of police supervisory training using a multivariate assessment of attitude change. *Journal of Police Science and Administration*, V. 5(1), March, 1877, 69-73.

Pugh, George : Situation tests and police selection. *Journal of Police Science and Administration*, V. 13(1) March, 1985, 30-35.

Pugh, George : California psychological inventory and police selection. *Journal of Police Science and Administration*, V. 13(2) June, 1985, 172-77.

Putti, Joseph and Aryee, Samuel and Tan, Seckkang : Personal values of recruits and officers in a law enforcement agency : An exploratory study. *Journal of Police Science and Administration*, V. 16(4) December, 1988, 249-54.

Pynes, Joan E. and Bernardin, H. John : Productive validity of an entry-level police officer assessment center, *Journal of Applied Psychology*, V. 74(5) October, 1989, 831-33.

Refky, David M. (and others) : Are police recruits cynical? *Journal of Police Science and Administration*, V. 4(3) September, 1976, 352-60.

Rajasthan University. Social Science Research Centre : Motivation and training of police personnel. Jaipur, the Centre, 1976.

Ramarao, C.V.S. : Some thoughts on recruitment policies (Paper, Seminar on recruitment and training of police officers,

August 1972). *Journal of the Society for the Study of State Governments*, V. 5(3-4) July-September-October-December, 1972, 264-69.

Rankin, J.H. : Psychiatric screening of police recruits. *Public Personnel Review*, July 1959, 191-96.

Rao, K.V. : A note on the need for strengthening the bureau of police research and training (Paper, Seminar on recruitment and training of police officers, August 1972). *Journal of the Society for the Study of State Governments*, V. 5 (3-4) July-September-October-December, 1972, 275-76.

Rao, K.V. : Recruitment, training and other related matters of Indian police (Paper) Seminar on the recruitment and training of police officers, August 1972, *Journal of the Society for the Study of State Governments*, V. 5(3-4) July-September-October-December, 1972, 179-205.

Reister, Mortin : Practical psychology for police officers. Springfield (III), Charles C. Thomas, 1973.

Rektor, B. : Police education in Hungary. *Police Journal*, April, 1972, 52-54.

Reynolds, Allen H. : Reliability of a scored oral interview of police officers. *Public Personnel Management*, V. 8(5) September-October, 1979, 324-28.

Rizer, Conard : Police Mathematics : A text book in Applied Mathematics for police. Springfield (III). Charles C. Thomas, 1954.

Rogers, J.H. : Officer training in the Australian and New Zealand forces. *Police Journal*, May, 1966, 259-62.

Saksena, N.S. : Impartial boards to choose police IG : Reforms urgently needed. *Times of India*, 9 April, 1979, 8.

Saksena, N.S. : What is wrong with police training. *Sardar Vallabhbhai Patel National Police Academy Magazine*, June, 1977, 7-10.

Sata, Lindbergh S. : Laboratory training for police officers. *Journal of Social Issues*, V. 31(1) 1975, 107-14.

Saxena, Anil Kumar : Programmed instruction in police training. *Indian Police Journal*, V. 29(3) January-March, 1983, 9-13.

Schachter, Hindy L. : Job-related examinations for police : Two developments. *Journal of Police Science and Administration*, V. 7(1) March, 1979, 86-89.

Schaeffer, Earl R. : Comparison of attitudes toward higher education held by police and fire students, other students, and police and fire non-students. *Dissertation Abstracts International*, V. 39(2-A) August, 1968, 613.

Schrager, Jules : Mental health training for state police officers. *Social Work*, April, 1964, 64-69.

Schwalb, Geraldine : Police-specific communication training : A practical approach to family crisis mediation. *Dissertation Abstracts International*, V. 37 (6-B) December, 1976, 3097.

Sen, Sankar : Training of police personnel. *Police Research and Development, Quarter I*, January-March, 1984, 28-30.

Sharma, Prabhu Datta : Recruitment and training of Sub-Inspectors of Police (Paper, Seminar on recruitment and training of police officers August 1972). *Journal of the Society for the Study of State Governments*, V. 5(3-4) July-September-October-December, 1972, 292-305.

Siegel, Arthur, Federman, Philip S. and Schultz, Douglas G. : Professional police human relations training. Springfield (III), Charles C. Thomas, 1963.

Simon, William E. (and others) : Psychological needs of a professional police personnel. *Psychological Reports*, V. 33(1) August, 1973, 313-14.

Singh, C.P. : Syndicate study on recruitment, training and development of constable in the civil police. *Transactions*, V. 29, 1979, 53-107.

Singhvi, G.C. : Indian police service : Recruitment. *C.B.I. Bulletin*, V. 11(6) June, 1977, 3-5.

Singhvi, G.C. : Police training : Innovations. *Indian Police Journal*, V. 31(3) July-September, 1984, 2-9.

Singhvi, G.C. : Police training perspectives. *C.B.I. Bulletin*, September, 1972, 4.

Singhvi, G.C. : Police training : Three innovations. *Indian Journal of Public Administration*, V. 31(2), April-June, 1985, 295-307.

Singhvi, G.C. : Refurbishing field training of IPS probationers. *Police Research and Development, Quarter I,* January-March, 1985, 24-26.

Singhvi, G.C. : What ails police training ? *Indian Journal of Public Administration,* V. 18(1) January-March, 1972, 51-66.

Srikanth Reddy, B. : Training police officers. In G. Ram Reddy and K. Seshadri (eds.) Developing Society and Police. Hyderabad, Osmania University, 1972.

Stebbins, Robert A. and Flynn, Colin : Police definitions of the situation : Evaluation of a diploma programme in law enforcement and community relations. *Canadian Journal of Criminology and Corrections,* V. 17(4) October, 1975, 334-53.

Stracey, E.L. : A century of police training. *National Police Academy Magazine,* October, 1961, 1-9.

Subramanian, S. : Pre-entry preparatory education for prospective entrants to police service. *Indian Police Journal,* V. 30(2) October-December, 1983, 2-5.

Subramaniam, S. : Training of police trainers. *C.B.I. Bulletin,* V. 18(3) March, 1984, 1-3.

Supnekar, N.M. : Training in attitudes formation in police. New Delhi, Department of Personnel and Administrative Reforms, 1978.

Talbert, Terry L. (and others) : A study of the police officer height requirement. *Public Personnel Management,* V. 3(2) March-April, 1974, 103-10.

Talley, Richard A. : New methodology for evaluating the curricula relevancy of police academy training. *Journal of Police Science and Administration,* V. 14(2) June, 1986, 112-20.

Taylor, M. : Undergraduate programmes in police studies. *Police Journal,* V. 56(2) April-June, 1983, 128-41.

Taylor, Maxwell : Psychology and police education. *Bulletin of the British Psychological Society,* V. 36, December, 1983, 406-07.

Teasley, C.E. and Wright T. Leonord : Effects of training on police recruit attitudes. *Journal of Police Science and Administration,* V. 1 (2) June, 1973, 241-48.

Thiruchitrambalam, S.I. : Recruitment and training of Sub-Inspectors and Inspectors (Paper, Seminar on recruitment and training of police officers, August 1972). *Journal of the Society for the Study of State Governments,* V. 5(3-4) July-September-October-December, 1972, 306-14.

Tobias, J.J. : Naught for your comfort : A study of police recruiting. *Police Journal,* July-September, 1974, 262-268.

Trikha, M.C. : Aspects of police training in the U.K. *Police Research and Development, Quarter III,* July-September, 1974, 37-43.

Tripathi, S.V.M. : Selection by extended interview in U.K. police. *National Police Academy Magazine,* November, 1973, 103-09.

Tuli, Vinod : Concept of specialisation in police functioning. *Indian Police Journal,* V. 29(2) October-December, 1982, 24-28.

Tyagi, A.R. : Recruitment and training of the police. *Journal of the Lal Bahadur Shastri National Academy of Police Administration,* Spring, 1973, 122-26.

Tyagi, A.R. : Recruitment and training of the police (Paper, Seminar on recruitment and training of police officers, August 1972). *Journal of the Society in the Study of State Governments,* V. 5(3-4), July-September-October-December, 1972, 285-91.

Veerabhadratah, H. : Some aspects of police training (Paper, Seminar on recruitment and training of police officers, August 1972). *Journal of the Society for the Study of State Governments,* V. 5(3-4) July-September-October-December, 1972, 278-84.

Veno, Arthur and Gardner, James M. : Evaluation of a community psychology approach to police training. *Journal of Community Psychology,* V. 7(3) July, 1979, 210-19.

Viteles, Morris B. : Psychological methods in the selection of policemen in Europe. *Annals of the American Academy of Political and Social Science,* November, 1949.

Vohra, V.K. : A syndicate study on the methods of police training, development and career planning of officers and changes that are required at any time in their service to modernise the outlook and to make the leadership of the force effective and morality strong. *Transactions*, V. 26, 1978, 160-196.

Walker, Ray O. : Performance measurement : Theory in criminal justice training. *Journal of Police Science and Administration*, V. 6(4) December, 1978, 471-78.

Weiner, Norman L. : Educated policeman. *Journal of Police Science and Administration*, December, 1976, 450.

Weiner, Norman L. : Effect of education on police attitudes. *Journal of Criminal Justice*, V. 2(4) Winter, 1974, 137-28.

Weston, P.B. : Police promotion quizzer. Springfield (III), Charles C. Thomas, 1958.

Winters, Clyde Ahmad : Problems of variance in the utility of the M.M.P.I. in the selection of metropolitan police. *Police Journal*, V. 63(2) April-June, 1990, 121-28.

Yunker, Rose M. : Police field training : The analysis of a socialization process. *Dissertation Abstracts International*, V. 38 (4-A) October, 1977, 2017.

Zacker, Joseph : Understanding one's clients : An attempt to improve sensitivity and morale in police recruits. *Psychological Reports*, V. 31(3) December, 1972, 999-1008.

Zacker, Joseph and Bard, Morton : Effects of conflict management training on police performance. *Journal of Applied Psychology*, V. 58 (2) October, 1973, 202-08.

11

Police Unrest

Abraham, A.S. : Police revolt in Gujarat : Making of an ominous trend. *Times of India*, 1 August, 1988, 6.

Adams, Horold, J. and Specier, Cathy A. : Humanism as repression : Counselors training police. *Counselor Education and Supervision*, V. 21(3) March, 1982, 181-86.

Agitated policemen and inept officialdom. *Link*, V. 9(37) 23 April, 1967. 19-24.

Army alerted as police stir turns violent in Madras. *Times of India*, 19 October, 1979, 1.

Army out in Gujarat to check police stir : Cracks down on union leaders : Stray incidents of violence and arson : Flag marches in some towns. *Times of India*, 25 July, 1988, 1.

Ayres, Richtiard M. : Case studies of police strike in two cities : Albuquerque and Oklahonia city. *Journal of Police Science and Administration*, V. 5(1) March 1977.

Bardhan, A.B. : Two faces of policemen. *New Age*, V. 30 (37) 12 September, 1982, 5.

Barely 30% A.P. police staff provided with houses. *Times of India*, 22 October, 1977, 9.

Bhaskara Rao, T. and Narshima Rao, T. : Police strike in India. *Indian Journal of Political Science*, V. 41(3) September, 1980, 507-20.

Bopp, William J. and Wiatrowski, Michael : Police strike in New Oriens : A city abandoned by its police. *Police Journal*, V. 55(2) April-July 1982.

Burdens of the policeman. *Thought*, V. 20(30) 27 July, 1968, 7.

Candeth, K.P. : Police agitation and the defence forces. *Indian Express*, 2 July, 1979, 6.

Chakravarty, Sukhamoy : Police revolt in West Bengal. *Janata*, V. 24(29) 10 August, 1969, 7-8.

Chary, S. : Some problems of police constable : An empirical study. *Journal of State Politics and Administration*, V. 1(1) January-June 1978, 74-80.

Eruption of police unrest. *Link*, V. 28(8) 3 October, 1982, 21-22.

Farah, S.A. : Delhi agitation. *Indian Nation*, 17 March, 1988.

Farah, S.A. : Police agitation. *Indian Nation*, July 19, 1988, 4

Firmen's pays : (Editorial). *Times of India*, July, 1988, 6.

Gammage, Allen Z. and Sachs, Stanley L. : Police unions. Springfield (Ill), Charles C. Thomas, 1972.

Ghosh, Sankar : Police discontent in West Bengal : Multiparty pressures. *Times of India*, 9 August 1969, 7.

Gill, Sucha Singh and Azad, Amar Singh : Policemen's struggle for rights. *Economic and Political Weekly*, V. 14(22), 3 June, 1979, 931-32.

Haryana accepts most demands of policemen. *Times of India*, 28 August, 1982, 1.

Haryana's police (Editorial). *Times of India*, 30 August, 1982.

Henstics. Earle : Police unions. Police year book (Washington, I.A.C.P. 1958) 45.

Inderjit : Parliament and the police revolt. *Tribune*, 10 July, 1979.

Inderjit : Police unrest : A way out. *Economic Times*, 31 August, 1982, 5.

Inderjit : Police unrest : A way out. *Tribune*, 31 August, 1982.

India, National Police Academy, Abu : Machinery for redress of policemen's grievances : Background, papers and proceedings of the seminar held on 11th, 12th and 13th Nov., 1967.

International Association of Chiefs of Police : Police union and other police organisations Washington, D.C., International Association of Chiefs of Police, 1944.

International Association of Chief of Police : Police Unions, Washington (D.C.), ACP, 1958.

Iyer, Radha : Reasons for police unrest. *Business Standard*, 18 June, 1979, 5.

Jain, Girilal : Bombay's mutinous police : Grievances must await normalcy. *Times of India*, 20 August, 1982, 6.

John, K.C. : Low credibility of Kerala police : Authorities embarrassed. *Times of India*, 5 May, 1977, 4.

Joshi, Prabhash : Punjab police unrest : Failure of the top. *Indian Express*, 23 May 1979, 6.

Joshi, V.I. : M.P. policemen back on warpath. *Times of India*, 30 October, 1979, 8.

Juris, Hevery, A. and Feuilles, Peter : Police unionism : Power and impact in public sector bargaining. Lexington, Lexington Books, 1973.

Kanetkar, V.G. : Police unrest and communication gap. *Free Press Journal*, 2 October, 1979.

Kearney, P.C. : Impact of police unionization on municipal budgetary outcomes. *International Journal of Public Administration*, V. 1(4) 1979, 361-79.

Krishnan, Jairam : Gujarat cops not indispensable. *Economic Times*, 31 July, 1983, 3.

Levine, Marging : A historical overview of police unionization in the United States. *Police Journal*, V. 81(4) October-December, 1988, 334-43.

M.P. policemen too on warpath. *Times of India*, 21 May, 1979, 1.

Maharashtra police union ultimatum to government. *Times of India*, 30 November, 1980, 1.

Maheshwari, S.R. : Outburst of long suppressed anger. *Hindu*, 6 June 1979, 8.

Maheshwari, Shriram : Unionism in the police : Redressal of police personnel's grievances. *Indian Journal of Public Administration*, V. 24(1) January-March, 1978, 68-86.

Malhotra, Inder : Grim portents from Punjab : Police defiance and after. *Times of India*, 17 May 1979, 8.

Mathur, K.M. : Police agitation in India : Causes and remedies : Some reflections. Seminar on police unrest—Working paper and background working papers. Hyderabad, Sardar Vallabhbhai Patel National Police Academy, 1980.

Mehra, Ajay K. : Dealing with police unrest. *Mainstream*, V. 21(12) 20 November, 1982, 23-25.

Mehra, Ajay K. : Fair pay, Yes; agitation never. A same approach to police problems. *Hindustan Times*, 17 June, 1979, 1.

Meyer, John C. Jr. : Discontinuity in the delivery of public service : Analyzing the police strike. *Human Relations*, V. 29(6) June, 1976, 545-57.

Misra, S.C. : Mounting police grievances. : Early action needed. *Times of India*, 23 June, 19'3, 6.

More about muting within the state forces. *Frontier*, V. 11(47) 21 July 1979, 4-5.

More forces for Gujarat. *Times of India*, 28 July, 1988, 1.

Mukherjee, D.P. : Discontent among policemen. *Capital*, V. 182(4564) 2 July, 1979, 6-7.

Nath, D.C. : Police : Roots of dissatisfaction. *Statesman*, 17 August, 1979.

Nath, T. : Police discontent. *Patriot* (*Mag*), 12 September, 1982, 1.

Nath, T. : Police muting and after. *Hindustan Times*, 20 June 1979, 9.

Nath, Tribhuvan : Grievance of Haryana police. *Times of India*, 14 September 1982, 6.

National Police Academy : Machinery for redress of policemen's grievances : Background papers and proceedings of the seminar held on 11th, 12th and 13th November, 1967, Abu, NPA, 1968.

Nayar, Kuldip : Echoes of police revolt. *Tribune*, 26 August, 1982, 4.

Negotiate with Delhi policemen (Editorial). *New Age*, V. 15(17) 23 April, 1967, 2.

One killed, 17 wounded : Troops called out in Lahore as striking policemen defy law. *Times of India*, 26 February, 1972, 1.

Patel's appeal to policemen to end stir. *Times of India*, 16 May, 1979 1.

Pfuhl, Erdwin H. : Police strikes and conventional crime : A look of the data. *Criminology : An Interdisciplinary Journal*, V. 21(4) November, 1983, 489-503.

Police agitation (Editorial). *Janata*, V. 34(18) 10 June, 1979, 1-2.

Police agitation. *Statesman*, 5 June, 1979.

Police agitation (Editorial). *Times of India*, 13 October, 1981, 8.

Police discontentment. *Link*, V. 21(42) 27 May, 1979, 16-17.

Police in the fray : Press comments. *Economic and Political Weekly*, V. 2(18) 6 May, 1967, 832.

Police politics (Editorial). *Economic Times*, 26 July, 1988, 5.

Police unrest (Editorial). *Times of India*, 1 June, 1971, 8.

Police violence (Editorial). *Times of India*, 9 July, 1972, 6.

Policemen on strike. *New Age*, V. 15(17) 23 April 1967, 1.

Policemen's agitation spreads in M.P. *Times of India*, 22 May 1979, 1.

Policemen's stir, (Editorial). *Times of India*, 5 October, 1981, 8.

Politicians exploiting Haryana police unrest. *Times of India*, 29 August, 1982, 9.

Pospielovsky, Dimitry : Russian police trade unionism : Experiment or provocations? London, Weidenfield, 1971.

Prasad Rao, V.G. : AIADMK handles police agitation skilfully. *Times of India*, 20 November, 1980.

Protest in police lines. *Organiser*, V. 20(36) 23 April, 1987, 3.

Provocation in Punjab. *Link*, V. 21(41) 20 May, 1979, 10-13.

Punjab sanctions rise in policemen's pay. *Times of India*, 15 May, 1979, 1.

Ramachandra Reddy, K. : Most neglected government employee : police unrest. *Patriot*, 17 July, 1979.

Ramachandra Reddy, K. : Police agitation : retrospect and prospect. *Indian Police Journal*, V. 26(1) July-September, 1979, 26-31.

Ranadive, B.T. : Police agitation and the Janata government. *People's Democracy*, V. 3(22) 3 June, 1979, 1-2.

Rangaswamy, K. : Police revolt in Uttar Pradesh. *Rising Sun*, 15 June 1973, 4-7.

Rau, N. Chalapathi : Unrest among policemen. *Link*, V. 21(44) 10 June, 1979, 9.

Richard, M. Ayres : Police strike. *Police Chief*, March, 1977.

Richard, K. Ayres : Police strikes : Are we treating the symptoms rather than the problem? *Police Chief*, March, 1977.

Sharma, J.M. : Policemen revolt. *Illustrated Weekly of India*, V. 100(21) 3 June, 1979, 33.

Shoot orders in Baroda : Army out. *Times of India*, 27 July, 1988, 1.

Singh, T.P. : Police unrest. *Hindustan Times*, October 25, 1988, 9.

Sub-Inspectors join M.P. police stir. *Times of India*, 28 May, 1979, 1.

Subramanian, K.S. : Police unrest in India : Notes towards an understanding. *Denouement*, V. 2(6 & 7) January-February, 1991, 17-21.

Tamil Nadu police unrest (Editorial). *Times of India*, 29 October, 1979, 8.

Upadhyay, B.B. : Police unrest. *C.B.I. Bulletin*, V. 14(12) December, 1980, 1-4.

Varma, Paripurnanand : Police agitation. *Pioneer*, 13 July, 1979.

Varma, Ravindra : Police discontent. *Janata* (*Special Number*), V. 37(28) 1982, 11-15.

Violence in Gujarat as police stir spreads. *Times of India*, 26 July, 1988, 1.

Vohra, K.B. : Syndicate study on police unions and associations. S.V.P. National Police Academy, 41 senior officers course, Ist May 1978 to 5th August 1978. *Transactions*, V. 28, 1979, 1-73.

Warier, K.U. : Kerala policemen get best pay in country. *New Age*, V. 27(25) 24 June, 1979, 14.

Welsh, Laurence : Pay negotiations in the police service. *Police Journal*, April-June, 1972, 161-64.

Whitaker, Ben : The case of the bent policemen. *New Society* V. 39 (750) 17 February, 1977, 327-29.

When the police ran amuck in Gujarat. *Link*, V. 30(53) 7 August, 1988, 9-11.

Why did M.P. policemen turn agitators? *Economic Times*. 1 June, 1979, 8.

Winfree, L. Thomas and Gehlen, Frieda : Police strike, public support and dissonance reduction during a strike by police. *Journal of Police Science and Administration*, V. 9(4) December, 1981, 451-62.

12

Police Leadership

Alderson, J.C. : Police leadership in times of social, economic and political turbulence. *Police Journal*, April-June, 1976, 87-92.

Ansaen, D.A. and Culley, P.R. : Police leader. Springfield, Illinois, Charles C. Thomas, 1971.

DeGrazia, Robert J. : Upgrading police leadership. *Police Journal*, V. 49(3) July-September, 1976, 150-57.

Horstmian, Preston : Leaderless group discussion as an assessment tool for supervisory and command promotions. *Journal of Police Science and Administration*, V. 2(1), March, 1974, 34-37.

Iyer, N. Rama : Leadership in police force (Paper). In second all India police science congress, Bombay, September, 1961.

Iyer, T.G.L. : Leadarship in police today. *C.B.I. Bulletin*, V. 24 (1) January, 1990, 13-15.

Jha, Sudhir Kumar : Juxtaposition of formal and informal leadership in police. *Indian Police Journal.* V. 32 (1) January-March, 1985, 56-58.

Kuykendall, Jack and Unsinger, Pelere : Leadership style of police managers. *Journal of Criminal Justice*, V. 10 (4) 1982, 311-21.

Lockley, T. : Police leadership. *Police Journal*, February, 1961, 94-100.

Malaviya, P.D. : Leadership at police station level. *Indian Police Journal*, V. 26 (2) October-December, 1979, 4-11.

Mishra, S.C. : Discipline and leadership. *National Academy Magazine*, November, 1970, 10-17.

Nayar, Kuldip : Police lacks leadership in crisis. *Indian Nation*, December, 15, 1983, 3.

Pell, Arthur R. : Police leadership. Springfield (Ill), Charles C. Thomas, 1967.

Potts Lee W. : Police leadership : Challenges for the eighties. *Journal of Police Science and Administration*, V. 10 (2) June, 1982, 181-88.

Singh, Jaspal : Aspects of negative leadership in police. *Indian Police Journal*, V. 28 (3) January-March, 1982, 20-23.

Votira, K.B. : A syndicate study on leadership styles in the police. *Transactions*, V. 26, 1978, 1-85.

Watt, Ian : Leadership in the police service. *Police Journal*, V. 62(1) January-March, 1989, 12-21.

13

Police Welfare

Ghosh, S.K. : Police welfare. Bhubaneswar, Home Department, Government of Orissa, 1966.

Menon, K. Sreekumara : Police welfare work. *Social Welfare*, V. 29(11) February, 1974, 83-84.

Police welfare machinery set up. *Haryana Review*, V. 13(7) July, 1979, 15.

Sharma, M.L. : Police welfare : A unique dimension, *C.B.I. Bulletin*, V. 17(5) May, 1983, 3-5.

Sharma, M.L. : Police welfare : A unique dimension. *Indian Police Journal*, V. 29 (3) January-March, 1983, 18-21.

Vadackumchery, Games : Police in social welfare. *Social Welfare*, V. 27 (9) December, 1980, 27-28.

14

Police Stress

Alkus, Stephen and Padesky, Christine : Special problems of police officers : Stress-related issues and interventions. *Counseling Psychologist*, V. 11 (2) 1983, 55-64.

Anson, Richard H. and Bloom, Mary E. : Police stress in an occupational context. *Journal of Police Science and Adn inistration*, V. 16 (4) December, 1988, 229-235.

Beley, Worren W. : American and Danish police "dropout" rates : Denmark's force as a case study in high job satisfaction, low stress and low turnover. *Journal of Vocatianal Behaviour*, V. 25 (1) August, 1984, 58-69.

Bhardwaj, Rupali, and Khandelwal, Preetam : Role stress among police personnel. *Indian Police Journal*, V. 6 (1) January-March 1989, 21-25.

Bhasker, Sarita : Measuring job stress of the Indian police : An empirical approach, *Abhigyan*, Spring, 1990, 30-44.

Burke, Ronald U. and Catherine, Kirchmeyer : Initial career orientations, stress and burnout in police workers. *Canadian Police College Journal*, V. 14 (1) 1990, 28-36.

Burke, Ronald J. and Catherine, Kirchmeyer : Present career orientations, stress and burnout in police workers. *Canadian Police College Journal*, V. 14 (1) 1990, 50-57.

Degenaro, Raymond T. : Sources of stress within a police organisation. *Indian Police Journal*, V. 27 (3) January-March, 1981, 47-54.

Dhillon, Paramjeet K. : Occupational stress and job satisfaction in relation to hierarchical position : A study of police personnel. *Social Science International*, V. 5 (1-2) January-July, 1989, 32-41.

Elliott, Michael L. (and others) : Marital intimacy and satisfaction as a support system for coping with police officer stress. *Journal of Police Science and Administration*, V. 14 (1) March, 1986, 40-44.

Gangopadhyay, Abhijit : A syndicate study on "alienation and stress among subordinate ranks of police". *Transactions*, V. 35, 120-208.

Gudjonsson, Gisli H. : Factors reducing occupational stress in police officers : Junior officers view. *Police Journal*, V. 56 (3) July-September 1983, 251-55.

Hageman, Mary J. : Responses to police officers to stress. *Journal of Police Science and Administration*, V. 10 (2) June, 1982, 235-43.

Hasek, John : Organizational stress in policing. *Royal Canadian Mounted Police Gazette*, V. 47 (9) 1985, 11-14.

Joseph, M.I. : Stress in police work : A preliminary study. *Psychological Studies*, V. 34 (1) March, 1989, 47-54.

Kirmeyer, Sandra and Dougherdy, Thomas W. : Work load tension and coping : Moderating effects of supervisor support. *Personnel Psychology*, V. 41 (1) Spring, 1988, 125-139.

Kores, W.H. (and others) : Job stress in policemen. *Journal of Police Science and Administration*, V. 2 (2) 1974, 145-55.

Larsson, Gerry (and others) : Appraisal and coping processes in acute time limited stressful situations : A study of police officers. *European Journal of Personality*, V. 2 (4) December 1988, 259-76.

Lester, David : Perceived stress in police officers and belief in locus of control. *Journal of General Psychology*, V. 107 (1) July 1982, 157-58.

Lester, David : Stress in American police officers : An American perspective. *Police Journal*, V. 56 (2) April-June, 1983, 188-90.

Lester, David : Subjective stress and self-esteem of police officers. *Perceptual & Motor Skills*, V. 63 (3) December, 1986, 1334.

Lester, David : Subjective stress and sources of stress for police officers. *Psychological Reports*, V. 50 (3, Part 2) June, 1982, 10-94.

Lester, David and Gallagher, Julie : Stress in police officers and department store managers. *Psychological Reports*, V. 46 (3, Part 1) June 1980, 882.

Lester, David and Leitner, Lewis A. : Stress and its management for police officers. *Police Journal*, V. 56 (4) October-December, 1983, 324-29.

Lester, David and Leitner, Lewis A. : Stress and its management for police officers. *Police Journal*, V. 57 (1) January-March, 1984, 31-35.

Lester, David and Mink, Stanley R. : Is stress higher in police officers? An exploratory study. *Psychological Reports*, V. 45 (2) October, 1979, 554.

Lester, David (and others) : A note on locus of control and stress in police officers. *Journal of Community Psychology*, V. 13 (1) January 1985, 77-79.

Lester, David (and others) : Effects of a stress management training programme on police officers. *International Review of Applied Psychology*, V. 33 (1) January, 1984, 25-31.

Lester, David and Solis, Anthony : Type A personality, stress, and job satisfaction in police officers. *Perceptual & Motor Skills*, V. 51 (3, Part 1) December 1980, 890.

Loo, Robert : Occupational stress in the law enforcement profession. *Canada's Mental Health*, V. 32 (3) September, 1984, 10-13.

Loo, Robert : Post-shooting stress reactions among police officers. *Journal of Human Stress*, V. 12 (1) Spring, 1986, 27-71.

Malloy, Thomas E. and Maya, G. Larry : Police stress hypothesis : A critical evaluation, *Criminal Justice and Behaviour*, V. 11 (2) June, 1984, 197-224.

Martelli, Theresa A. (and others) : Police stress survey : Reality and relation to job satisfaction and organizational commitment. *Psychological Reports*, V. 64 (1) February, 1988, 267-73.

Martin, Catherine A. (and others) : Post-traumatic stress disorder in police and working with victims : A pilot study. *Journal of Police Science and Administration*, V. 14 (2) June 1986, 98-101.

Maynard, Peter E. and Maynard, Nancy E. : Stress in police families : Some policy implications. *Journal of Police Science and Administration*, V. 10 (3) September, 1982, 302-14.

Mcnulty, S. (and others) : Use of hormone analysis in the assessment of the efficacy of stress management training in police recruits. *Journal of Police Science and Administration*, V. 12 (2) June, 1984, 130-32.

Mills, Robert B. : Simulated stress in police recruit selection. *Journal of Police Science and Administration*. V. 4 (2) June, 1976, 179-86.

Moyer, Imogene : An exploratory study of role distance as police responses to stress. *Journal of Criminal Justice*, V. 14 (4) 1986, 363-73.

Nordlicht, Stephen : Effects of stress on the police officer and family. *New York State Journal, of Medicine* V. 79 (3) March, 1979, 400-01.

Oyefese, Adenekan O. : Occupational stress and attitude to work in the Nigerian police force. *Indian Journal of* Behaviour, V. 13 (2) April, 1989, 14-22.

Pendleton, Michaol (and others) : Stress and strain among police fire-fighters and government workers : A comparative analysis. *Criminal Justice and Behaviour*, V. 16 (2) June, 1989, 196-210.

Perrier, David C. and Toner, Reginald : Police stress : The hidden foe. *Canadian Police College Journal*, V. 8 (1) 1984, 15-26.

Ramachandran, G. : Can't we reduce stress factors on the police? *Nirnay*, V. 2 (2) September, 1987, 1-10.

Reiser, Mortin : Some organisational stresses on policemen. *Journal of Police Science and Administration*, V. 2 (2) June, 1974, 156-59.

Sarason, Irwing (and others) : Helping police officers to cope with stress : A cognitive-behavioural approach. *American Journal of Community Psychology*, V. 7 (6) December, 1979, 593-603.

Schaefer, Robert B. : Stress in police working. *C.B.I. Bulletin*, V. 19 (12), December, 1985, 10-12.

Sigler, Rober T. and Wilson, Charles N. : Stress in police work : Comparing police stress with teacher stress. *Journal of Police Science and Administration*, V. 16 (3) September, 1988, 151-62.

Singleton, Gory W. : Effects of job-related stress on the physical and psychological adjustment of police officers. *Dissertation Abstracts International*, V. 38 (5-B) November 1977, 2384.

Somadevilla, S.A. : Stress management programme for law enforcement officers. *C.B.I. Bulletin*, V. 17 (2) February, 1984, 12-13.

Territo, Leonard and Vetter, Harold J. : Stress and police personnel. *Journal of Police Science and Administration*, V. 9 (2) June, 1981, 195-208.

Terry, W. Clinton, III : Police stress : The empirical evidence. *Journal of Police Science and Administration*, V. 9 (1) March, 1981, 61-75.

Violanti, John M. and Marshall, James R. : Police stress process. *Journal of Police Science and Administration*, 11 (4) December, 1983, 389-94.

Violanti, John M. (and others) : Stress, coping and alcohol use : The police connection. *Family of Police Science and Administration*, V. 13 (2) June, 1985, 106-10.

White, Jacquelyn W. (and others) : Factors of stress among police officers. *Criminal Justice and Behaviour*, V. 12 (1) March, 1985, 111-128.

15

Police Discipline

Bhattacharyya, P. : Discipline in constabulary. Central Police Training College, Abu, 3rd Advanced Course, June-December, 1961.

Bose, A.C. : Police indiscipline and politics. *Amrita Bazar Patrika*, 9 September, 1969, 6.

Denning, Lord : Discipline of law. London, Butterworths, 1979.

Dhavan, Rajeev : Police and Judges : Nadial case. *Hindustan Times*, 23 September, 1991, 7.

Gourley, G. Douglas : Police discipline. *Journal of Criminal Law and Criminology*, May-June, 1950.

Kulkarni, V.B. : New threat to democracy : Politicians responsible for police indiscipline. *Indian Express*, 31 August, 1969, 6.

Mudaliar, N. Murugesa : Government and police discipline. *Swarajya*, V. 14 (12) 20 September, 1969, 19.

Nath, D.C. : Roots of police indiscipline. *Police Research and Development, Quarter II*, April-June, 1985, 4.

Police indiscipline (Editorial). *Times of India*, 4 February, 1969, 8.

Reddy, G.K. : Police indiscipline worries centre. *Hindu*, 15 May, 1980.

Rosha, P. : Strengthening police discipline. *Indian Express*, 17 September, 1988, 8.

Rustamji, K.F. : Police indiscipline : Everyone to blame. *Hindustan Times*, 5 August, 1988, 9.

Saksena, N.S. : Anatomy of police indiscipline. *Times of India*, 26 May, 1979, 8.

Sen, A.K. : Indian poliee and discipline. *Swarajya*, V. 11 (47) 20 May, 1976, 9-10.

16

Police and Citizen

Adams, Thomas F. : Law enforcement : An introduction to the police role in community. Englewood Cliffs (N.J.), Prentice Hall, 1968.

Agarwal, K.P. : Police-public relations. *C.B.I. Bulletin*, September, 1973, 1-3.

Ahren, James F. : We don't know what we want from the police. *Centre Magazine*, July-August, 1973, 32-35.

Akshey Kumar : Police in a changing society. *C.B.I. Bulletin*, V. 23 (6) June, 1989, 8-12.

Akshey, Kumar : Police in the society. *Indian Police Journal*, March, 1983, 22-27.

Akshey Kumar : Police response as a catalyst in police-community relations. *Indian Police Journal*, V. 36 (1) January-February, 1989, 26-32.

Alderson, John C. : Police and public order. *Public Administration*, V. 63 (4) Winter, 1985, 435-44.

Alper, Geeffrey P. and Dunham, Roger G. : Community policing. *Journal of Police Science and Administration*, V. 14 (3) September, 1986, 212-22.

Ames, Walter L. : Police in the community. *Police Journal*, V. 52 (3) July-September, 1979, 152-59.

Amiruddin, Parween : Role of police in the enforcement of social legislation. *Indian Journal of Criminology* (*Suppl.*), V. 7(2) July, 1979, 197-201.

Ananthachari, T. : Police in a changing society. *Indian Police Journal*, V. 31(4) October-December, 1984, 14-22.

Arul, F.V. : Police in the enforcement of social legislation. *C.B.I. Bulletin*, V. 17(5) May, 1983, 1-2.

Arul, F.C. : Police in the enforcement of social legislation. *Indian Journal of Criminology* (*Suppl.*), V. 7(2) July, 1979, 187-89.

Ashenhust, P.M. : Police and the people. Springfield (III) Charles C. Thomas, 1956.

Avasthi, A. : Police-public relations : Some aspects. *Administrative Change*, V. 5(2) January-June, 1978, 179-83.

Bacon, Ranulph : Four ways to help the police. *Police Journal*, V. 56(3) July-September, 1983, 210-20.

Banerjee, D. : A syndicate study on "community control of police". S.V.P. National Police Academy, Hyderabad, *Transactions*, V. 28, 1979, 136-198.

Banton, Michael : Policy-community relations. London, Collins, 1973.

Banton, Michael : Policemen in the community. London, Tavistock, 1964.

Baumann, Donald J. (and others) : Citizen participation in police crisis intervention activities. *American Journal of Community Psychology*, V. 15(4) August, 1978, 459-481.

Bawa, P.S. : Police and public co-operation against crime. *Police Research and Development, Quarter III*, July-September, 1984, 1-6.

Bawa, P.S. : Citizen and the police. Calcutta, Rupa, 1987.

Bawa, P.S. : Crime : Citizen and the police. Calcutta, Rupa Publications.

Bawa, P.S. : Police and public cooperation against crime. *Police Research and Development, Quarter III*, 1984, 1-6.

Bawa, P.S. : Strategy for public relations. *Police Research and Development, Quarter III*, July-September, 1986, 1-3.

Bayley, David H. : Police and society. California, Sage Publications, 1977.

Belson, William : Public and the police. London, Harper and Row, 1975.

Benson, Paul R. : Political alienation and public satisfaction with police service. *Pacific Sociological Review*, V. 24(1) January, 1981, 45-64.

Bent, A.E. and Rossum, R.A. : Police, criminal justice and the community. New York, Harper & Row Publishers, 1976.

Berkley, George : Democratic policeman. Boston, Beacon Press, 1969.

Bhambhari, C.P. and Mathur, Kuldeep : Students, police and campus unrest : A study of images and perceptions. Jaipur, H.C. Mathur State Institute of Public Administration, 1972.

Bhatia, K.L. : Role of police in a changing society. *Lawyer*, July, 1978, 149-53.

Bhowmik, Shant K. : Police and society. *Economic and Political Weekly*, V. 21(6) 8 February, 1986, 241-43.

Bidwai, Praful : Police connection helps gangs. *Times of India*, December 16, 1981, 1.

Black, Algernon D. : People and the police. New York, McGraw Hill Book Company, 1968.

Blaram, A. : Police and the citizen : Working out a meaningful relationship. *C.B.I. Bulletin*, August, 1978, 5-7.

Bopp, William J. : Police community relationships. Springfield, Charles C. Thomas, 1972.

Bose, Sukumar and Dasgupta, Snehanshu K. : Study on the attitude of adolescents towards police of Calcutta. *Indian Journal of Criminology*, V. 13(1) January, 1985, 34-40.

Brandslatte, A.F. and Redelet, Louis A. : Police-community relations : A source book. California, Beverley Hills, 1968.

Brown, James and Howles, Graham (eds.) : Police and the community. Farnborough (Hants), Saxon House, 1975.

Cain, Maureen E. : Society and policeman's role. London, Routledge & Kegan Paul, 1973.

California University : Police and the community. Washington (D.C.), Government Printing Office, 1966.

Chamanlal, Bikshu : Policeman your friend. New Delhi, The Author, 1971.

Chinnappareddy, O. : Police, the public and the law. In Ram Reddy and K. Seshadri (eds) Developing society and police. Hyderabad, Osmania University, 1972, 1-12.

Chakrabarti, Nirmal Kanti : Non-crime services. *Indian Police Journal*, V. 36(2) April-June, 1989, 18-24.

Chakrabarty, S.K. : Social acceptability of the police. *Indian Police Journal*, V. 26(1) July-September, 1979, 3-8.

Channappa Reddy, O. : Police, the public and the law. In G. Ram Reddy and K. Seshadri (eds) Developing society and police. Hyderabad, Osmania University, 1972.

Chappell, Duncan and Wilson, P.R. : Police and the public in Australia and New Zealand. St. Lucia, University of Queensland Press, 1968.

Chattopadhyay, Gouranga P. : Children of the Kapos. (Paper) Presented in all India seminar on the role of the police in changing Indian society. Calcutta, 1985. *Management and Labour Studies*, V. 11(4) October, 220-26.

Chaturvedi, S.K. : Pathology of police-public relationship : Causes and cure. *Indian Police Journal*, V. 31(3) July-September, 1985, 39-42.

Cizanckas, Victor I. and Feist, Fritzi : A community's response to police change. *Journal of Police Science and Administration*, V. 3(3) September, 1975, 284-91.

Clark, Roberts : Police and the community : An analytic perspective. New York, New Viewpoints, 1979.

Clifford, William : Integrity of the police. *Public Administration*, (*Kanpur*) October, 1974, 5.

Coates, Robert B. : Dimensions of police citizen interaction : A social psychological analysis. *Dissertation Abstracts International*, V. 33(8-A) February, 1973, 4553.

Coates, Robert B. and Miller, Alten D. : Patrolmen and addicts : A study of police perception and police-citizen interaction. *Journal of Police Science and Administration*, V. 2 (3) September, 1974, 308-21.

Coffey, Alan, Eldefonso, Edward and Hartinger, Walter : Police-community relations. Englewood Cliffs (NJ), Prentice Hall, 1971.

Cook, Judith : A good guy policeman. V. 50(895) 29 November, 1979, 492-93.

Cromwell, Paul F. Jr. and Keefer George (eds.) : Police-community relations, St. Paul, Minn, West, 1973.

Curb the police. (Editorial) *New Age*, V. 26(23) 4 June, 1978, 2.

Das, Dilip K. : Understanding police-human relations. Metuchen, Scarecrow Press, 1987.

Dasgupta, Ranjit : Police-people relationship in contemporary India. *Indian Journal of Public Administration*, V. 32(4) October-September, 1986, 1036-42.

Dean, M. : Finger on the policeman's collar *Political Quarterly*, V. 93(2) 1982.

Decker, Scott H. : Citizen attitudes toward the police : Review of past findings and suggestions for future policy. *Journal of Police Science and Administration*, V. 8(1) March, 1981, 80-87.

Decker, Scott H. and Wagner, Allen E. : Impact of patrol staffing of police : Citizen inquiries and dispositions. *Journal of Criminal Justice*, V. 10(5) 1982, 375-82.

Deriega, J. (and others) : Officer friendly : changing children's attitude about the police. *Journal of Community Psychology*, V. 7(3) July, 1979, 220-27.

Dev, Jai : Men and policemen. *Patriot* (*Mag*), 20 June, 1982, 1.

Devlin, Lord : Police in a changing society. *Police Journal*, February, 1966, 75-86.

Dewan, V.N. : Security guide for police and public. New Delhi, Newman Group of Publishers.

Dharmaraj, J. : Pollce and people, *C.B.I. Bulletin*, June, 1974, 1-2.

Diamond, Michael Jay and Lobitz, W. Charles : When familiarity breeds respect, the effects of an experimental depolarization program on police and student attitudes towards each other. *Journal of Social Issues*, V. 29(4) 1973, 95-109.

Diaz, S.M. : Police in the service of the police. *Indian Journal of Criminology*, V. 6(2) January, 1978, 49-52.

Diaz, S.M. : Public expectations, perceptions and attitudes to police in India. *Indian Journal of Criminology*, V. 17 (1) January, 1979, 42-52.

Diaz, S.M. : University students' perception of serious crime and related police responses. *Indian Journal of Criminology*, V. 12(2) July, 1984, 79-86.

Dinakar, C. : Effective police interaction with the people representatives. *Transactions*, V. 25, April, 1977, 131-146.

Doig, Jameson W. : Police in a democratic society. *Public Administration, Review*, September-October, 1968, 393-406.

Dube, S.C. (ed) : Public service and social responsibility. New Delhl, Vikas Publishing House, 1979.

Durai, A.P.: The constabulary : Key to better police-public relation. *Indian Police Journal*, V. 29(4) April-June, 1983, 10-13.

Dutt, Tushar : Pollce and labour. *Sardar Vallabhbhai Patel National Police Academy Magazine*, July, 1976, 64-76.

Earle, Howard H. : Police-community relations : crisis in our times. Springfield, Charles C. Thomas, 1976.

Edwards, George : Police on the urban frontier : A guide to community understanding. New York, Institute of Human Relations Press, 1968.

Eisenberg, Terry (and others) : Police-community action : A program for change in police community behaviour patterns. New York, Praeger, 1973.

Erayol, Alphonse S. and James, Vadakumcheri : Police and society. Trivandrum, Kairali Books, 1985.

Erez, Edna : Self-defined "desert" and citizens' assessment of the police. *Journal of Criminal Law and Criminology*, V. 75 (4) Winter, 1984, 1276-99.

Farah, S.A. : In defence of police. *Indian Nation*, June 21, 1988.

Farah, S.A. : Police-public relations. *Indian Nation*, 21 July, 1987.

Fein, Edith and Knaut, Susan A. : Crisis intervention and support: Working with the police. *Social Case Work*, V. 17(2) May, 1986, 276-82.

Fleisher, Leslie A. : Police-community relations. Chapel Hill (N.C.), Institute of Government, University of North Carolina, 1967.

Foulger, R.E. : Police and the police. *Corona*, May, 1959, 165-67.

Friedmann, Robert R. and Sharer, Moshe : Effect of different policing strategies upon citizens' attitudes toward the police and their community. *Canadian Police College Journal*, V. 8 (1) 1984, 27-35.

Galvin, Raymond and Redelet, Louis : A national survey of police and community relations. East Lansing, Michigan State University, 1967.

George, K.N. : Role of police in the enforcement of social legislation. *Indian Journal of Criminology* (Suppl.) V. 7(2) July, 1978, 190-92.

Germann, A.C. : Problem of police-community relations : A report prepared for the task force on the law enforcement. Washington (D.C.) National Commission on the causes and prevention of violence, 1968.

Ghosh, S.K.: Police and the public. Bhubaneshwar, Home Department, Government of Orissa, 1965.

Gibson, I.R.: Police organised boys clubs. *Indian Police Journal*, V. 26(4) April-June, 1980, 53-56.

Glauser, Michael J. and Tullar, William L. : Citizen satisfaction with police officer/citizen interaction : Implications for the changing role of police organizations. *Journal of Police Psychology*, V. 70(3) August, 1985, 514-27.

Gore, M.S. : Police and society. *Decision*, V. 13 (3) July, 1986, 149-55.

Gourg, Douglas : Public relations and the police. Springfield, Illinois, Charles C. Thomas, 1953.

Gourley, G. Douglas : Police and the public. Springfield (III), Charles C. Thomas, 1963.

Gourley, G. Douglas : Public relations and the police. Springfield (III), Charles C. Thomas, 1953.

Graf, Francis A. : Relationship between social support and occupational stress among police officers. *Journal of Police Science and Administration*, V. 14(3) September, 1986, 178-86.

Great Britain, Working Group for England and Wales : The handling of complaints against the police. London, 1974 (Cmnd. 5582, Chairman : A.D. Gorton Brown).

Great Britain : Working group for Scotland. Handling of complaints against the police. Edinburgh, 1974 (Cmnd. 5583 Chairman : W.K. Fraser).

Greenweld, Judith E. : Aggression as a component of police-citizen transactions : Differences between male and female police officers. *Dissertation Abstracts International*, V. 37 (2-8), August, 1976, 1034.

Gregory, G.D. : Public relations and the police. *Police Journal*, October, 1970.

Griffith, Rodger W. and Cadderty, Thomas P. : Police and citizen value systems : Some cross-sectional comparisons. *Journal of Applied Social Psychology*, V. 7 (3) July-September, 1977, 191-204.

Groves, Theodore (and others) : An approach to problems in police community relations. *Journal of Community Psychology*, V. 8(4) October, 1980, 357-63.

Gupta, Ranjit : Police and public order. *Times of India*, 14 April, 1980, 6.

Hain, Peter (ed) : Policing in the police. London, John Calder, 1979.

Haldar, Dipak : Police-community relations during unusual conditions. *Police Research and Development, Quarter IV*, October-September, 1986, 1-3.

Hann, Harlon (ed) : Police in urban society. Beverly Hills (Cal), Sage Publications, 1971.

Hennessy, James J. : Use of civilians in police work. *Police Chief*, April, 1976, 36.

Hewitt, William H. and Newman, Charles L. : Police-community relations : An anthology and bibliography. New York, Foundation Press, 1970.

Higgins, A.C. : Basis and the quality of relationships between the police and the public. *Police Journal*, V. 49 (4) October-December, 1976, 285-89.

Hilton, Jennifer : Psychology of police-public relations. *Police Journal*, July-September, 1973, 233-41.

Hodge, Robert W. : Public, the police and the administration. Chicago, National Opinion Research Center, 1965.

Holdaway, Simon : Police and social work relations : Problems and possibilities. *British Journal of Social Work*, V. 16 (2) April, 1986, 137-60.

Hooda, R.K. : Police-public relations. *National Police Academy Magazine*, November, 1968, 28-31.

Hooja, B. : Public-police relations. *Prashasnika*, V. 7(3-4) July-December, 1978, 106-11.

Hooja, G.B K. : Police and social service. *C.B.I. Bulletin*, V. 15 (4) April, 1981.

Hughes, Patrick H. (and others) : Addicts, police and the neighbourhood social system. *American Journal of Orthopsychiatry*, V. 44 (1) January, 1974, 129-41.

Hunt, R.A. Police and public communication. *Police Journal*, April-June, 1973, 167-77.

Ignatiaff, Michael : Police and people : The birth of Mr. Peel's 'blue locusts'. *New Society*, V. 40 (882) 30 August, 1979, 443-45.

India, Ministry of Home Affairs. Bureau of Police Research and Development : The IV workshop-cum-seminar on police-public relations. Bombay (8-9 October, 1990), 37-39.

Inefficient police wants to disarm public. *Modern Review*, V. 129(2) August, 1971, 85-86.

Innaiah, N. : Police in democratic set up. *Radical Humanist*, V. 49 (2) May, 1984, 22-23.

Innaiah, N. : Police Vs. people. *Radical Humunist*. V. 42 (3) June, 1978, 31-32.

International City Managers Association : Police community relations programs. Washington, (D.C.), ICMA, 1967.

Jackson, Keith and Lansley, John : Police in the community : experiment in police university co-operation. *Police Journal*, October-December, 1971, 294-301.

Jacques, D.N.O. and Mctchell, A.J. : Social and community involvement for police cadets. *Police Journal*, October-December, 1975, 266-67.

Jaidev : Men and policeman. *Patriot*, 20 June, 1981, 1.

Jha, Sudhir Kumar : Social legislation and police. *Indian Police Journal*, V. 27 (3) January-March, 1981, 12-28.

Jha, Sudhir Kumar : Social legislation and police. Souvenir, 10th Symposium of all India principals police training college, Dated 22.10.1981 to 24.10.1981, Patna, 21-24.

Jonikas, Journe : Police and you : A public relation program. *Indian Journal of Criminology and Criminalistics*, V. 1(2-3) June-September, 1981.

Joshi, G P. : Police-public relations. *Indian Police Journal*, V. 20(4) April-June, 1974, 13-18.

Kanetkar, V.C. : Police-public cooperation. *C.B.I. Bulletin*. V. 18(10) October, 1984, 2-4.

Katju, K N. : Police and the people. *Public Administration*, March, 1963, 24-26.

Katzman, Marvin S. : Police labour relations : Where labour organizations and employers stand. *Police Journal*, V. 56(2) April-June, 1983, 183-87.

Kaul, D N. : Police and the changing society. *Akashvani*, 21 May, 1978, 15-16.

Kaul, D.N. : Police-community relations : Scope for improvement. *Man and Development*, V. 2 (1) March, 1980, 44-47.

Kaul, Gautam : Why we don't help others. *Indian Police Journal*, April-June, 1976, 20-22.

Kaushal, R.S. : Police and the public. Ambala, Standard Publishers, 1954.

Kelly, Joseph A. and O'rourke, Thomas W. : An appraisal of the attitudes of police officers toward the concept of police-community relations. *Journal of Police Science and Administration*, V. 1(2) June, 1973, 224-31.

Kettle, Martin : Guns, the police and the citizen. *New Society*, V. 50(894) 22 November, 1979, 431-32.

Khan, M.Z. and Krishna, K.P. : Adolescents and the police : A study in attitudinal change. *Indian Journal of Public Administration*, V. 28(4) January-March, 1982, 45-54.

Khan, M.Z. and Krishna, K.P. : Adolescents and the police : A study in attitudinal change. *Police Research and Development, Quarter I*, January-March, 1981, 5-7.

Khan, M.Z. and Krishna, K.P. : Attitude of adolescents to police. New Delhi, Institute of Criminology and Forensic Science, 1980.

Khan, M.Z. and Krishna, K.P. : Development of a scale to measure public attitude towards police. *Indian Journal of Criminology*, V. 13(2) July, 1985, 85-95.

Khullar, Surrinder : People versus police. *Indian Nation*, 13 August, 1969, 4.

Khullar, Surrinder : Police and the public. *Assam Tribune*, 13 August, 1969, 4.

King, E.M. : Officer speaks in public. Springfield, Charles C. Thomas, 1968.

Kistaiah, M. : Police and public relations. *Mainstream*, V. 22(17) 24 December, 1983, 3-4.

Knights, P.D. : Police in a changing society. *Police Journal*, December, 1966, 608-18.

Kreps, Gary A. and Weller, Jack M. : Police-community relations movement. *American Behavioural Scientist*, V. 16(3) January-February, 1973, 402-412.

Krishna, K.P. and Khan, M.Z. : Personal, familial and international antecedents of adolescents' attitude towards police. *Indian Journal of Psychology*, V. 55(3-4) September-December, 1980, 138-56.

Krishna, K.P. (and others) Police-community relations : A study in images. *Indian Journal of Criminology*, V. 9(1) January, 1981, 14-22.

Krishna Murthy, S : Syndicate study on implementation of the protection of civil rights acts. *Transactions*, V. 30, 1980, 22-69.

Krishnan, R.S : Police in a democracy. *Hindu*, 14 June, 1977, 8.

Krishnan, R.S. : Police in a democracy. *Hindu*, 15 June, 1977, 6.

Krishnaswamy, N. : How aloof are the police from the people. *Hindu*, 31 October, 1976.

Krishnaswamy, N. : How aloof are the police from the people. *Indian Police Journal*, V. 23(4) April-June, 1977, 8-14.

Krishnaswamy, N. : Police-public interaction. *Indian Police Journal*, V. 24(1) July-September, 1977, 11-14.

Kroeker, Larry L. (and others) : Evaluation of a police-youth human relations program. *Professional Psychology*, V. 5 (2) May 1974, 140-54.

Kulkarni, V.B. : Police and the citizen. *Indian Express*, 6 February, 1975, 4.

Kumar, Akshey : Dignity of the individual and security of the society : Dilemma for the police. *C.B.I. Bulletin*, V. 17(11) November, 1983, 1-4.

Kumar, Akshey : Police in a changing society. *C.B.I. Bulletin*, V. 23(6) June, 1989, 8-12.

Kumar, Akshey: Police in the society. *Indian Police Journal*, V. 29 (3) January-March, 1983, 22-27.

Lakshmanna, C. : Changing social structure and the police. In G. Ram Reddy and K. Seshadri (eds.) Developing society and police. Hyderabad, Osmania University, 1972.

Lester, David : The prestige of policemen around the world. *Police Journal*, V. 55(2) April-July, 1982, 110-12.

Levi, M. and Jones, S. : Public and police perceptions of crime seriousness in England and Wales. *British Journal of Criminology*, V. 25(3) July, 1985, 234-50.

Lohman, Josepl and Gordon, E. Misner : Police and the community. Berkeley (Cal.), University of California, School of Criminology, 1966.

Loree, Donald J. : Police in a plural society. *Canadian Police College Journal*. V. 9(4) 1985, 391-412.

Lundman, Richard J. : Domestic police citizen encounters. *Journal of Police Science and Administration*, V. 2(1) March, 1974, 22-27.

Maharashtra : Improving relations between the police and the public. *Capital*, V. 176 (4397) 22 January, 1976, 134.

Mahmood Bin Muhammad : Delinquency in affluent societies and the police. *Police Research and Development, Quarter III & IV*, July-December, 1972, 1-5.

Mahmood Bin Muhammad : Problems of youth are the problems of the police. *Police Research and Development, Quarter II*, April-June, 1972, 1-4.

Malaviya, P.D. : Why don't police change? *Sardar Vallabhbhai Patel Natianal Police Academy Magazine*, June, 1977, 36-52.

Malimath, S.P. : Police-public relations. *Indian Police Journal*, V. 23(2) October-December, 1979, 64-67.

Masterson, K.W. : Projecting the police role in Society. *Police Journal*, V. 62(1) January-March, 1989, 4-12.

Mathivanan, Shri N. : Police-public relations : Problems and prospects. *Police Research and Development, Quarter II*, April-June, 1986, 1-4.

Mathur, K.M. : Dignity of the individual and security of the society. *Indian Police Journal*, V. 29(1) July-September, 1982, 6-12.

Mathur, K.M. : Problems of police in a democratic society. Jaipur, RESA Publishers, 1987.

Mathur, Krishna Mohan : Community control of police : The implications of decentralisation of police functions. *Police Research and Development, Quarter-II*, April-June, 1979, 8-11.

Mathur, Krishna Mohan : State of police community relations in India today : How to improve it. *C.B.I. Bulletin*, V. 18(1) January, 1984, 7-12.

Mays, John Barron : Crime and the social structure. London, Faber and Faber, 1963.

Mccabe, Sarah : Police and the public. *Police Journal*, V. 53 (4) October-December, 1980, 357-66.

Mckenna, James S., Mark Brever and Singer, Ralph B. : Police social services. *C.B.I. Bulletin*, V. 15(4) April, 1981, 9-10.

Mclaren, Peter : Does society expect too much from its police. *Police Journal*, V. 52(3) July-September, 1979, 218-28.

Measures to improve ties between police and public. *Times of India*, 9 September, 1970, 3.

Mehra, Ajay K. : Public and the police : Need for fresh thinking. *Decision*, V. 13 (3) July, 1985, 191-92.

Mehra Preeti : Human factor. *Economic Times*, 12 April, 1981, 4.

Merricks, David L. : Attitudes of normal and educable mentally related children toward police officers. *Dissertation Abstracts International*, V. 34(1-A) July, 1973, 193-94.

Merricks, F.R. : Development of community relations in the metropolitan police. *Police Journal*, January, 1970, 239-35.

Michaels, Rhoda A. and Trager, Harvey : Social work in police departments. *Social Work*, V. 18(5) September, 1973, 67-75.

Michigan State University : A national survey of police and community relations. Washington (D.C.) Government Printing Office, 1967.

Mir, Mehrajuddin : Public cooperation in police work. *Indian Police Journal*, V. 28(3) January-March, 1982, 48-52.

Mishra, B.B. : Miscellaneous services by the police and public relations. *C.B.I. Bulletin*, V. 16(C) April, 1982, 1-3.

Misra, S.C. : Police and the problem of student unrest. *Prashasnika*, October-December, 1974, 49-54.

Misra, S.C. : Police-public relations. *Orissa Review*, October, 1971, 39-42.

Mohapatra, Taraprasad : Securing public cooperation in police work. *Indian Police Journal*, V. 26(3) January-March, 1980, 28-33.

Morris, Elaine B. : Citizen perception of police service delivery : A look at some consequences. *Political Studies*, V. 29 (3) September, 1981, 352-64.

Muir, A.A. : Police and its public. *Police Journal*, May 1963, 207-13.

Mukhoty, Gobinda : Police and the public. *Mainstream*, V. 16(43), 24 June, 1978, 12-14.

Mullick, B.N. : Police-public relationship. *Indian Police Journal*, V. 15(1) July, 1968, 3-12.

Muniswamy, R.K. : Police-public relations. *Deccan Chronicle*, 5 April, 1976, 4.

Munn, Names, R. and Renner K. Edward : Perceptions of police work by the police and by the public. *Criminal Justice and Behaviour*, V. 5(2) June, 1978, 165-80.

Nagarkar, V.V. : Police and the people. *Radical Humanist*. V. 47 (11) February, 1983, 17-23.

Nagla, B.K. : Police-public relations in contemporary society. *Social Defence*, V. 18(69) July, 1982, 30-40.

Najmi, Mohammad : Police and the public : A two way traffic. *Social Welfare*, V. 32 (5) August, 1985, 30-31.

Nandy, Raj : Police and the community. *Hindustan Times*, 2 March, 1980, 1.

Narasimhan, C.V. : Police, judiciary and the public. *Decision*, V. 13 (3) July, 1986, 161-64.

Narasimhan, C.V. : Police-public relations : A case study. *Vidura*, February, 1979, 32-33.

Narayan, Rao A. : Police and the public. *Indian Police Journal*, V. 25(1) July-September, 1978, 74-77.

Nath D.C. : Police in a changing society. *Decision*, V. 13 (3) July, 1986, 226-32.

Nath, D.C. : Social responsibilities of the police force : Scope and limitations. *Indian Police Journal*, V. 27(3) January-March, 1981, 29-38.

Nath, T. : Police and public relations. *Nagpur Times*, 6 December, 1976.

National Center on Police and Community Relations : A national survey of police and community relations. Washington (D.C.) Government Printing Office, 1967.

National Police Academy : Seminar on public grievances against the police (Report by G.K. Kasture). *National Police Academy Magazine*, November, 1967, 108-22.

Niederhoffer, A. : Behind the shield : The police in urban society, New York, Doubleday & Co., 1967.

Niederhoffer, Arthur and Smith, Alexander B. : New directions in police-community relations. San Francisco, Rinehart Press, 1974.

Nigam, R.L. : Police and the people. *Radical Humanist*. V. 47(11) February, 1983, 9-12.

Ohri, R.K. : Police-community relations : A systems overview. *Indian Police Journal*, V. 22 (1), July-September, 1975, 33-41.

Olmos, Ralph A. : An introduction to police-community relations. Springfield (Ill), Charles C. Thomas, 1974.

Pal, H. Bhisham : Police and public. *C.B.I. Bulletin*, V. 21 (1) January, 1987, 7-9.

Pal, H. Bhisham : Police and public. *C.B.I. Bulletin*, V. 21 (2) February, 1987, 7-10.

Pandian, S. Ratnavel : Police in the enforcement of social legislation. *Indian Journal* of *Criminology* (Suppl.), V. 7(2) July, 1979, 181-86.

Pant, N.C. : Role of police in promoting secularism. *Secular Democracy*, April 1972, 14.

Paramaguru, Pon : Police in the enforcement of social legislation. *Indian Journal of Criminology* (Suppl.), V. 7(2) July, 1976, 202-04.

Parker, W.H. : Police role in community relations. Chicago, National Conference of Christians and Jews, 1955.

Parkinson, Gary C. : Cooperation between police and social workers : Hidden issus. *Social Work*, V. 25(1) January, 1980, 12-18.

Patrick, Clarence H. : Police, crime and society, Springfield, Illinois, C.C. Thomas, 1972.

Peek, Charles W. (and others) : Comparative evaluation of the local police. *Public Opinion Quarterly*, V. 42(3) Fall, 1978, 370-79.

Peoples, Edward E. : Analyzing police-citizen transactions : A model for training in communications. *Journal of Police Science and Administration*, V. 5(2), June, 1977, 202-17.

Perry, David C. and Sornoff, Paula A. : Politics at the street level : The select case of police and the community. Boverly Hills, Sage Publications, 1973.

Police and the public (Editorial). *Thought*, V. 23(4) 20 November, 1971, 6.

Pomrenko, Norman E. (ed.) : Police-community relations. Chabel Hill (N.C.), Institute of Government, University of North Carolina, 1966.

Portune, Robert G. : Changing adolescent attitudes toward police. Cincinnati, W.H. Anderson, 1971.

Potholm, Christian P. and Morgan, Richart E. : Focus on police. Police in American society. New York, John Wiley, 1976.

Prasad, J.M. : Police-public relationship. Souvenir. 10th Symposium of All India Principals Police Training College. Dated 22.10.1981 to 24.10.1981, Patna, 73-80.

Punch, Maurice and Naylor, Tevor : Police : A social survey. *New Society*, 17 May, 1973, 358-61.

Purcell, Cannon William : British police in a changing society : Increased role of women in police work. London, Mowbrays, 1984.

Puri, Rakshat : Police and the public. *Hindustan Times*, 24 May, 1978.

Quadirali, M. : Police cooperation in youth movement. *National Police Academy Magazine*, September, 1960, 59-66.

Radelet, Lousis A. and Reed, Hoytcoe : Police and the community. Encino (Cal.), Glencoe, 1980.

Rajgopal, P.R. : Police and the judiciary in the context of social change. *Decision*, V. 13(3) July, 1986, 157-59.

Ramalingam, R. : Public role in police activity in prevention and control of mob-violence. *Resource Material Series*, No. 3, UNAFEI, Japan, March, 1972, 75-85.

Rana, N.S. : A grass-roots model of public grievances : A case study for Delhi. *Indian Police Journal*, V. 32 (1) January-March, 1985, 49-54.

Rath, Radhanath : Citizens and the policeman. *Orissa Review*, Ocober, 1971, 27-30.

Ravindra Nath, A. : Police-public relations : Some suggestions for improvement. *National Police Academy Magazine*, November, 1972, 74-80.

Reddi, C.V. Narasimha, : Police-public relations : A case study. *Vidura*, V. 16(1) February, 1979, 32-33.

Reddy, G. Ram and Seshadri, K. : Developing society and police. Hyderabad, Osmania University, 1972.

Reiss, Albert J. : Police and the public. New Haven, Yale University Press, 1971.

Roberts, Alberts R. : Police social workers : A history. *Social Work*, V. 21(4) July 1976, 294-99.

Roemer, Dereck V. : Commentary on "An approach to problems in police-community relation's". *Journal of Community Psychology*, V. 8(4) October, 1980, 364-65.

Rolph, C.H. Psued (i.e., Cecil Raph Hewitt) : Police and the public : An enquiry. London, Heinemann, 1962.

Ruthnaswamy. M. : Police and the public. *Assam Information*, V. 19(9) December, 1968, 25-29.

Sahai, S.B. : Police and the public. *Decision*, V. 13(3) July, 1986, 169-77.

Samra, A.S. : How to improve police-community relations. *Indian Police Journal*, V. 28(3) January-March, 1982, 17-19.

Sarolia, Shankar : Crime, society and the police. *Indian Police Journal*, V. 28(3) January-March, 1982, 24-36.

Schaffer, Evelyn B. : Community policing. London, Groom Helm, 1980.

Sen, Sankar : Crime, society and the police. *Decision*, V. 13 (3) July, 1986, 193-98.

Sethi, H.S. : Much-maligned police force. *Hindustan Times*, 26 November 1978, 3.

Shane, Paul G. : Police and people. Missouri, C.V. Mosby, Bombay, 1980.

Sharma, K.K. : Citizen-police relations : an empirical exploration. *Indian Journal of Public Administration*, V. 31(1) January-March, 1985, 150-13.

Sharma, P.D. : Administration and the police : Police-citizen relationship. *Indian Journal of Public Administration*, V. 21(3) July-September, 1975, 421-33.

Sharma, P.D. : Community participation. *Seminar*, No. 252 : August, 1980, 32-35.

Sharma, P.D. : Dilemmas inhibiting community participation in police work. *C.B.I. Bulletin*, V. 13(9) September, 1979, 1-2.

Sharma, P.D. : Dilemmas inhibiting community participation in police work. *C.B.I. Bulletin*, V. 13(10) October, 1979, 1-3.

Sharma, P.D. : Police and the community, *C.B.I. Buletin*, March, 1974, 1-7.

Sharma, P.D. : Police and the people. *Indian Police Journal*, V. 28(2) October-December, 1981, 59-66.

Sharma, P.D. : Police, polity and people in India. New Delhi, Uppal Publishing House, 1981.

Shernock, Stan K. : An empirical examination of the relationship between police solidarity and community orientation. *Journal of Police Science and Administration*, V. 16(3) September, 1988, 182-94.

Shukla, K.S. and Malaviya, P.D. : Juvenile and police units. *Police Research and Development, Quarter III & IV*, July-December, 1972, 6-20.

Siegel, Arthan I. (and others) : Police and public : American style. Springfield (III), Charles C. Thomas, 1964.

Simey, Margaret : Can the public share the optimism of the police. *Municipal Review*, February, 1980, 261-62.

Singer, Henry A. : Police action—community action. *Journal of Social Issues*, V. 3(1) 1975, 99-106.

Singer, Ming S. and Singer, Alan E. : Self and other perceptions of the police and University students in New Zealand. *Journal of Social Psychology*, V. 125(6) December. 1985, 729-33.

Singh, Mohinder : New police perspective. *Hindustan Times*, 19 Arpil, 1972, 5.

Singh, Nand Kumar : Police accountability to the law and the people. *Sardar Vallabhbhai Patel National Police Academy Magazine*, November, 1978, 121-33.

Singh, Pratap : A syndicate's study "role of the police in the implementation of social legislation." *Transactions*, V. 24, 1977, 35-80.

Singh, Sita Ram : Role of police in modern society. *Indian Journal of Criminology*, V. 15(1) January, 1987, 37-42.

Singhvi, G.C. : Police-public relations : Issues and management, V. 12(4) January-March, 1981, 336-44.

Singhvi, G.C. : To whom should the police be responsible. *Indian Journal of Public Administration*, V. 24 (1) January-March 1978, 113-122.

Sinha, B.M. : Police and the society. *Hindustan Times*, 21 February 1984, 9.

Sinha, K.C. : Police community relations : Practical methods of gaining public support in police work. *C.B.I. Bulletin*, August, 1974, 1-4.

Skogen, W.G. : Citizen satisfaction with police services. In R. Boker and F.A. Meyer (eds.), Evaluation alternative law enforcement policies. Lexington, M.A. D.C. Health, 1979.

Smith, Alexander and Niederhoffer Arthur : Police-community relations programmes. A study of depth. Washington (D.C.), Government Printing Office, 1970.

Som, Nirupom : Police and public. *Statesman*, 21 March, 1989, 6.

Spalding, Alan : A model police : Public relations systems in Australia. *Indian Police Journal*, October, 1975, 45-49.

Srivastava, R.G. : Police-public cooperation in the context of crime prevention. *Social Defence*, V. 11(44) April, 1976, 11-15.

Srivastava, S.P. : Police-public relationship : Policeman's point of view. *Indian Journal of Criminology and Criminalistics*, V. 1(2-3) June-September, 1981.

Steadman, Robert F. : Police and the community. Baltimore, Johns Hopkins University Press, 1972.

Strackey, E.L. : Police-public relations. *Indian Journal of Criminology*, V. 5(2) July 1977, 70-73.

Subramanayan, K.V.V. : Police and society. *Sardar Vallabhbhai Patel National Police Academy Magazine*, November, 1978, 115-20.

Sullivan-Taylor, Lois : Policemen and nursing students : Crisis intervention teams. *Journal of Psychological Nursing and Mental Health Services*, V. 23(9) September, 1985, 26-30.

Tarnopolsky, Walter Surma : Police-community relations and the administration of justice. *C.B.I. Bulletin*, April, 1975, 6-7.

Tarun Kumar : Police and society. *Indian Express*, 26 November, 1967, 6.

Thapar, Romesh : Living with the police. *Illustrated Weekly of India*, V. 107(26) 22 June, 1986, 28-29.

Thurston, Robert W. : Police and people in Moscow 1906-1914, *Russian Review*, V. 39(3) Jula, 1980, 320-28.

Tomlin, Mourice : Police and public. London, Longmans, Green, 1936.

Tripathi, S.V.M. : Credibility gap : Police. *Sardar Vallabhbhai Patel National Police Academy Magazine*, November, 119-24.

Tyler, L.G. : Church and police in a changing society. *Police Journal*, December 1969, 554-56.

Tyler, Tom R. and Folger, Robert : Distributional and procedural aspects of satisfaction with citizen-police encounter. *Basic and Applied Social Psychology*, V. 1(4) December 1980, 281-92.

Vajpayee, Dhirendra K. : Public opinion of bureaucratic performance in U.P. and its impact in social change and modernisation, 1966-76. *Indian Journal of Public Administration*, V. 23(4) December, 1977.

Varma, L S. : Police and the people. *Indian Police Journal*, V. 24(4) April-June, 1978, 8-11.

Venkateswaran, V. : Code of conduct for police-public relations. *Hindu*, 24 January, 1979, 8.

Venugopal Rao, S. : Crime, society and the police. *Indian Express*, 9 June, 1977, 4.

Venugopal Rao, S. : Crime, society and the police. *Indian Express*, 10 June, 1977, 4.

Venugopal Rao, S. : Crime, society and the police. *Indian Express*, 11 June, 1977, 6.

Venugopal Rao, S. : Crime, society and the police. *Indian Police Journal*, V. 23(4) April-June, 1977, 28-42.

Venugopal Rao, S. : Police-public ties : Some relations. *Indian Express*, 27 March, 1979, 6.

Verma, Suresh : Police go to the people. *Times of India* (*Magazine*), 10 April, 1977, 11.

Viano, C. and Reiman, J.M. : Police in society. Massachusetts, Lexington Books, 1975.

Vigilance India Report : Relations between police and the public. *Mainstream*, V. 17(15) 9 December, 1978, 16-19.

Viswanathan, Gita : Police in the enforcement of social legislation. *Indian Journal of Criminology*, (Suppl.), V. 7(2), July, 1979, 193-96.

Vohra, K.B. : The extent of support and cooperation to the police may legitimately expect from the public in performance of the functions. *Transactions*, 24 April, 1970, 31-94.

Vollmer, August : Police and modern society. London, Cambridge University Press, 1936.

Walsh, J M. : Co-operation between the public and police. *Australian Police Journal*, January, 1977, 3.

Watson, Nelson A. : Improving the officer-citizen contact. Washington (D.C.), International Association of Chiefs of Police, 1968.

Watson, Nelson A. (ed.) : Police and the changing community. Washington, D.C. International Association of Chiefs of Police, 1965.

Wells, W.T. : Public control and the police. *Political Quarterly*, April-June, 1959, 141-48.

Wertheimer, R. : Are the police necessary? In Viano, C. and Retman, J.M. (eds.) The Police in Society, Mass, Lexington Books, 1975.

Whisenand, Paul M. (ed) : Police-community relations : Readings in the development of effective environmental relations. Pacific Palisades, California, Goodyear Publishing Company, 1974.

Whitaker, Ben : Police and the public. *New Statesman*, 8 January, 1971, 37-38.

Whitaker, Ben : Police in society. London, Eyre Methuen, 1979.

White, Mervin F. and Menke, Ben A. : On assessing the mood of the public toward the police : Some conceptual issues. *Journal of Criminal Justice*, V. 10(3) 1982, 211-30.

Who is to guard the guardians. *Economics and Political Weekly*, V. 14(25) 23 June, 1979, 1028-29.

Wiatrowski, Michael D. : Formal and informal social control : The police and the community. *Police Journal*, V. 41(2) April-June, 1988, 100-9.

Wiatrowski Michael D. and Vardalis, James : An experiment in community policing in Detray Beach, Florida. *Police Journal*, V. 63(3) April-June, 1990, 134-41.

Wiley, Mory Glenn and Hudik, Terryl : Police citizen encounters : A field test of exchange theory. *Social Problems*, October, 1974, 119-27.

Willman, Mark T. and Snortum, John R. : A police program for employment of youth gang members. *International Journal of Offender Therapy and Comparative Criminology*, V. 26(3) 1982, 207-14.

Winfree, L. Thomas and Williams, Lerry E. : Call security : Effect of fear and public image of staff security contacts in a public hospital. *Journal of Police Science and Administration*, V. 13(14) December, 1985, 310-320.

Young, David : Public relations and police. *Police Journal*, April, 1966, 195-99.

17

Police Image

Allegations against police officers, *Link*, V. 24(27), 14 Feb., 1982, 25-26.

Banergea, D. : Procedure for enquiry into complaint against police. *Transactions*, V. 26, 1978, 86-125.

Bhambhari, C.P. and Mathur, Kuldeep : Students and the policemen : Image and counter-image. *Economic and Political Weekly*, 13 January, 1973, 79-81.

Cairae, S.M. : General insurance as a means for improving image and functioning of police. *C.B.O. Bulletin*, V. 17(3) March, 1983, 6-8.

Chowdhury, Noorga : Poor image of the police constable. *Hindustan Times*, 28 January, 1979, 1.

Corrigan, Robert S. (and others) : Perception of danger by police officers. *Perceptual & Motor Skills*, V. 50(1) February, 1980, 284.

Das, Dalip K. : Image of American police in comparative literature. *Police Journal*, V. 64(3) July-September, 1986, 265-79.

Das, Dalip K. : Image of American police in comparative literature in police studies. *International Review of Police Development*, V. 8(2) Summer, 1985, 78.

Eight-point plan to tone up police image : Union Home Minister's letter to Chief Ministers. *Indian Express*, 5 March, 1976, 4.

Farah, S.A. : Beware of policemen. *Indian Nation*, May 29, 1986, 4.

Giljam, D.M. : Police image. *Indian Police Journal*, January-March, 1974, 24-31.

Gurevitch, Michael (and others) : Image of police in Israel. *Law and Society Journal*, February, 1971, 367-88.

Haldane, R. : Improving the police image. *Indian Police Journal*, V. 26(3) January-March, 1980, 1724.

Handoo, G.K. : Police : Image and reality. *Indian Nation*, 15 August, 1979.

Hodges, D.R. : Improving the image. *Police Journal*, V. 60(3), July-December, 1987, 188-99.

Johnston, Eric : Complaints against police : Why the system should not change. *Times (London)*, 12 March, 1976.

Joshi, G.P. : Poor image of the police : Role of corruption and cruetly. *Times of India*, 1 August, 1981, 8.

Kakkar, T.R. : Image of police and administration of criminal justice in India. *Indian Journal of Criminology*, V. 4(3) July, 1976, 126-30.

Karunakaran, K. : New image for the police. *Hindu*, 4 October, 1975, 4.

Kewaltamani, R.D. : Changing the police image. *Police Research and Development, Quarter II*, April-June, 1981, 190.

Khan, M.A. and Krishna, K.P. : Police image amongst adolescents, *Indian Journal of Criminology and Criminalistics*, V. 1(2-3) June-September, 1981.

Krishna, K.P. : Improving the police image. *Indian Journal of Criminology*, V. 10(2) July, 1982, 140-47.

Krishna, K.P. (and others) : Police-community relations : A study in images. *Indian Journal of Criminology*, V. 9(1) January, 1981, 14-22.

Krishnan, B. Sesha : Socio-economic position of police in a city of Andhra Pradesh : A research study. *Social Defence*, V. 11(43) January, 1976, 32-43.

Lester, David : Improving the police image by changing police attitudes. *Police Journal*, V. 55(4) October-December, 1982, 352-54.

Marini. R.G. : Politics and police image *INFA Feature*, 26 May, 1977.

Misra, S.C. : Police image. *C.B.I. Bulletin*, February 1974, 1-3.

Nath, Trilok : Indian police : A case for a new image. New Delhi, Sterling, 1978.

Nath, Trilok : Police image : Educating people the prime job. *Patriot (Mag.)* 28 November, 1983, 1.

Noorani, A.G. : Investigating complaints against police. *Economic and Political Weekly*, V. 18(8) 19 February, 1983, 255.

Page, Robert W. and Swanton, Bruce : Complaints against police in New South Wales : Administrative and political dimensions. *Australian Journal of Public Administration*, V. 42(4) December, 1983, 503-28.

People unsafe in police hands, says Magistrate. *People Democracy*, V. 7(38) 19 September, 1971, 1.

Rao, P.S. Rammohan : Image of the police in a changing society. In G. Ram Reddy and K. Seshadri (eds.) Developing society and police. Hyderabad, Osmania University, 1972, 57-68.

Rao, P.S. Rammohan : Image of the police in a changing society. *Indian Police Journal*, October, 1973, 13-18.

Regen, D.E. : Complaints against the police. *Political Quarterly*, October-December, 1971, 402-13.

Russell, Kenneth V. : Complaints against the police : An international perspective. *Police Journal*, V. 51(1), January-March, 1978, 34-44.

Sarkar, Subhash Chandra : Redressing grievances against police. *Commerce*, 3 May, 1980, 759.

Saksena, N.S. : Police unpopularity : causes and remedies. *Indian Police Journal*, October-December, 1974, 7-17.

Singh, R.D. : Police image : An analysis of causes and cures. *Indian Journal of Criminology and Criminalistics*, V. 1(2-3) June-September, 1981.

Singhvi, G.C. : Citizen's grievances against police : Dimensions and strategies. *Indian Journal of Public Administration*, V. 21(3) July-September, 1975, 421-33.

Singhvl, G.C. : People's grievances against the police : Dimensions and strategies. *Indian Journal of Criminology and Criminalistics*, V. 1(2-3) June-September, 1981.

Sinha, R.N. : What should be done to improve the image of our policeman. *Indian Nation*, 15 August, 1985, 5.

Srivastava, Saraswati : Image of the police. *B.H.U. Survey*, 1972.

Srivastava, Saraswati : Public image of the police (Paper, seminar on recruitment and training of police officers, August 1972) *Journal of the Society for the Study of State Governments*, V. 5(3-4) July-September-October-December, 1972, 243-63.

Tisseyre, Charles : Image and attitude of young people towards the police. *International Child Welfare Review*, No. 30-31, September-December, 1976, 94-105.

Yadav, H.S. : Our policemen need a new image. *Times Weekly*, 26 August, 1973, 10.

18

Police Cynicism

Chandler, Ernest V. and Jones, Claude S. : Cynicism : An inevitable police work. *Journal of Police Science and Administration*, V. 7 (1) March, 1979, 65-69.

Crank, John P. (and others) : Measurement of cynicism among police chiefs. *Journal of Criminal Justice*, V. 15 (1) 1987, 37-48.

Langworthy, Robert H. : Police cynicism : What we know from the Niederhoffer scale. *Journal of Criminal Justice*, V. 15 (1) 1987, 17-35.

Lester, David : Cynicism of police and job satisfaction. *Psychological Reports*, V. 54 (2) April, 1984, 558.

Lester, David : Job satisfaction cynicism, education and belief in an internal locus of control in police. *Psychological Reports*, V. 50 (3, part 2) June, 1982, 1214.

Lotz, Roy and Regoli, Robert M. : Police cynicism and professionalism. *Human Relations*, V. 30 (2) 1977, 175-82.

O'connell, Brianj (and others) : Police cynicism and the modes of adaptation. *Journal of Police Science and Administration*, V. 14 (4) December, 1981, 307-13.

Regoli, Robert M. : Effects of college education on the maintenance of police cynicism. *Journal of Police Science and Administration*, V. 4 (3) September 1976, 340-45.

Regoli, Robert M : Toward an understanding of police cynicism. *Dissertation Abstracts International*, V. 36 (8-A) February, 1976, 5570.

Wilt, G. Marie and Bannon, James D. : Cynicism or realism : A critique of Niederhoffers research into police attitudes. *Journal of Police Science and Administration*, V. 4 (1) March, 1976, 38-45.

19

Policc and Media

Abdur Rahim : Mutual interaction vital in press-police relations. *Indian Journal of Communication Arts*, V. 4 (5-6), January-February, 1979, 22-24.

Abdur Rahim : Mutual interaction vital in press-police relations. *Indian Express*, December, 1978, 17-18.

Bhatia, V.B. and Rahman, Rafiqur : Crime and press. *Indian Journal of Social Work*, V. 36(1) April, 1975, 87, 91.

Bhupal, K. : Police and the media. *Vidura*, V. 18 (6) December, 1981, 396-97.

Dhillon, K.S. : Police and the media in India, *C.B I. Bulletin*, V. 18 (6) June, 1984, 1-4.

Hetherington, Alastair : Press, police and public interest, *Vidura*, V. 11 (2), April, 1974, 565-68.

Iyer, T.G.L. : Police, public and the press. *Indian Police Journal*, V. 28 (1) July-September, 1981, 37-41.

Malaviya, P.D. : Press and the public. *Policc Research and Development*, *Quarter III und IV*, 1974, 2-5.

Murphy, Pathrick V. : Police-press relations. In A.F. Brandstatter and Louis A. Redelet (eds) Police and community relations : A source book. California, Glencoe Press, 1968. 435-39.

Noorani, A G. : Police and the press. *Economic and Political Weekly*, V. 16 (52) 26 December, 1981, 2121-22.

Pandes, S.K. : Police, press and the people. *Secular Democracy*, February, 1979, 13-14.

Parmar, R.S. : Relations with the press. *Transactions of the National Police Academy*, Mt. Abu, V. 10, 1968, 107-18.

Rustamji, K.F. : Police and the press : Need for imaginatic public relations. *Monthly Commentary on Indian Economic Conditions*, V. 22 (1) August, 1980, 41-49.

Rustamji, K.F. : Unremitting hostility : Press-police relations. *Vidura*, V. 17(1) February, 1980, 32-33.

Sahay, S. : Police and the press. *Statesman*, 5 January 1984, 6.

Sahay, S. : Hazards of grassroots journalism. *Telegraph*, August, 9, 1989.

Saksena, N.S. : Relations between the police and press in the capital. *National Police Academy Magazine*, September 1960, 25-30.

Sarkar, Chanchal : Police and the media. *Deccan Herald* 13 March, 1979.

Scuro, Joseph E. : Police media relations. *C.B.I. Bulletin*, V. 19 (10), October, 1985, 8-9.

Singh, Prakash : Police and media. *Decision*, V. 13 (3) July, 1986, 205-07.

Vohra, B.L. : Police and the press. *Indian Police Journal*, April-June, 1976, 31-35.

Wilson, Jerry V. and Fuqua, Paul Q. : Police and the media. Boston, Educational Associates, 1975.

20

Police and Weaker Section

Another case of police rape. *People's Democracy*, V. 3 (44), 4 November, 1979, 5.

Banzon, Michael : Social integration and police authority, *Police Chief*, V. 13 (4) April, 1963.

Barse, Sheela : Policing the weaker sections : The role of IPS officers. *Decision*, V. 13 (3) July 1986, 187-90.

Bayley, David H. and Mendelson, Horld : Minorities and the police. New York, Macmillan, 1969.

Burger, Angela S. : Policing a communal society : the case of Sri Lanka, *Asian Survey*, V. 27 (7) July, 1987, 827-33.

Chandra, Prabhat : Police and the weaker sections. *Journal of Social Studies*, January, 1983, 148, 56.

Engineer, Asghar Ali : Communal violence and police terror *Economic and Political Weekly*, V. 21 (9), 1 March, 1986, 382-83.

Engineer, Asghar Ali : Grim tragedy of Bhagalpur riots : Role of police criminal nexus. *Economic and Political Weekly*, V. 25 (26) February 10, 1990, 305-307.

Engineer, Asghar Ali : Role of the police in communal riots. *Radical Humanist*, V. 46 (11) February, 1983, 35-36.

Farooqi, Vimla : A.P. police vendetta against a woman. *New Age*, V. 26 (46) 12 November, 1978, 5.

Haldar, Niranjan : Police bias against minorities, *Janata*, V. 32 (44) 18 December, 1977, 3-4.

Hiranyappa, G.S. : How Bangalore police foil communal plots of the secular tribe. *Organiser*, V. 31 (28) 2 December, 1979, 7-14.

Hooda, R.K. : Communal disturbances and the police (Paper) In 7th Police Science Congress, Jaipur, 1968.

Janeksela, G.M. and Deming, R.R. : Police—minority conflict and conflict resolution. *International Journal of Group Tensions*, V. 6 (3-4) 1976, 47-56.

Jones, Sandra and Levi, Michael : Police and the majority : The neglect of the obvious? *Police Journal*, V. 55 (4) October-December, 1983, 351-63.

Kannabiram, Vasantha : The police and Shakila : Findings of a women's group. *Economic and Political Weekly*, V. 14 (45) 10 November, 1979, 1829.

Katz, Myron : Family crisis training : Upgrading the police while building a bridge to the minority community. *Journal of Police Science and Administration*, V. 1 (1) March, 1973, 30-35.

Killer rapist police go scot free. *New Age*, V. 29 (14) 5 April, 1981, 5.

Kumar, Santh : A syndicate study on communal disturbances. National Police Academy, Hyderabad, *Transactions*, V. 27, 1979, 199-282.

Life and death of Khairunisa Begum. *Economic and Political Weekly*, V. 14 (48) 1 December, 1979, 1946-47.

Lopamundra : Rape by police and new law. *Indian Nation*, February 19, 1984, 111.

Mass rape by cops alleged. *Free Press Journal*, 14 June, 1982, 5.

Nath, Trilok : Police and the scheduled castes. *Hindustan Times*, 29 October, 1978, 1.

Police and women. *Economic and Political Weekly*, V. 18 (4) 22 January, 1983, 99-100.

Police atrocities on Harijan women. *Economic and Political Weekly*, V. 14 (13) 18 August, 1979, 1414.

Police guilty in Siswan rape case. *Indian Express*, 27 June, 1982, 1.

Police rape of minor husted up. *Times of India*, 14 August, 1983, 9.

Prasad, P.S.N. : Police and Rameeza Bee : Muktadar Commission's findings. *Economic and Political Weekly*, V. 14 (35) 1 September, 1979, 1484.

Rao, B. Mallikarjuna : A.P. police on rape-loot spree. *New Age*, V. 29 (10) 8 March, 1981, 3.

Rapists in uniform (Editorial). *Times of India*, 31 March, 1936, 8.

Ray, Sandimoy : Bhagalpur carnage in perspective. *Mainstream* V. 28 (20), March 10, 1990, 15-17.

Reddy, M. Gopinath : Police and the weaker sections of rural society. *Social Action*, V. 40 (1), January-March, 1990, 87-93.

Rustamji, K.F. : Police and communal violence. *Indian Express*, 23 September, 1983, 6.

Rustamji, K.F. : Communalism and the police. *Radical Humanist*, V. 47 (11) February, 1983, 15-16.

Saksena, N.S. : Police and communal riots. *Radical Humanist*, V. 47 (11) February, 1983, 25-28.

Saksena, N.S. : Police and women : Norms of conduct. *Times of India*, 11 April, 1980, 6.

Saksena, N.S. : Why are the police communal? *Indian Express* (*Mag*) 17 January, 1988, 1.

Sanwal, Mukal : Dealing with communal riots : Strategic issues. *Indian Journal of Public Administration*, V. 34 (2) April-June, 1988, 276-283.

Sarkar, Lalita (and others) : Women and custodian violence. *Mainstream*, V. 18 (38) 17 May, 1980, 24-27.

Sinha, Ramesh : On the spot report on police bestility shame of Siswan. *New Age*, V. 30 (28) 11 July, 1982, 4.

Subramanian, L.S. : Violence against the scheduled castes in India : Overview, problems, prospects. New Delhi, Nehru Memorial Museum and Library, 1985.

Thakur, K.N. : Role of the police in protecting the weaker sections. *Indian Police Journal*, V. 25 (1) July-December, 1978, 70-73.

Tripathi, Srinivas : Basti rape case : NFIW calls for campaign to punish guilty police. *New Age*, V. 29 (22) 31 May, 1981, 15.

Tripathi, Srinivas : Rapist police continues offensive in Basti village. *New Age*, V. 29 (25) 21 June, 1981, 5.

Venugopal Rao, S. : Police and communal violence. *Indian Express*, 28 December, 1978, 6.

Walkout in Parliament against police atrocities on women. *New Age*, V. 28 (28) 13 July, 1980, 1.

Yanik, A. : Police and black people in U.K. *Times of India*, 2 May 1979, 8.

21

Police Corruption

Anatomy of corruption. *Illustrated Weekly of India*, V. 104 (13) 27 March, 1983, 12-13.

Aultman, M.G. : A social psychological approach to the study of police corruption. *Journal of Criminal Justice*, V. 4 (4) Winter, 1976, 323-32.

Bahn. Charles : Psychology of police corrupation. *Police Journal*, V. 48 (1) January-March, 1975.

Barker, Thomas and Roebock, Julian : Empirical typology of police corruption : A study in organizational deviance. Springfield (Ill), Charles C. Thomas, 1973.

Beral, Harold and Sisk, Marcus : Administration of complaints by civilians against the police. *Harvard Law Review*, January, 1964, 499-519.

Conference of Inspectors General of Police, 1962 : Report of the committee of Inspectors General of Police on corruption in police service. New Delhi, 1962, (Convenor : S.P. Varma).

Goldstein, Herman : Police corruption : A perspective on its nature and control. Washington (D.C.), Police Foundation, 1975.

Hari Mohan : Corruption in the police service. Central Police Training College, Abu. 3rd Advanced Course, June-December, 1961.

Jelhan, Promilla : Cops and corruption. *Hindustan Times*, 19 November, 1972, 4.

Jerath, Arati R. : Delhi : A haven for corrupt policemen. *Indian Express*, 16 August, 1980,

Jerath, Arati R. : The most corrupt are the most efficient. *Indian Express*, 17 August, 1980.

Mcnamara, Joseph D. : Impact of bureaucratic dysfunctions on attempts to prevent police corruption. *Police Journal*, V. 48(1) January-March, 1975, 37-44.

Misner, Gordon E. : Organization and social setting of police corruption. *Police Journal*, V. 48(1) January March 1975.

Nath, D.C. : Police lawlessness : How to police in police. *Indian Police Journal*, V. 28(2) October-December, 1981, 37-45.

P.M. exhorts police to end corruption. *Times of India*, 19 April, 1985, 1.

Roebuck, Julian B. and Barker, Thomas : A typology of police corruption. *Social Problems*, V. 2 (3) 1974, 423-37.

Saksena, N.S. : Growing crime on railway : Corruption and unionized police main factor. *Times of India*, November 7, 1980, 8.

Sheraman, Lawrence W. (ed.) : Police corruption : A sociological perspective. Gardencity (N. Y.) Doubleday, 1974.

Singh, C.P. : Managerial steps to check corruption in the police. *Transactions*, V. 33, 1981, 1-50.

Sinha, Eshava Pratap : Police and corruption : An old hat looks at the cadre. *Indian Nation*, December 10, 1987, 4.

Stesd. Philip John : Some notes on English police corruption. *Police Journal*, V. 48(1) January-March, 1975, 24-29.

Ward, Richard H. : Police corruption: An overview. *Police Journal*, V. 48(1) January-March, 1975.

22

Police, Crime and Criminals

Abdi, S.N.M. : A mafia runs this country today. *Illustrated Weekly of India*, V. 110(35) 27 August, 1989, 10-19.

Abhayyanand : Economics of crime. *Indian Police Journal*, V. 32(1) January-March, 1985, 18-25.

Abrahamsen, David : Psychology of crime. New York, John Wiley & Sons, 1960.

Adward, S.M. : Crime in India. London, Oxford University Press, 1924.

Ahuja, Ram : Crime, criminal and society. *Modern Review*, V. 117(1) January, 1965, 67-71.

Alam, M. Jabbar : Ministerial patronage for criminals. *New Age*, V. 30 (31) 1 August, 1982, 51.

Alam, M. Jabbar : Political patronage for Bihar criminals. *New Age*, V. 35(26) 28 June, 1987, 8.

Andreano, Ralph and Siegfred (eds.) : Economics of crime. Cambridge, John Wiley and Sons, 1969.

Arul, F.V. : Some aspects of criminology, *C.B.I. Bulletin*, V. 23(5) May, 1989, 1-2.

Attar, U.A. : Urbanisation and crime. *Social Welfare*, V. 22(3) June, 1975, 1-3.

Bajpai, G.S. : Conception of deviant victim : An approach to de-victimization. *Indian Journal of Criminology*, V. 15(2) July, 1987, 89-94.

Bajpai, G.S. : Study in motive behind criminal victimization. *Indian Journal of Criminology*, V. 16(2) July 1988, 116-18.

Banerjee, Sivadas : Plans to further reduce crime rate in West Bengal. *Times of India*, 16 April, 1976, 6.

Banerjee, Sivadas : War against crime in West Bengal : Evolving a new strategy. *Times of India*, 2 December, 1975, 4.

Banik, Sunil : Criminality in the Philippines. *Economic Studies*, V. 10(8) February, 1970, 461-70.

Barlow, High D. : Introduction to criminology. Toronto, Little Brown and Company, 1981.

Barnes, Harry Elmer and Teeters, Negley K. : New horizons in criminology. New Delhi, Prentice-Hall of India, 1966.

Barse, Sheela : A voice from deathrow. *Indian Express (Mag.)* 3 April, 1983, 5.

Barthwal, R.R. and Nair, K.N.S. : Development, intensity of crimes and size of states in India. *Economic Affairs*, V. 21 (12) December, 1976, 441-47.

Basu, Kajal: Crime pays and bow. *Times of India*, 9 August, 1981, 8.

Bayley, David H. : Crime, culture and change. *Indian Journal of Social Work*, V. 41(1) April, 1980, 1-9.

Ben-Aron, M.H. (and others) : Clinical criminology. Toronto, University of Toronto, 1985.

Bhadauria, Y.S. : A sociological study of history sheeters. *Social Welfare*, V. 26(1) April, 1979, 13-14.

Bhadauria, Y.S.: Reactions of history sheeters. Towards police servillance. *Indian Journal of Social Work*, V. 41(1) April, 1980, 45-50.

Bhanot, M.L. and Misra, Surat : Criminality amongst women in India : A study of female attenders and female convicts. *Police Research and Development, Quarter III*, July-September, 1978, 1-14.

Bhattacharya, P. : Management of crime foreseeing : The emerging crime pattern. *Police Research and Development, Quarter II*, April-June, 1980, 5-8.

Bhattacharya, P.K. : Conditioning of crime. *Social Welfare*, V. 15(3) June, 1968, 4-6.

Bhattacharya, Sauren : Criminal law amendment ordinance. *Call*, V. 30(12) December, 1980, 18-19.

Bhattacharya, S.K. : Concept and areas of social defence. *Social Welfare*, V. 17(9) December, 1970, 4-6.

Brantingham, Paul and Brantingham, Paticia : Patterns in crime, New York, Macmillan, 1984.

Caramazza, I.F. : Phenomenology of kidnappings in Sardinia. Rome, Pratelli Palambi Editori, 1984.

Chaitanya : Are we attracted to crime? *Times of India*, 9 November, 1975, 8.

Chambias, William J. : Crime in capitalist and socialist societies. *Indian Journal of Criminology and Criminalistics*, V. 1(1) March, 1981, 13-18.

Chand, Tek : Fertile crop of crime. *Tribune* (*Sunday Mag.*), 6 November, 1988, 1.

Chockalingam, K. : A study of relationship between friendship and past crime life among recidivists. *Indian Journal of Criminology*, V. 7(1) January, 1979, 62-64.

Church, Albert M. : Compensation of victims, criminal deterrence, and economic efficiency. *Southern Economic Review*, V. 4(4) April, 1975, 227-35.

Clark, Ramasy : Crime in America. New York, Podub Books, 1971.

Clinard, Marshall B. : Crime in developing countries : A comparative perspective. New York, John Wiley & Sons, 1973.

Conklin, J.E. : Criminal violence. Lexington, D.C. Health, 1974.

Crime and caste. *Economic and Political Weekly*, V. 16 (41) 10 October, 1981, 1644-45.

Crime and police : A crisis. *Link*, V. 17(44) 15 June, 1975, 29-31.

Crime and politics nexus in Bihar. *Time of India*, 15 July, 1986, 1.

Criminal legislators bane of Bihar politics. *Link*, V. 32(32), 18 March, 1990, 14-15.

Criminals of grassroots (Editorial). *Times of India*, 2 October, 1988, 6.

Dang, Satpal : Law and order situation in Punjab worsening. *New Age*, V. 26(45) 5 November, 1978, 6.

Dave, P.N. : Crime statistics for 1970 and changes being introduced from 1971. *Police Research and Development, Quarter II*, April-June, 1971, 23-24.

Deb, R. : Principles of criminology, criminal law and investigation. Sarkar, 1968.

Deogaonkar, S.G. : Tribal exploitation : A study of victims of crime and bondedness. Delhi, Manas Publications, 1991.

Devdutt : Criminalisation of the polity. *Janata*, V. 37(7) 21 March, 1982, 5-7.

Dhanagare, D.N. : Urbanism and crime. *Economic and Political Weekly*, V. 4 (28-30) July, 1969, 1239-42.

Dutt, Ashok K. (and others) : Variation of the spatial patterns of crime in Ajmer, India. *Indian Journal of Criminology*, V. 13(1) January, 1985, 57-72.

Edwards, S.M. : Crime in India. London, Oxford University Press, 1924.

Engelmann, Hugo O. : Crime : Deviation or institution ? *Indian Journal of Social Research*, 3 December, 1964, 265-70.

Evans, Peter : Are criminals born ? *Times of India* (*Sunday Rev*), 10 August, 1986, IV.

Fernandes, Allwyn : How safe are our cities ? *Times of India* (*Sunday Review*), 21 May, 1989, I.

Gandhi, Arun : One murder every 30 minutes. *Illustrated Weekly of India*, V. 94(22) 3 June, 1973, 6-9.

Gandhi, Rajmohan : Crime and corruption. *Statesman*, June 21, 1981, 6.

Glaser, Daniel : Routinizing evaluation : Getting feedback on effectiveness of crime and delinquency programmes. Maryland, National Institute of Mental Health, 1976.

Gokhale, S.D. : Contemporary criminology : An evaluation. *Indian Journal of Criminology*, V. 14(2) July, 1986, 104-13.

Gokhale, S.D. : Youth crime and social control. *Social Defence*, V. 11 (42) October, 1975, 19-32.

Gonklin, J.E. : Impact of crime. New York, Macmillan, 1975.

Goppinger, H. : Life style and criminality. New York, Veriag, 1987.

Gray, Charles M. (ed.) : Cost of crime. London, Sage Publications, 1979.

Gupta, Anandswarup : Crime and police in India (Up to 1861). New Delhi, Sahitya Bhawan, 1974.

Gurr, Ted Robert : Politics of crime and conflict. A comparative history of four cities. London, Sage Publications, 1977.

Haikerwal, Bejoy Shanker and Mukerjee, Radha Kamal : Economic and social aspects of crime in India. London, Allen and Unwin, 1934.

Haldar, M.K. : Criminalisation of politics or politics of the criminals ? *Radical Humanist*. V. 48(12) March, 1985, 27-29.

Halloran, Richard : Crime wave in the U.S. *Times of India*, 29 August, 1970, 6.

Handberg, Roger (and others) : Crime, punishment and deterrence : The impact of an execution on attitudes toward the death penalty. *Indian Journal of Criminology*, V. 11(1) January, 1983, 18-27.

Hodges, Donald Clark : Primitiveness as a philosophy of crime. *Indian Journal of Social Research*, 3 December, 1964, 271-78.

Hood, R.F. : Crime, criminology and public policy. New York, Free Press, 1974.

India. Ministry of Home Affairs : National Crime Records Bureau : Crime in India 1988. Faridabad, Government of India Press, 1990.

Intosh, Mary Mc. : Thieves and fences : Markets and power in professional crime. *Police Research and Development, Quarter III*, July-September 19 6, 6-10.

Islam, R.K. : Planning and crime. *Social Welfare*, V. 22(4) July, 1975, 171.

Jagdish, B.V. : Crime : Can community be a passive onlooker. *Social Welfare*, V. 30(9) December, 1983, 4-5.

Jamuar, K.K. and Misra, V.D. : A comparative study of some personality traits of first offender and non-criminals. *Social Welfare*, V. 17(66) October 1981, 19-22.

Jamuar, K.K. and Mishra, V.D : Aggression and criminality. *Indian Journal of Criminology*, V. 9(1) January, 1981, 9-13.

Jha, Amiya : Champaran : Where crime is big business. *Hindustan Times* (*Mag.*) 23 February, 1986, 1.

Jha, Prem Shankar : Black money and crime : Twin threats to Indian state. *Times of India*, 7 December, 1981, 6.

Joshi, G.P.: Crimes and crime figures. *Indian Police Journal*, V. 28(2) October-December, 1981, 12-19.

Joshi, G.P. and Sharma, J.K. : Crime in India in 2000 AD : Some projections. New Delhi, Bureau of Police Research and Development, 1989.

Kapur, Sohaila : Modus operandi. *Economic Times*, 12 April, 1981, 5.

Karlekar, Haranmy : Land of the rising gun. *Indian Express* (*Mag.*) 20 February, 1983, 1.

Kassebhaum, Gene : Crime and economic development. *Indian Journal of Social Work*, V. 43(1) April, 1982, 1-10.

Kathpalia, Virendra : Alternative to logic of science-error in criminology : revisited. *Indian Journal of Criminology*, V. 15 (2) July, 1987, 103-06.

Keating, William F. and Kennedy, John P. : New thrust in organized crime. *C.B.I. Bulletin*, V. 17(1) January, 1983, 8-10.

Kenetkar, V.G. : Checking the rising crime. *Lok Rajya*, V. 24(2) 16 May, 1968, 12-13.

Khan, M.Z. : Criminology in India : Problems and prospects. *Indian Journal of Criminogy*. V. 12 (2) July, 1984, 69-78.

Khan, M.Z. and Krishnan, K.P. : An analysis of crime and population in India during 1966-76. *Indian Journal of Criminolagy* V. 10(1) January, 1982, 4-11.

Krishna Iyer, V.R. : From Macaulay to Mahatma : In Indian criminological odyssey. *Indian Journal of Criminology*, V. 16 (2) July, 1988, 88-105.

Kulkarni, R.S. : Crimes, criminals and cops. New Delhi, Vikas Publishing House, 1989.

Kulkarni, Ramakant S. : On the crime beat. *Times of Indian* (*Sunday Review*), 14 May, 1989, 4.

Kumar, Anoop and Chandra, S.S. : Importance of sex and age in medicolegal cases. *C.B.I. Bulletin*, V. 23 (7) July, 1989, 11-24.

Lal, Nathoo : Crime in the context of socio-economic development in India. *Indian Police Journal*, V. 27 (2) October-December, 1980, 39-44.

Laver, M. : Crime game. Oxford, Martin Robertson, 1982.

Lieser, Burton M. : Liberty, justice and morals : Contemporary value conflicts, Macmillan, 1973.

Lobo, John : Criminal who gave himself up. *Goa Today*. V. 16 (6) January, 1982, 16.

Lodex-Rey, Manuel: Institutional violence and crime. *Social Defence*, V. 18 (72) April, 1983, 5-20.

Lowe, Sunaina When the reader turns detective. *Times of India*, 23 August, 1981, 8.

Lunden, Walter A. : Crimes and criminals. Iowastate, University Press, 1967.

Makandar, Mohammad Ali : Rise of critical criminology. *Indian Journal of Criminolgy*, V. 13(1) January, 1985, 54-56.

Makkar, S.P. Singh : Developing concept of crime. *Indian Journal of Criminology*. V. 16 (2) July, 1988, 106-09.

Malik, Surendra : Complete Supreme Court criminal digest. Lucknow, Eastern Book Company, 1985.

Mannheum, Hermann : Comparative criminology : A text book. London, Routledge Kegan Paul, 1965.

Mars, Gerals : Cheats of work : An anthropology of work place crime London, Allen & Unwin, 1983.

Mathew, George : Criminalisation of politics : A sociological view. *Radical Humanist*, V. 48 (12) March, 1985, 23-26.

Matthew, Mammen : Kidnapping industry. *Hindustan Times*, September 15, 1991, 4.

Matthew, Mammen : What causes violence in Bihar, *Hindustan Times*, 19 June, 1987.

Mehra, Ajay K. : Collective violence and the police. *Mainstream*, V. 24 (32) 12 April, 1986, 26.

Mehrajuddin, Mir : Police and correction of offenders. *Social Defence*, V. 17 (65) July, 1981, 31-37.

Menon, N.R. Madhava : Satwalogy : The natural law response to the challenge of crime. *Indian Journal of Criminology* V. 10 (2) July, 1982, 76-90.

Mishra, Amarendra and Rai, Markandey : An appraisal of the crime figures in Bihar. *Journal of Social and Economic Studies*, V. 9(2) September, 1981, 319-26.

Mishra, V.D. : Need pattern of criminals and non-criminals. *Social Defence*, V. 17 (65) July, 1981, 38-43.

Mohan, Vidhu and Singh, Arvinder : Effect of caste and education on the nature of crime. *Indian Journal of Criminology*, V. 5 (2) July, 1977, 92-95.

Mohanty, S. (and others) : Importance of instigation in crime commission with special reference to muder : an empiric analysis. *Indian Journal of Criminology*, V. 14 (2) July, 1986.

Mohideen, Nebeel : Other side of the beat. *Times of India* (*Sunday Review*), 4 June, 1989, I.

Mookerjee, Sabyasachi : Urban goondas—Calcutta. *Illustrated Weekly of India*, V. 97 (12) 21 March, 1976, 8-13.

Mukherjee, Arun : Crime and criminals in nineteen century Bengal, 1861-1904. *Indian Economic Social History Review*, V. 21 (2) April-June, 1984, 153-83.

Mukherjee, K.M. : The murderers. *Police Research and Development*, *Quarter I*, January-March, 1972, 19-21.

Mukherjee, Kalyan : Bhagalpur : The other side of the river. *Hindustan Times* (*Mag*), 26 May 1985, I.

Mukherjee, Satyanshu K. : Crime trends in twentieth century Australia. Australia, Australian Institute of Criminology, 1981.

Mukherjee, Satyanshu K. : Dimensions in assessing consequence of crime. *Indian Journal of Criminology and Criminalistics*, V. 1 (1) March, 1981, 22-27.

Mukherjee, Satyanshu K. : On crime statistics. *Indian Journal of Criminology*, V. 8(1) January, 1980, 7-11.

Mukherjee, Satyanshu K. (and others) : Source book of Australian criminology and social statistics : 1930-1980. Australia, Australian Institute of Criminology, 1982.

Mukhopadhyay, Chandidas : Crime and criminals among the Kharias of Purulia. *Asian Studies*, V. 7 (2) April-June, 1989, 63-74.

Murthy, Hosur Narayan : Crime and temperament. *Psychological Studies*, V. 11 (1) January, 1966, 15-22.

Nagarkar, V.V. : Crime and politics in India. *Radical Humanist*, V. 48(12) March, 1985, 13-17.

Nagpaul, Hans : Crime problem in American society. *Indian Journal of Social Research*, V. 21 (1) April, 1980, 58-76.

Nayar, Baldev Raj : Violence and crime in India. Delhi, Macmillan, 1975.

Noor, Mohammad : Slum house and crime. *Indian Journal of Criminology*, V. 11 (1) January 1983, 38-41.

Owomero, Basil O. : Development performance and crime in Kenya. *Indian Journal of Criminology*, V. 16(2) July, 1988, 126-36.

Panda, N.L. : Study of crimes in U.P. *Agra University Journal of Research*, V. 22(2) July, 1974, 25-29.

Paul, C.J.R. : Crime and modern trends in punishment. *Social Defence*, V. 10 (40) April, 1975, 15-24.

Pillai, Syed Mohammad : Crime : How far society is responsible ? *Social Welfare*, V. 18(6) September, 197 , 8-10.

Police and politics. *Mainstream*, V. 7 (47), 9 August, 1969, 6-8.

Politics, police and crime. *Economic and Political Weekly*, V. 16(34) 22 August, 1981, 1366.

Ponnaiya, T. : Simhachalam temple dacoity. *Indian Police Journal*, V. 26(4) April-June, 1980, 45-52.

Prasad, Ishwari: Ganga jal campaign : Bihar. *Janata (Annual Number)*, V.36 (1), 8 February, 1981, 51-59.

Quadri, S.M. Afzal : Individulization of treatment. *Commercial Law Gazette*, V. 6 (28), 12 August, 1983, 2.

Radzinowiez, L. : Ideology and crime. London, Heinemann, 1966.

Rajendra Prasad : Traits of effective leadership as perceived by criminals. *ISPI Journal of Research*, V.2 (2) July, 1978, 112-18.

Rajagopal, P.R. : Bihar : The grapes of wrath. *Illustrated Weekly of India*, July 20, 1986.

Rajagopal, P.R. : Violence and response : New Delhi, Uppal Publishing House, 1988.

Rao, P. Kamalakara : Crime in urban society. *Indian Journal of Criminology*, V.13 (1) January, 1985, 73-75.

Rao, P. Kamalakara (and others) : Some correlates of crime trends in India. *Indian Journal of Criminology and Criminalistics*, V.3 (1-2) March-June, 1983, 7-12.

Rathi, S. and Rai, G.C. : Certain psycho-social aspects of murders, assailants and thieves. *Indian Journal of Criminology*, V.15 (2) July, 1987, 131-44.

Ray, A.S. : Fresh approaches in criminology. *Social Defence*, V.14 (56) April, 1979, 12-23

Reddy, O. Chennappa : Society, law and crime. *Mainstream*, V. 21(11) 15 November, 1982, 17-19.

Reid, Sue Titus : Crime and criminology. New York, Holt, Rinehart and Winston, 1976.

Sahaya, Jai Narayan : Crime and power politics. *Radical Humanist*, V. 48(12), March, 1985, 35-38.

Sampurnanand : Popular attitude towards crime and the criminal. *Lok Rajya*, V. 24(4) 1 July, 1968, 8-9.

Sandhu, Harjit S. : Low rates of delinquency and crime in India : A case of strong social controls. *Indian Journal of Criminology*, V. 15(1) January, 1987, 9-16.

Saksena, N.S. : Crime rates and misleading data. *Times of India*, 25 April, 1980, 6.

Saksena, N.S. : High incidence of crime in China. *Times of India*, 23 January, 1980, 6.

Saksena, N.S. : How China fights crime. *Times of India*, 31 October, 1981, 8.

Sangar, S.P. : Crime and punishment in Mughal India. New Delhi, Sterling, 19(8.

Saksena, N.S. : Rise in murder rate in India : Some major factors. *Times of India*, 4 September, 1978, 6.

Saksena, N.S. : Ten fold rise in crime in Britain. *Times of India*, 3 September, 1979, 6.

Sarker, Subhash Chandra : Crime in India. *Modern Review*, V. 26(3) March, 1970, 178-82.

Saksena, N.S. : Main reasons for increase in crime in India in recent years. *Indian Journal of Public Administration*, V. 21(4), October-December, 1975, 678-93.

Schnelder, Hans Joachim : Crime and its control in Japan and in the federal republic of Germany. *Indian Journal of Criminology*, 17(1) January, 1989, 31-41.

Sen, Sankar: Crimes in modern societies. *Indian Police Journal*, V. 29(3) January-March, 1983, 9-13.

Senapati, G.C. : Socio-economic dimensions of white collar crime. *Police Research and Development, Quarter II*, 1986, 5-8.

Senapati, R.N. : Crimes in the tribal society : A case study of Kathiwara block in Madhya Pradesh. *Administration*, V. 23(1) September, 1978, 173-80.

Sethana, J.M.J. : Society and the criminal. Bombay, Tripathi, 1989.

Shanmugam, T.E. : Delinquency and crime in India. *Indian Journal of Criminology*, V. 8(1) January, 1980.

Shanmugam, T.E. : Influence of mass media on crime and delinquency. *Indian Journal of Criminology*, V. 6(2) Janurary 1978, 27-28.

Sharma, Mahendra Bhushan : Law of bails and disposal of property in criminal cases. *Prashasnika*, V. 16(3-4) July-December, 1987, 57-65.

Shekar, Sanober : Ameliorating criminal's role or prisons. *Economic Times (Suppl.)*, 23 January, 1982, 11.

Shukla, K.S. : Criminal violence. *Seminar*, No. 252, August 1980, 12-16.

Shukla, K.S. (ed.) : Collective violence : Genesis and response. New Delhi, Indian Institute of Public Administration, 1988.

Shur, E.M. : Crime without victims. Englewood Cliffs (N.J.) Prentice Hall, 1965.

Siddique, Ahmed : Criminology : Problems and perspectives. New Delhi, Eastern Book Co., 1976.

Siddiqui, Aziz Ahmad : Supreme Court referencer on crimes. Indore, Lawyers Home, 1986.

Simhadri, Y.C. : Ex-criminal tribes and criminolgical theories. *Indian Journal of Social Work*, V. 34(2) July 1973, 107-12.

Singh, Amar Kumar : Criminal : Guilty or victim? *Social Change*, V. 12(3) September, 1982, 11-21.

Singh, Balwant : Perspective on police, crime, law and order-2000. *Police Research and Development, Quarter III*, 1985, 1-6.

Singh, D.R. : Decriminalisation : A social dilemma. *Social Defence*, V. 16(22) October, 1980, 17-24.

Singh, D.R. and Khan, M.Z. : Crime : Urbanisation linkage in India. *Indian Journal of Social Work*, V. 44(3) October 1983, 243-51.

Singh, Indra J. : Sciences of man and definition of crime : A third man approach. *Indian Journal of Criminology*, V. 17(2) July, 1986, 109-17.

Singh, J.D. : Scotland yard gets a bad name : Two murders unsolved. *Times of India*, 16 April, 1975, 4.

Singh, M.K. : A decade of crime—sociological analysis. *Indian Journal of Criminology*, V. 12 (2) Juny, 1984, 87 97.

Singh, Udai Pratap : Intelligence in criminals. *Indian Journal of Social Work*, V. 27 (4) January, 1917, 393-98.

Singh, Udai Pratap (and others) : Extraversion, neuroticism and criminality : a comparative study of different criminal groups. *Indian Journal of Social Work*, V. 46 (2) July, 1985, 259-66.

Sinha, Anand Vardhan : Crime and criminology : A perspective. Souvenir. 10th symposium of all India principals police training college, dated 22-10-1981 to 24-10-1981. Patna, 29-32.

Sinha, B.P. : Cops and crime. *C.B.I. Bulletin*, V. 20 (5) May, 1986, 1-4.

Sinha, Birendra Prasad : For a thousand years more. *Times of India*, (Sunday Rev.), 18 December, 1983, VI.

Sivamurthy, A. : Crime diversity. *Indian Journal of Criminology*, V. 14 (2) July, 1986, 139-43.

Sivamurthy, A. : Pattern of public perceptions of crime in Madras. *Indian Journal of Criminology*, V. 17 (2) July, 1989, 130-37.

Sivamurthy, A. : Town size and crime. *Indian Journal of Criminology*, V. 14 (1) January, 1986, 17-21.

Sivamaurthy, A. : Urban structure and crime. *Indian Journal of Criminology*, V. 16 (2) July, 1988, 110-15.

Smith, J.C. and Hogan, Brian : Criminal Law : Case and materials. Bombay, International Book House.

Sodhi, Sunita : Towards a theoretical explanation of crime. *Social Defence*, V. 14 (56) April, 1979, 30-42.

Somasundaram O. : Depressive illness and crime. *Indian Journal of Criminology*, V. 7 (2) July, 1929, 153-56.

Somasundaram, O. and Romadess, R. : Criminals who forget their crimes. *Indian Journal of Criminology*, V. 4 (1) January, 1976, 7-15.

Sri Rao : Survey of crime in India in 1975. *Mysore Economic Review*, V. 65 (6) June, 1980, 6-7.

Srivastava, R.N. : Modern trends in criminology and steps toward correctional administration. *Indian Journal of Social Research*, V. 23 (2) August, 1982, 177-85.

Srivastava, S.P. : Modern trends in criminology and corrections. *Social Defence*, V. 15 (59) January, 1980, 22-29.

Srivastava, S.S. : Towards a rational criminology in Indian context. *Indian Journal of Criminology*, V. 15 (2) July 1987, 79-83.

Sukla Das : Crime and punishment in ancient India. New Delhi, Abhinav Publications, 1977.

Sundar Rajan, K.R. : Crime and commonsense. *Overseas Hindustan Times*, 28 September, 1978.

Sutherland, E.H. : White collar crime. New York, Reinhart and Winston, 1961.

Sutherland, E.H. and Creassey, D.R. : Crime principles of criminology. Philadelphia, J.B. Lippincott, 1978.

Sweeping lawlessness, daring crime. *Link*, V. 19 (5) 24 July, 1977, 8-13.

Talwar, H.R.K. : Offences and offenders beyond the reach of law. *Indian Police Journal*, V. 27 (1) July-September, 1980, 19-24.

Tandon, P.K. : Real face of anti-goonda campaign of the police. *People's Democracy*, V. 3 (37) 16 September, 1979, 5.

Tandon, Snehlata : Approach towards the denotified tribes and the habitual offenders : Some issues. *Indian Journal of Criminology*, V. 10 (2) July, 1982, 132-39.

Teslaye, Andargatchew : Patterns and trends of crime in Ethiopia : A comparative analysis of the crime in the pre and post-revolution periods. *Indian Journal of Crimology*, V. 14 (1) January, 1986, 66-85.

Tirilogachander, A.C. : Movies and crime. *Indian Journal of Criminology*, V. 6 (2) January, 1978, 29-31.

Tripathi : Society and the criminal. Bombay, Sethna, 1988.

Trivedi, B.V. : Statistics of crime and justice in India : A need for fresh look. *C.B.I. Bulletin*, V. 23 (1) January, 1989, 9-12.

Trivedi, D.B. : Law and order in upper India : A study of Oudh 1856-1877. Delhi, Manas Publications, 1991.

UNESCO : Violence and its causes. Paris, Unesco, 1981.

Varma, Paripurnand : Correct or convict. *Social Welfare*, V. 15 (11), February, 1969, 3.

Varma, Paripurnand : Increase in female criminality. *Police Research and Development, Quarter I*, January-March, 1985, 6-7.

Venugopal Rao, S. : Crime in our society : A politics perspective. New Delhi, Vikas Publishing House, 1983.

Venugopal Rao, S. : Dynamics of crime : Spatial and socio-economic aspects of crime in India. New Delhi, Indian Institute of Public Administration, 1981.

Venugopal Rao, S. : Facets of crime in India. New Delhi, Allied Publishers, 1967.

Venugopal Rao, S. : Perspective in criminology, Shimla, Indian Institute of Advanced Study, 1985.

Venugopal Rao, S. : Power and criminality : A survey of famous crimes in Indian history. New Delhi, Allied, 1978.

Venugopal Rao, S. : Victims of crime. New Delhi, Allied Publishers, 1989.

Vukur-Quarashie, G.N. : Additional posers in the provocation law of Nigeria. *Indian Sociological Legal Journal*, V. 14 (1-2) 1988, 1-4.

Walker, Nigel : Crimes, courts and figure : An introduction to criminal statistics. Penguin Book, 1971.

Wilson, J.Q. : Thinking about crime. New York, Atheneum, 1975.

23

Police and Criminal Justice

Abadinsky, Howard : Social service in criminal justice. New Jersey, Prentice Hall, 1979.

Adam, Thomas F. : Law enforcement : An introduction to the police role in the criminal justice system. Englewood Cliffs, N.J. Prentice Hall, 1973.

Ali, S. Murtaza Fazal : Judicial approach. *Indian Journal of Criminology and Criminalistics*, V. 1 (1) March, 1981, 1-6.

Allen, Francis A. : Borderland of criminal justice. London, University of Chicago Press, 1969.

Anandhachari, T. : Police and criminal administration in India : Need for a system approach. *Indian Journal of Public Administration*, V. 24 (1) January-March, 1978, 169-72.

Baldwin, John and Bottomley, Keith (eds.) : Criminal justice : Selected readings. London, Sage Publications, 1980.

Banerjee, Phanindra Nath : Some aspects of criminal justice in medieval India. *Quarterly Review of Historical Studies*, V. 13(2) 1973-74, 81-86.

Baxi, Upendra : Crisis of the Indian legal system. New Delhi, Vikas Publishing House, 1982.

Benjamin, Ward (ed.) : Improving management in criminal justice. London, Sage Publications, 1980.

Bhagwati, P.N. : Human rights in the criminal justice system. *Journal of Indian Law Institute*, V. 27(1) January-March, 1985, 1-22.

Chakrabarti, Nirmal Kant : Admonition in criminal justice. *Cochin University Law Review*, V. 13(4) December, 1989, 37-82.

Chinnappa, O. : Criminal law, police and justice. *Indian Police Journal*, V. 27(3) January-March, 1981, 55-60.

Clifford, William and Gokhale, S.D. (eds.) : Innovations in criminal justice in Asia and the Pacific. Canberra, Australian Institute of Criminology, 1979.

Coffey, Alan (and others) : An introduction to the criminal justice system and process. New Jersey, Prentice Hall, 1974.

Cohn, Alvin W. (ed.) : Criminal justice planning and development. London, Sage Publications, 1977.

Cole, George F. (ed.) : Major criminal justice systems. London, Sage Publications, 1981.

Criminal Justice Administration : Planning for the future. *Indian Police Journal*, V. 27(2) October-December, 1980, 23-28.

Criminal Justice System—Correctional process, problems and possible remedies (Editorial). *Indian Journal of Criminology*, V. 9(2) July, 1981, 81-85.

David, R. and Brearly, J.E. : Major legal systems in the world today. London, Free Press, 1968.

Davies, Christie : Indians and British criminal justice. *Quest*, No. 93, January-February, 1975, 25-32.

Deb, R. : Criminal justice in a free society. *Social Defence*, V. 15 (59) January, 1989, 30-43.

Diaz, S.M. : Challenges facing the criminal justice system of India in the context of social change and development. *Police Research and Development, Quarter II*, April, June, 1990, 11-17.

Diaz, S.M. : Public policies and practices proper to the organization making up the criminal justice system. *Indian Journal of Criminology*, V. 12(1) January, 1984, 37-42.

Duffee, David (and others) : Criminal justice : Organization structure and analysis, New Jersey, Prentice Hall, 1978.

Eisanstein, F. and Jacob, H. : Felony justice : An organisational study of criminal courts. Boston, Little Brown, 1977.

Folk, Gerhard : Blind moloch : In the criminal justice industry, guilt is our most important product. *International Review of History and Political Science Review*, V. 19(2) May, 1982, 59-72.

Gibbons, Donc (and others) : Criminal Justice Planning : An introduction. New Jersey, Prentice Hall, 1977.

Glaser, Daniel : Strategic criminal justice planning. Maryland, National Institute of Mental Health, 1976.

Gokhale, S.D. : Criminal justice system : A review. *Social Defence*, V. 14(55) January, 1979, 5-13.

Hagan, John Ed. : Quantitative criminology : Innovations and applications. California, Sage Publications, 1982.

Hageman, Mary J. : Authoritarianism and dogmatism in criminal justice research : Themes over times. *High School Journal*, V. 68(4) April-May, 1985, 429-37.

Iyer, V.R. Krishna : Minorities, civil liberties and criminal justice. New Delhi, People's Publishing House, 1980.

Iyer, V.R. Krishna : Reforms in criminal justice : Issues and problems in decision making. *Indian Journal of Criminology*, V. 9(1) January, 1981, 3-8.

Jacob, Herbert (ed.) : Potential reform of criminal justice. London, Sage Publications, 1974.

Jain, S.N. : Public participation in criminal justice process : Indian experience. *Journal of Indian Law Institute*, V. 18(1) January-March, 1976, 134-48.

Joshi, G.P. : Cost of criminal justice system in India. *Police Research and Development*, *Quarter III*, 1990, 1-16.

Khan, M.Z. : Criminological research in India. *Social Change*, V. 12(3) September, 1982, 3-10.

Khan, M.Z. and Intezar : Jawaharlal Nehru and criminal justice system. *Indian Journal of Criminology*, V. 16(1), January, 1983, 3-9.

Khanna, H.R. : Some reflections on criminal justice. *Journal of Indian Law Institute*, V. 12(4) October-December, 1974, 505-15.

Lopez-Rey, Manuel : Crime, criminal justice and criminology : An inventory. *Social Defence*, V. 17(68) April, 1982, 5-15.

Lopez-Rey, Manuel : Need for a new international-national criminal justice order. *Social Defence*, V. 12(2) July, 1984, 118-21.

Maheshwari, S.R. : Crime and punishment : Failures of the police judiciary. *Statesman*, January 23, 1982, 8.

Marsh, Merry : Implementing criminal justice problems. California, Sage Publications, 1983.

Mir, Mehrajuddin : Crime and criminal justice system in India. New Delhi, Deep & Deep Publications, 1984.

Nagel, Stuart S. (ed.) : Modelling the criminal justice system. London, Sage Publications, 1977.

Nair, Sadasivan : Prison justice and the court. *Cochin University Law Review*, V. 2(3) September, 1978, 331-47.

Narayanaswami, K. and Ramchandran, S. : Impact of science on the administration of criminal justice. *C.B.I. Bulletin*, V. 20(3) March, 1986, 1-4.

Nathoo Lal : Police as a system of criminal justice in Japan. *Indian Police Journal*, V. 27(4) April-June, 1981, 43-55.

Oretuyl, S.A. : Plea of autrefois acquit or convict in Nigerian criminal law. *Indian Sociological Legal Journal*, V. 14(1-2) 1988, 59-66.

Pandey, D.C. : Release on bail : Law and practice. Bombay, N.M. Tripathi & Co., 1986.

Patro, H.C.M. : Criminal liability of the state. *Cochin University Law Review*, V. 11(2) June, 1987, 186-94.

Pillai, V.N. : Crime and the criminal justice system in the next decade in developing countries. *Indian Journal of Social Work*, V. 38(2) July, 1977, 99-112.

Price, B.R. and Baunach, Phyllis : Criminal justice research : New models and findings. London, Sage Publications, 1980.

Rajagopal, P.R. : Violence and response : a critique of the Indian criminal justice system. New Delhi, Uppal Publishing House, 1989.

Rajan, V.N. Whither criminal justice police. New Delhi, Sagar Publications, 1983.

Rajan, V.N. : Functional accountability syndrome in criminal justice administration. *Indian Journal of Public Administration*, V. 29(3) July-September, 1983, 612-22.

Rajan, V.N. and Khan, M.Z. : Delay in the disposal of criminal cases in the sessions and lower courts in Delhi. New Delhi, I.C.F.S., 1982.

Razdan, Usha : Supreme Court on humanizing juvenile justice. *Cochin University Law Review*, V. 14(2) January, 1990, 165-192.

Ram Reddy, P. : Criminal rules of practice and circular orders. Hyderabad, Asia Law House, 1966.

Reddy, O. Chinnappa. : Criminal law, police and justice. *Indian Police Journal*, V. 27(3) January-March, 1981, 55-60.

Reddy, O. Chinnappa : Criminal law, police and justice. *Mainstream*, V. 19 (10) 8 November, 1980, 7-8.

Reddy, O. Chinnappa : Society, law and crime. *Mainstream*, V. 21(11) 13 November 1982, 17-19.

Rossum, Ralph A. : Politics and the criminal justice system : An organisational analysis. New York, Dekkar, 1981.

Roy, Jaytilak Guha : New dimensions in criminal justice administration. *Indian Journal of Criminology*, V. 17 (1) January, 1989, 26-30.

Rustomji, K.F. : Reform criminal justice before it is too late. *Decision*, V. 13(3) July, 1986, 183-84.

Saksena, N.S. : Rival system of criminal justice. *Times of India*, 24 May, 1980, 6.

Sanwal, Mukul : Reorganising criminal administration. *Economic and Political Weekly*, V. 16 (5) 31, January, 1981, 142-44.

Sebastin, V.S. : Legal aid and criminal justice. *Cochin University Law Review*, V. 5(4) December, 1981, 401-407.

Seena, Joseph J. and Siegel, Larry J. : Introduction to criminal justice. Minnesota, West Publishing Co.

Shah, Saleem A. : Diversion from the criminal justice system. Maryland, National Institute of Mental Health, 1973.

Sharma, Girja Shankar : Dissecting the law relating to probation of offenders : The first correctional step in the field of administration of criminal justice. *Indian Sociogical Legal Journal*, V. 11(1-2) 1985, 51-67.

Sharma, J.K. : Crime, punishment and justice. *Social Welfare*, V. 28 (9) December, 1981, 27-29.

Sharma, P.D. : Police and criminal justice administration in India. New Delhi, Uppal Publishing House, 1989.

Shukla, K.S. : Criminal justice : Emerging issues and challenges. *Indian Journal of Public Administration*, V. 31(3) July-September, 1985, 840-55.

Singh, Indra J. : An approach to comprehensive criminal justice planning for a developing country India. *Indian Journal of Criminology*, V. 4 (2) July, 1976, 104-10.

Singhvi, G.C. : Separation of prosecution from police : A new dimension to rule of law. *Management in Government*, V. 4(2) July-September, 1972, 125-38.

Sirohi, J.P.S. : Probation officers investigation report in the realm of criminal judicial administration. *Journal of Indian Law Institute*, V. 21(3) July-September, 1979, 313-35.

Smith, Alexander B. and Pollack, Harnol : Criminal justice : An overview. U.S.A., Holt Reinhart and Winston, 1980.

Troganwicz, Robert and Dixon, Samuel : Criminal justice and the community. Englewood Cliff (N.J.), Prentice-Hall, 1974.

Turk, A. : Criminality and legal order, Chicago, Rand McNally, 1969.

Vadactumchery, James : Reliability of witness : Testimony. *Police Research and Development, Quarter II*, April-June, 1981, 1-4.

Vandenltaag, E. : Punishing criminals. New York, Basic Book, 1975.

Varghni, Dhirendra (ed.) : Criminal trial and judgement. Lucknow, Eastern Book Co., 1981.

Venugopal Rao, S. : Criminal justice administration : Planning for the future. *Indian Journal of Public Administration*, V. 26(3) July-September, 1980, 618-30.

Venugopal Rao, S. : Criminal justice problems and perspective in India. Delhi, Konark Publisher, 1991.

Venugopal Rao, S. : Dynamics of crime : Spatial and socio-economic aspects of crime in India, New Delhi, IIPA, 1981.

Venugopal Rao, S. : Perplexities in criminal justice. *Journal of Indian Law Institute*, V. 27(3) July-September, 1985, 458-68.

Walkar, M.R. : Criminal justice system and the community. *Social Defence*, V. 13(49) July, 1977, 6-16t.

Whitaker, Gordon P. and Phillips, Charles David (eds.) : Evaluating performance of criminal justice agencies. New Delhi, Sage Publications, 1983.

Wicks, Rober J. and Josephs, Ernest H. : Psychology of leadership for criminal justice officer : A basic programmed text. Springfield (Ill), Charles C. Thomas, 1973.

Wright, R. Gene and Mario, John A. : Police officer and the criminal justice. New York, McGraw-Hill, 1970.

Zuekic, Ugliesa and Mattel, Aurello : Research and international cooperation in criminal justice. Rome, UNSDRI, 1987.

24

Police Operation

Aaron, Thomas J. : Control of police discretion : the Danish experience. Springfield (Ill) Charles C. Thomas, 1966.

Abdi, S.N.M. : Trail of blood. *Illustrated Weekly of India*, V. 109(2), 16 January 1988, 44-45.

Adam, Hargrave L. : Police work from within : With some reflections upon women, the law and lawyers. London, G. Bell, (n.d.).

After killing 23 Gundu Rao climbs down. *New Age*, V. 28 (31) 3 August, 1980, 1.

Ahern, James E. : Police in trouble : A frightening crisis in law enforcement. New York, Hawthorn, 1972.

Albanese, Jays : The outer limits of law enforcement. *Journal of Police Science and Administration*, V. 12 (1) March 1984, 27-31.

Alderson, J. : Case of community policing. In Cowell, D. Jones, T. and Young J. (eds.) Policing the riots. London, Junctions Books, 1982.

Alderson, J. : Policing freedom. Plymouth, Macdonal and Evans, 1979.

Alderson, John : A force for power. *Police Journal*, July-September, 1978, 230-42.

Aleem, Shamin : Police on the University campus : A study in urban unrest. *Prashasnika*, V. 12(3) July-September, 1983, 37-42.

Ali, S. : Kanpur killings. *Sunday*, 12 February, 1978, 15-17.

All for peace. *Economic and Political Weekly*, V. 16(41) 10 October, 1981, 1630.

Ananthachari, T. : Police and criminal administration in India : Need for a system approach. *Indian Journal of Public Administration*, January-March 1978, 169-72.

Ananthachari, T. : Policing of tribal areas. *Indian Police Journal*, V. 27 (1) July-September, 1980, 12-18.

Anderton, James : Policing to same purpose. *Indian Police Journal*, V. 26 (3) January-March, 1980, 34-42.

Anita : Increasing participation of woman in agitations and role of police. *Prashasnika*, V. 16(3) July-December, 1987, 41-44.

Arcuri, Alan F. : You can't take fingerprints of water : Police officer's views toward cop television shows. *Human Relations*, V. 30(3) March, 1977, 237-47.

Arm, Walter : Policeman : An inside look at his role in modern society. New York, E.P. Dutton, 1969.

Army called out as widespread rioting rocks Siliguri town. *Times of India*, January, 1970, 1.

Arnold, David : Police and colonial control in south India. *Social Scientists*, V. 4 (1?) July, 1976, 3-16.

Arnold, David : Police power and colonial rule. Madras (1859-1947). New Delhi, Oxford University Press, 1986.

Arthur, Gary L. (and others) : Domestic disturbances : A major police dilemma and how one major city is handling the problem. *Journal of Police and Administration*, V. 5 (4) December, 1977, 421-29.

Arthur, Paul : Policing and crisis politics : Northern Ireland is a case study. *Parliamentary Affairs*, V. 39(3) July, 1986, 341-53.

Asnani, Hari Singh U. : Handling law and order situations. *Prashasnika*, V. 16(3-4) July-December, 1987, 83-86.

Atthreya, N.H. : A delivery end point of view : A note. *Indian Journal of Public Administration*, V. 23 (1) January-March, 1978, 224-233.

Axelberd, Mark and Valle, Jose : Development of the behavioural scale for measuring police effectiveness in domestic disputes, *Crisis Intervention*, V. 9 (2) 1978, 69-80.

Azen, Statey P. (and others) : A longitudinal predictive study of success and performance of law enforcement officers. *Journal of Applied Psychology*, V. 57(2) April, 1973, 190-92.

Bahadur, B.N. : Treatment of dangerous or habitual offenders. *Social Defence*, V. 15(57) July, 1979, 4-16.

Bajpai, K.D. : A syndicate study on management problems in dealing with student agitations. *Transactions*, V. 32, 1981, 65-123.

Bajpai, K.D. : Syndicate study on policing a major city : Pattern and nature of law and order problems faced by the city police and how handled. *Transactions*, V. 37, 1983.

Bajwa, S.S. : Some of the handicaps under the police work. *Sardar Vallabhbhai Patel National Police Academy Magazine*, November, 1978, 74-84.

Baker, Marytt (and others) : Impact of a crime wave : Perceptions, fear and confidence in the police. *Law and Society Review*, V. .7(2) 1983, 319-35.

Balagopal, K. : Revival of encounters in Andhras. *Economic and Political Weekly*, V. 16(38) 19 September, 1981, 1524-25.

Balaram, A. : Police functions unrealistic. *Hindu*, 2 June, 1981, 17.

Balkin Joseph (and others) : Police in college : The value gap revisited. *Psychological Reports*, V. 41(3, Part 2) December 1977, 1023-29.

Bammi, Deepak and Thomepulos, Nick T. : A predictive model for the response function. *Operation Research Quarterly*, V. 27(1) 1976, 15-30.

Bandy, Carole (and others) : Police performance in resolving family disputes : What makes the difference? *Psychological Reports*, V. 58(3) June 1986, 743-765.

Banerjea, D. : A syndicate study on police role in the vindication of civil right and social justice in India. *Transactions*, V. 25, April, 1977, 95-130.

Banerjea, D. : Syndicate study on "evaluation of the police role in social defence". *Transactions*, V. 33, 1981, 86-91.

Banerjea, D. : Sydicate study on problem of beggary : Enforcement of the related laws and the role of the police. A study with particular reference to the uuion territory of Delhi. *Transactions*, V. 29, 1979, 108-199.

Banerjea, D. and Husain, Ahmed : Syndicate study on arrest and police discretion under the law. *Transactions*, V. 34, 1981, 30-56.

Banerjee, Sivadas : How effective are our police: Calcutta's cops are coercive. *Illustrated Weekly of Indla*, V. 99(45) 26 November, 1978, 13.

Banerjee, Sivadas : Projecting the rural poor : Bengal police handicap. *Times of India*, 5 February, 1976, 6.

Bangalore bandh complete : Police kills six. *New Age*, V. 29(4) 25 January, 1981, 1-2.

Banton, Michael: Policing a divided society. *Police Journal*, October-December, 1974, 304-21.

Barahiya firing. *Link*, V. 20(5) 11 September, 1977, 18-19.

Barooah, M.K. : Preserving the frontiers : A proud job for policeman. *Assam Information*, V. 19(3) June, 1968, 23-26.

Batria, Puran : Policing in tribal areas. *Indian Police Journal*, October-December, 1971, 51-60.

Batria, Puran : Role of police in curbing prostitution. *Indian Police Journal*, V. 24(3) January-March, 1978, 35-38.

Bawa, P.S. : Policing for people. Calcutta, Rupa.

Bayley, David H. : A world perspective on the role of the police in social control. In Rita Donelan (ed.) Maintenance of order in society Canada, Canadian Police College, 1982.

Beck, Kenneth H. (and others) : Police officer attitudes toward Marijuana : A descriptive analysis. *American Journal of Drug and Alcohol Abuse*, V. 9(2), 1982-83, 183-93.

Beck, Kenneth H. and Summons, Terry G. : Police officer attitudes toward Marijuani : A replication and confirmation. *American Journal of Drug and Alcohol Abuse*, V. 10(4) 1984, 519-28.

Belknap, Jaonne, Morash, Merry and Trosanowicz, Robert : Implementing a community policing model for work with juveniles : An exploratory study. *Criminal Justice and Behaviour*, V. 14(2) June 1987, 211-245.

Ben-Dor, Gabriel : Role of the police in political development. *Police Journal*, April-June, 1974, 101-14.

Bennett, R.R. (ed.) : Police at work : Policy issues and analysis. London, Sage Publications, 1983.

Berg, Bruce L. (and others) : Police, riots and alienation. *Journal of Police Science and Administration*, V. 12(2) June 1984, 186-90.

Berk, Richard A. (and others) : Cops on call . Summoning the police to the scene of spousal violence. *Law and Society Review*, V. 18(3) 1984, 479-98.

Beutler, Larry E. (and others) : Parameters in the prediction of police officer performance. *Professional Psychology : Research and Practice*, V. 16(2) April, 1985, 324-35.

Beyond the call of duty. *Economic Times*, 12 April, 1981, 4.

Bhambhari, C.P. : Making police force more effective. *Times of India*, January 28, 1982, 4.

Bhattachary, Dipankar : Myth and reality of Barkakana police firing. *Other Side*, 86, March, 1989, 30-31.

Bhattacharya, P.K. : Beggar problem and the police. *Transactions of the National Police Academy*, November, 1969, 1-23, 1983.

Biderman, Albert D. (and others) : Report on a pilot study in the district of Columbia on victimization and attitudes towards law enforcement and administration of justice : Report to the presidents commission on law enforcement and administration of justice. Washington (D.C.), Bureau of Social Science Research, 1967.

Biles, David and Braithwaite, John : Crime victims and the police. *Australian Psychologist*, V. 14(3) November, 1979, 345-55.

Birch, Roger : Policing Europe in 1992. *Police Journal*, V. 62(3) July-September, 1989, 203-10.

Bittner, E. : Functions of the police in the modern society. Maryland, National Institute of Mental Health, 1970.

Black, Donald J. and Riess, Albert J. : Police and citizen behaviour in field encounters : Some comparisons according to the race and social class status citizens. Ann Arbor, University of Michigan Press, 1966.

Bloch, Peter B. : Policemen on patrol : Final report. Washington, Urban Institute, Police Foundation, 1974.

Bloodshed at Nipani (Editorial). *Times of India*, 8 April, 1982, 6.

Bose, A.C. : Immobilisation of policemen. *Amrit Bazar Patrika*, 9 July, 1969, 6.

Bose, P.K. : Police in independent India : Functional confusions and needs. *Current Events*, August, 1978, 46-48.

Bowes, Stuart : Police and civil liberties. London, Lawrence and Wishart, 1956.

Bozza, Charles M. : Motivations guiding policemen in the arrest process. *Journal of Police Science and Administration*, V. 1(4) December, 1973, 468-76.

Bracki, Mare A. and Connor, Gregory : Survey of police attitudes toward rape. Illinois. *Crisis Intervention*, V. 6(3) 1975, 28-42.

Braiden, Christopher : Bank robberies and stolen bikes : Thoughts of a street cop (French). *Canadian Police College Journal*, V. 1C(1) 1986, 1-35.

Braj Mohan : Police negligence in Delhi the worst crime. *Sunday*, 24 September, 1978, 43-45.

Brent, Edward E. and Sykes, Richard E. : Mathematical model for symbolic interaction between police and suspects. *Behavioural Science*, V. 24(6) November, 1979, 388-402.

Britt, David W. and Little, Charles R. : Crime rates and police behaviour : A test of two hypotheses. *Social Forces*, V. 54(2) December, 1975, 441-51.

Brodsky, Standley L. and Williamson, Glenda D. : Attitudes of public towards violence. *Psychological Reports*, V. 57(3) Part 2, December 1985, 1179-1180.

Brown, Karin and Coulter, Philip B. : Subjective and objective measures of police service delivery. *Public Administration Review*, V. 43 (1) January-February, 1983, 50-58.

Brown, Michael F. : Use of deadly force by patrol officers : Training implications. *Journal of Police Science and Administration*, V. 12(2) June 1984, 133-40.

Buchanan, Dale R. : Enhancing eye witness identification : Applied Psychology for law enforcement officers. *Journal of*

Police Science and Administration, V. 13(4) December, 1985, 303-09.

Buchanan, Dale R. and Chasnoff, Pati : Family crisis intervention programs : What works and what doesn't. *Journal of Science and Administraion*, V. 14(2) June, 1986, 161-68.

Buoh, M.H. : Reversing the tide of lawlessness. *Times of India*, 25 April, 1986, 8.

Burke, Ronald J. : Burnout in police work : An examina- of the cherniss model. *Group and Organization Studies*, V. 12(2) June 1987, 174-188.

Burris, Carole A. and Jaffe, Peter : Wife abuse as a crime : The impact of police laying charges. *Canadian Journal of Criminology*, V. 25(3) July, 1983, 309-18.

Campbell, Don : Police, the exercise of power. Estover (Plymouth), Macdonald & Evans, 1978.

Carlson, Helen M. and Sutton, Markleys : Development of attitudes as a function of police roles. *Personality and Social Psychology Bulletin*, V. 1(1) 1974, 113-15.

Carnage of Bailadilla mines. *New Age*, V. 26(16) 16 April, 1978, 1-2.

Carr, Adam F. (and others) : Outcome measures of police performance : Some steps towards positive accountability. *Journal of Community Psychology*, V. 82(2) April 1980, 165-71.

Carter, David L. : His panic perception of police performance : An empirical assessment. *Journal of Criminal Justice*, V. 13(6) 1985, 487-500.

Cascio, Wayne F. and Valenzi, Enzo R. : Relations among criteria of police performance. *Journal of Appliea Psychology*, V. 63(1) February, 1978, 22-28.

Central Police Training College, Abu : 2nd Advanced Course, 1961 : Status and role of police.

Centrai Police Training College : Centre's role in police functions : Background papers and proceedings of the seminar held on 9th to 21st November, 1965, Abu CPTC, 1966.

Chakraberty, C. : Student indiscipline and the police. *Transactions of the National Police Academy*, Mt. Abu, V. 10, 1967, 84-106.

Chapman, Jeffrey L. : Impact of police of crime and crime on police : A synthesis of the economic and ecological approaches. Los Angels, Institute of Government and Public Affair, University of California, 1973.

Charan Singh : Changing role of the police. *Indian Police Journal*, V. 24(1) July-September, 1977, 3-10.

Chaturvedi, B.L. : Face to face with criminals. Delhi, Pocket Books, 1970.

Chaturvedi, S.K. : Police and emerging challenges. Delhi, B.R. Publications, 1988.

Chemani, G.D. : Police and the young offenders. *Social Welfare*, March 1971, 1-2.

Chhabra, Rami : Blame not only police. *Statesman*, 2 Sept. 1978, 3.

Chitale, K.A. : Ensure laws effective enforcement. *M.P. Chronicle*, 4 February, 1980.

Chwast, Jacob : Value conflict in law enforcement : In A. Niederhoffer and Arthur, S. Blumberg (eds.) Ambivalent force : Perspectives on police. U.S.A., Genn and Co., 1970, 113-20.

Cingranelli, David L.: Effects of neighbourhood-context on evaluations of police services. *Journal of Urban Affairs*, V. 5(4) Fall, 1983, 355-61.

Clark, D.J. : Policemen's duties : Problems of definition and enforcement. *Hong Kong Journal of Public Administration*, V. 1(1) June, 1979, 30-55.

Clarke, R.V.G. and Hough, J.M. (ed.) : Effectiveness of policing. Fornborough, Gower, 1980.

Clements, Carl B. : School relations bureau : A programme of police intervention. *Criminal Justice and Behaviour*, V. 2(4) December, 1975, 358-71.

Clifford, Brain : Police as eyewitnesses. *New Society*, V. 36(707) 22 April, 1976, 176-77.

Clifford, W. : Crime control in Japan. Lexington, D.H. Health, 1976.

Clift, Raymond E. : A guide to modern police thinking : An introduction policing. Cincinnati, W.H. Anderson, 1970.

Contractor, Jal B. : Bombay police social service squads. *Indian Police Journal*, July-September, 1976, 54-59.

Costa, Benedict : Who will police the policeman? *Illustrated Weekly of India*, V. 101(35) 31 August, 1980, 8-12.

Courley, G. Douglas and Bristow, Allen P. : Patrol Administration. Springfield (Ill), Charles C. Thomas, 1961.

Courtis, M. and Dusseyer, I. : Attitudes toward crime and the police in Toronto : A report on some survey findings. Toronto, Centre of Criminology, University of Toronto, 1970.

Covey, Herbert C. and Menard, Scott : Response to rapid social change : The case of boomtown law enforcement. *Journal of Police Science and Administration*, V. 12(2) June, 1984, 164-69.

Cowan, D. : Team work in policing. *Royal Canadian Mounted Police Gazette*, V. 50(6) 1988, 11-12.

Cowell, D. (and others) : Policing in riots. London, Junction Books, 1982.

Cox, Edmund Charles : Police and crime in India. London, S. Paul, 1911.

Cox, Edmund Charles : Police and crime in India. New Delhi, Manu Publications, 1976.

Crime and punishment (Editorial). *Times of India*, 5 December, 1980, 8.

Crime control is no picnic. *Illustrated Weekly of India*, V. 104(13) 27 March, 1983, 13-14.

Crime without punishment (Editorial). *Economic and Political Weekly*, V. 13(40),7 October, 1978, 1681-82.

Cullen, Francis T. (and others) : Paradox in policing : A note on perceptions of danger. *Journal of Police Science and Administration*, V. 11(4) December, 1983, 457-62.

Curran, James T. (and others) : Police and law enforcement. New York, Ams. Press, 1973.

Curry, J.E. and King, Glen D. : Race tensions and the police. Springfield (III), Charles C. Thomas, 1962.

Dang, Satyapal. : Police and terrorists. *Mainstream*, V. 22 (45) 7 July, 1984, 6.

Datta-Ray, Sunanda K. : Policing the state : Shift from force to service. *Statesman*, January 15, 1990.

Datta-Ray, Sunanda K. : Protector or violator : Restoring dignity to the police. *Statesman*, 3 April, 1984, 6.

Dear, G.J. : Law and order : the war ahead. *Police Journal*, January-March, 1980, 62-71.

Deb, R. : Malpractices in law enforcement. *Indian Police Journal*, V. 19(3) 1973.

Deb, R. : Police and juvenile delinquent. *National Police Academy Magazine*, November, 1970, 27-33.

Deb, R. : Police and law enforcement. Calcutta, S.C. Sarkar & Sons, 1988.

Deb, R. : Police and law enforcement, *Journal of Criminology and Criminalistics*, V. 1 (2-3), June-September, 1981.

Deb, R. : Role of police in social defence. *Assam Information*, V. 19(6) September, 1968, 13-15.

Delprino, Robert P. and Bahn, Charles : National survey of the extent and nature of psychological services in police departments. *Professional Psychology : Research and Practice*, V. 19(4) August, 1988, 421-25.

Deshmukh, Rajguru V. : Pushing the police around. *Indian Express*, 2 September 1979, 13.

Desmed T., John C. : Use of force paradigm for law enforcement. *Journal of Police Science and Administration*, V. 12(2) June, 1984, 170-76.

Deters, Gary and Dalre, Gary : No fault policing : Generating community interest to share prevention responsibility. *C.B.I. Bulletin*, V. 11(10) October, 1977, 9-10.

Dewan, V.N. : Security guide for police and public : Techniques of criminals and counter measures for safety. Newsman Group Publications, 1978.

Dhagamwar, Vasudha : Policing the police. *Mainstream* (Annual Number), V. 19(1-5) 1980, 69-71.

Dhar, M.K. : Policing the police. *Hindustan Times*, April 4, 1981, 9.

Diaz, S.M. : Impact of social change on police role and functions in India, *Sardar Vallabhbhai Patel National Police Academy Magazine*, V. 35, November, 1975, 13.

Diaz, S.M. : New dimensions to police role and functions in India. Abu, *Sardar Vallabhbhai Patel National Police Academy*, 1977.

Diaz, S.M. : Police responsibility to the criminal trial process. *Indian Journal of Criminology*, V. 4(2) July, 1976, 111-16.

Diaz, S.M. : Public violence vis-a-vis public order. *Inaian Journal of Criminology*, V. 4(1) January, 1976, 37-43.

Diaz, S.M. : Sensitisation of the police for effective role performance. *Denouement*, V. 2(6 and 7) January-February, 1991, 25-32.

Diaz, S.M. : Towards a better police service. *Akashvani*, 21 January 1977, 7-9.

Dixit, Mahesh Dutt : Roles and functions of the police in a changing society. *Resource Material Series*, No. 10, UNAFEI, Japan, October, 1975, 38-44.

Dogra, Bharat : Terrorism and police repression. *Economic and Political Weekly*, V. 24(41) 14 October, 1989, 2296.

Dolon, Ronald (and others) : Police practices and attitude toward domestic violence. *Journal of Police Science and Administration*, V. 14(3) September, 1986, 187-92.

Domash, M.A. (and others) : Police and prosecution system : An analysis of a police criminal case preparation program. *Journal of Applied Behaviour Analysis*, V. 13(3) Fall, 1980, 397-406.

Domash, Michele A. : Behavioural prosthetics : Preparation of police reports for criminal prosecution. *Dissertation Abstracts International*, V. 39(11-B) May, 1979, 5608-09.

Donelan, Rita (ed.) : Maintenance of order in society. Canada, Canadian Police College, 1982.

Douthit, Nathan : Enforcement and non-enforcement roles in policing : A historical inquiry. *Journal of Police Science and Administration*, V. 3(3) September, 1975, 336-45.

Dubey, K.P. : On encounter with criminal. *Indian Nation*, April 8, 1974 (Sunday Mag.) II.

Duncon, M.D.G. : Effective use of police resources. *C.B.I. Bulletin*, V. 17(12) December, 1983, 2-9.

Dutt, G.C. : Reflections on crowd control. *Indian Police Journal*, April, 1960, 22.

Dwivedi, J.N. : Police powers and duties. Allahabad, Allahabad Law Agency, 1950.

Dwivedi, S.C. : A syndicate study on "the role of police in natural calamities." *Transactions*, V. 22, April, 19/6, 87-113.

Dynes, Russell R. (and others) : Police perspectives and behaviour in a campus disturbance. *Journal of Police Science and Administration*, V. 2(3) September, 1974, 344-51.

Dynes, Russell (and others) : Police perspectives and behaviour in a campus unrest : In Donald, E.J. Macnamara and Marc Ridel (eds.) Police : Perspectives, problems, prospects. New York, Praeger Publishers, 1974, 53-64.

Easley, Mary Pipines : What police and prosecutors need from each other. *Popular Government*, 47(3) Winter, 1982, 17-21.

Elmes, Frank : Police and commercial security. *Police Journal*, January-March, 1971, 55-60.

Encounter shown to be murder. *Economic and Political Weekly*, V. 13(34) 26 August, 1978, 1965-66.

Encounter with outrage (Editorial). *Economic Times*, 28 April, 1986, 8.

Erez, Edna and Tontodonato, Pamela : Patterns of reported parent-child abuse and police response. *Journal of Family Violence*, V. 4(2) June, 1989, 143-59.

Ericson, Richard V. : Patrolling the facts : Secrecy and publicity in police work. *British Journal of Sociology*, V. 40(2) June, 1989, 205-26.

Experts' views on powers of police. *Times of India*, 8 Nov., 1969, 3.

Farah, S.A. : G.P. robbery and after. *Indian Nation*, 8 May, 1988.

Farah, S.A. : Police patrolling. *Indian Nation*, July 28, 1988, 4.

Farah, S.A. : Third degree method. *Indian Nation*, 27 June, 1988.

Feltham, Rob : Validity of a police assessment centre : A 1-19 year follow-up. *Journal of Occupational Psychology*, V. 61(2) June, 1988, 129-44.

Fichter, Joseph H. : Police handling of arresties (a research study of police arrests in New Orleauns), Loyala University of the South, 1964.

Field, Hurbert S. : Attitudes toward rape : A comparative analysis of police, rapists, crisis counselors, and citizens.

Journal of Personality and Social Psychology, V. 36(2) February, 1978, 156-79.

Finnimore, Peter : How should the effectiveness of the police be assessed? *Police Journal*, V. 55(1) January-March, 1982, 55-56.

Flanagan, Timothy, J. : Consumer perspectives on police operational strategy. *Journal of Police Science and Administration*, V. 13(1) March, 1985, 10-21.

Franz, Verl and Jones, David M. : Perceptions of organizational performance in suburban police departments : A critique of the military model. *Journal of Police Science and Administration*, V. 15(2) June, 1987, 153-161.

Fraser, Lord : Police in the judicial process. *Police Journal*, October-December, 1972, 265-78.

Fyfe, James J. : Blind justice : Police shootings in maphis. *Journal of Criminal Law and Criminology*, V. 37(2) Summer, 1982, 707-22.

Fyfe, James J. : Who shoots? A look at officer race and police shootings. *Journal of Police Science and Administration*, V. 9(4) December, 1981, 367-82.

Gabard, E. Caroline and Kenney, John P. : Police writing. Springfield (III), Charles C. Thomas, 1957.

Gandhi, Rajmohan : Parallel raj of the underworld. *Indian Express*, 24 March 1980.

Ganganagar firing toll now eight. *Times of India*, 9 January, 1970, 1.

Garner, Peter, E. : Policing in Lesotho. *Police Journal*, January-March, 1971, 41-47.

Gautam, D.N. and Trivedi, B.N. : Unnatural deaths of married women with special reference to dowry deaths : A sample study of Delhi. New Delhi, Government of India Press, 1986.

Geller, William A. : Officer restraint in the use of deadly force : The next frontier in police shooting research. *Journal of Police Science and Administration*, V. 13(2) June, 1985, 153-71.

Germann, A.C. : Law enforcement : A look into the future. *Police Journal*, October-December, 1977, 340-47.

Germann, A.C. : What is the developing mission of the American police ? *Police Journal*, February, 1970, 97-104.

Ghate, Prabhakar, : Law and order : A holding operation. *Indian Journal of Public Administration*, V. 19(4) October-December, 1973, 472-94.

Ghosh, S.K.: Anti-terrorism handbook : A practical guide to counteraction planning and operations for individual, business and government. Delhi, Manas Publications, 1991.

Ghosh, S.K. : Gangsterism I : A national menace. *Hindustan Times*, July 31, 1990, 7.

Ghosh, S.K. : Gangsterism II : Dealing with crime. *Hindustan Times*, August 1, 1990, 7.

Ghosh, S.K. : Law and order : From the police point of view. Calcutta, Eastern Law House, 1972.

Ghosh, S.K. : Law enforcement in retrospect. *Indian Journal of Public Adrr instration*, V. 24 (1) January-March, 1978, 123-26.

Ghosh, Sadhan Kumar : Naxalites and policemen. *Swarajya*, V. 15(17) 24 October, 1970, 13.

Gill, Raj : Callous cops give a rude shock. *Hindustan Times*, 4 September, 1978, 3.

Gill, Raj : Police department in dock. *Hindustan Times*, 1978, 3.

Gill, Y.S. : Police shoots to kill impact Kotdwara. *New Age*, V. 29 (16) 19 April, 1981, 1-2.

Gilling, Paulette M. (and others) : What do police officers really want from the mental health system ? *Hospital and Community Psychiatry*, V. 41 (6) June, 1990, 663-65.

Gleizal, J.J. : Police, law and security in France : Questions of method and political strategy. *International Journal of the Sociology of Law*, V. 9(4) November, 1981, 361-82.

Golden, Kathryn M. : police role : Perceptions and preferences. *Journal of Police Science and Administration*, V. 10 (1) March, 1982, 108-11.

Goldstein, Herman : Police policy formulation : A proposal for improving police performance. *Michigan New Review*, V. 65(6) April, 1967, 1123-1146.

Goldstein, Herman : Police response to urban crisis. *Public Administration Review*, September-October, 1968, 417-22.

Goldstein, Herman : Policing a free society. Massachusettes, Ballinger Publishing Company, 1977.

Gondolf, Edward W. and Mcferron, J. Richard : Handling battering men : Police action in wife abuses. *Criminal Justice and Behaviour*, V. 16(4) December, 1989, 429-39.

Goswami, Biswa : Repressive measures in Assam. *Janata*, V. 38 (5) 13 March, 1983, 5-7.

Gottdiener, Mark : Suburban crime : Testing the police hypothesis. *Journal of Police Science and Administration*, V. 10 (4) December, 1982, 425-34.

Goudar, K.M. : Crime : Its administration in Mysore state. *Journal of the Karnatak University (Social Sciences)*, 1971, 166-73.

Gourley, G. Douglas and Bristow, Allan B.: Patrol administration. Springfield (III), Charles C. Thomas, 1961.

Grant Douglas : Policing then and now. *Police Journal*, January-March, 1980, 55-61.

Greenbaum, Charles W. and Zemach, Mina : Role playing and change of attitude toward the police after a campus riot : Effects situational demand and justification. *Human Relations*, V. 25(1) February, 1972, 87-89.

Gregory, Eric and Turner, Peter : Unit beat policing in England. *Indian Police Journal*, July-September, 1970. 55-64.

Gribble, Leonard : Famous stories of police and crime. London, Arthur Barker, 1972.

Griffin, Johan I : Statistics essential for police efficiency. Springfield (III), Charles C. Thomas, 1958.

Gross, Leonard : "Is there a samoritan in the neighbourhood" ? *Indian Police Journal*, V. 14(3) January, 1968, 64-57.

Gupta, Anandswarup : Crime and police in India (Up to 1861). Agra, Sahitya Bhawan, 1974.

Gupta, Anandswarup : How to avoid misuse of the police. *Indian Police Journal*, V. 25(1) July-September, 1978, 37-47.

Gupta, Pranab K. Das : Role of police in a changing society in India : Maintenance of public order in pre-literate and modern society, *Decision*, V. 13(3) July, 1986, 199-203.

Gupta, R.G. : Methods of crowd control. *Police Research and Development, Quarter III*, July-September, 1981, 1-6.

Gupta, Ranjit : Guarding the people. In S.K. Ghosh (ed.) Police administrators : Reminiscences. Delhi, Ashish Publishing House, 1989, 90-106.

Gwynn, Charles William : Imperial policing. London, Macmillan, 1934.

Hall, S. (and others) : Policing the crisis : Mugging the state and law and order. London, Macmillan, 1978.

Hamilton, Peter : Police and the security industry. *Police Journal*, June, 1968, 261-67.

Hamilton, Peter : Police and the security industry, *Police Journal*, July, 1968, 297-303.

Hampton, Ross : Labelling theory and the police decision to prosecute juveniles. *Australian and New Zealand Journal of Sociology*, V. 11(3) October, 1975, 64-66.

Hazer, John T. : Longitudinal relationship between role perception, role ambiguity and police performance. *Dissertation Abstracts International*, V. 37(11-B) May 1977, 5869.

Hearn, C.V. : Duty to the public : A frank assessment to today's police force. London, Frederickmuller, 1965.

Heywood, R.N. : Some thoughts on police roles. *Indian Police Journal*, April-June, 1976, 10-12.

Hogan, Robert and Kurtines, William : Personalogical correlates of police effectiveness. *Journal of Psychology*, V. 91(2) November, 1975, 289-95.

Holcomb, R.L. : Police patrol. Springfield (Ill), Charles C. Thomas, 1952.

Hollinger, Richard C. : Race occupational status and proactive police arrest for drinking and driving. *Journal of Criminal Justice*, V. 12(2) 1984, 173-83.

Holman, Mary : Police officer and the child. Springfield (Ill) Charles C. Thomas, 1962.

Holzworth, R. James and Pipping, Catherine B. : Drawing a weapon : An analysis of police judgement. *Journal of Police Science and Administration*, V. 13(3) September, 1985, 185-94.

Homan, Robert J. and Kennedy, Daniel B. : Police perceptions of spouse abuse : A comparison of male and female officers. *Journal of Criminal Justice*, V. 33(1) 1985, 29-47.

Hooda, R.K. : Problems of the police in the area of crowd control and violence : Also difficulties in relation to the University of Bombay- *Journal of the University Bombay (New Sense)*, No. 37, October, 1968, 229-53.

Howard, Mary K. : Police encounters with juvenile offender. *Dissertation Abstracts International,* V. 34(3-A) September, 1973, 1382-83.

Iengar, H.V.R. : Use and abuse of police power. *Indian Express*, 18 April 1968, 4.

Igbinovia, Patrick, Edobor : Pattern of policing in Africa. The French and British connections. *Police Journal,* V. 54(2) April-June, 1981, 123-56.

Imbert, Peter : Policing London. *Police Journal,* V. 61(3) July-September, 1988, 199-208.

India, National Police Academy, Abu : The expanding role of the police : Background papers and proceedings of the Seminar held on 6th and 7th November, 1968.

India, National Police Academy : Need for motivational techniques in police service : Background papers and proceedings of the seminar held on 15th and 16th November, 1972.

Iyer, T.G.L. : System approach to law and order. *Police Research and Develcpment, Quarter IV,* October-December, 1975, 7-12.

Iyer, T.G.L. : Avoiding failures in policing. *Indian Police Journal*, V. 36(2) April-June, 1989, 39-42.

Iyer, T.G.L. : Towards better policing. *Indian Police Journal*, V. 25(1) July-September, 1978, 103-8.

Iyer, T.G.L. : 20 point programme and the police. *Indian Police Journal*, January-March, 1976, 12-16.

Jackson, R.M. : Enforcing the law. London, Macmillan, 1967.

Jacobs, David : Inequality and police strength : Conflict theory and coercive control in metropolitan area. *American Sociological Review*, V. 44(6) December, 1979, 913-25.

Jacobs, David and Brit, David : Inequality and police use of deadly force : An empirical assessment of a conflict hypothesis. *Social Problems*, April, 1979, 403-12.

Jaffe, Pater (and others) : Impact of police charges in incidents of wife abuse. *Journal of Family Violence*, V. 1(1) March, 1986, 37-49.

Jain, R.B. : Changing police functions. *Seminar*, No. 250, June, 1980, 38-40.

Jaipur firing. *Administrator*, V. 26(4) Winter, 1981, 645-56.

Jayasingh, J. Viruvathas : Changing perspectives and police services. *Indian Police Journal*, V. 14(3) January-March, 1978, 43-45.

Jayewardhene, C.H.S. : Contextual constraints on police action. *Indian Journal of Criminology*, V. 10(2) July, 1982, 100-07.

Jayewardhene, C.H.S. : Control of crime in developing countries. *Indian Journal of Social Work*, V. 42(4) January, 1982, 381-92.

Jayewardhene, C.H.S. : Internal organisational constraints on police efficiency. *Indian Police Journal*, V. 31(3) July-September, 1984, 10-16.

Jayewardhene, C.H.S. and Mc Watt, F.E. : Police and the female delinquent. *Canadion Police College Journal*, V. 8(3) 1984, 203-17.

Jerath, Arati R. : High acquittals due to police inefficiency. *Indian Express*, 20 December, 1980.

Jeyasingh, J. Visuvathas : Changing perspectives in police services. *Indian Police Journal*, V. 24(3) January-March, 1978, 43-45.

Jha, Akhileshwar : Police on the campus. *Hindustan Times*, 26 December, 1980.

Jha, Jagadanand : Role of police in welfare state. Souvenir, 10th symposium of all India principals police training college. Dated 22.10.1981 to 24.10.1981. Patna, 50-56.

Jobson, J.D. and Schneck, Rodney : Constituent views of organizational effectiveness : Evidence from police organizations. *Academy of Management Journal*, V. 25(1) March, 1982, 25-46.

Johnson, Elmer Hubert : Crime, correction and society. Homewood, Dorsey Press, 1974.

Johnston, T. Eric St. : British police experience. *Police Journal*, November, 1969, 486-508.

Jones, J. Meruyn : Organizational or victim needs : The implications for a policing by objectives strategy. *Police Journal*, V. 36(3) July-September, 1983, 276-90.

Jorgensen, James D. : Crime in a free society : Choice or challenges. *Federal Probation*, V. 34(1) March, 1970, 14-18.

Joshi, G. P. : Basis of police authority cannot be mere law: It has to be public trust too. *Sardar Vallabhbhai Patel National Academy Magazine*, November, 1977, 80-90.

Kakalk, James S. and Wildhorn, Sorel : Aids to decision-making in police patrol : A report prepared for department of housing and urban development. Santa Monica (Cal.), Rand Corporation, 1971.

Karnik, V. B. : Role of police in a democracy. *Radical Humanist*, V. 47 (ii) February, 1983, 7-8.

Keane, Carl, Gills, A. R. & Hagan John : Deterrence and amplification of juvenile delinquency by police contract : Importance of gender and risk orientation. *British Journal of Criminology*, V. 29(4) Fall, 1989, 336-352.

Keefe, M. L. : Police and the rape victim in New York. *Victimology*, V. 1(2) Summer, 1976.

Kelly, William and Kelly, Nora : policing in Canada. Toronto, Macmillan of Canada, 1976.

Kenetkar, V. G. : Police and prohibition. *Indian Express*, 4 January, 1978, 6.

Kenney, John P. and Pursuit, Dan G. : Police work with juveniles and the administration of juvenile justice. Springfield (III), Charles C. Thomas, 1970.

Kernish, Robert : Working environment and role variation : The case of the suburban police. *Dissertation Abstracts International*, V. 37 (12-A, Part 1) June, 1977, 8008-09.

Khan, A. N. : Recognition of vicarious liability for the wrongful acts of a police officer. *Police Journal*, July-September, 1977, 240-47.

Khan, Akbar Ali and Mohiddin, Ahmed. Charminar Police Division, Hyderabad : A case study in the working of police field unit. *Journal of Social Studies State Governments*, V. 6 (1) January-March, 1973, 18-33.

Khan, Sultan Akbar : Police, power and public. Kurukshetra, Vikas Publications, 1983.

Khan, Zillur R. and Spragens. William C. : American and Pakistan policemen's attitudes towards law enforcement. *Western Political Quarterly*, September, 1970, 579-88.

Khandelwal, Brij : Our police and our civil liberties. *Point of View*, 17 February, 1973, 25-28.

Khandelwal, Brij : Police and the total revolution. *Janata*, V. 33(2) 12 February, 1978, 14-16.

Khanna, K.C. : Decimation of the police : Politics takes its roll. *Times af India*, 20 December, 1983, 6.

Khanna, K.C. : Maintaining public peace. *Times of India*, 17 August, 1984.

Khemani, G.D. : Police and the young offenders. *Social Walf. re*, V. 17(12), March, 1971, 1-2.

Khullar, Surrinder : Policing the people. *Times of India*, 6 February, 1972, 6.

Kissiah, Carl W. : Development of an objective rating instrument for campus police officers. *Dissertation Abstracts International*, V. 34(6-B) December, 1973, 2902.

Klien, Herbert : Police : Demand if they do, and demand, if they don't. New York, Crown Publishers, 1968.

Khigths, Philip : Ultimate command : The responsibilities of chief constables in the 1980's. *Police Journal*, V. 54(4) October-December, 1981, 331-39.

Koenig, Daniel J. : Police, perceptions of public respect and extra-legal use of force : A reconsiderating of folk wisdom and pluralistic ignorance. *Canadian Journal of Sociology*, V. 1(3) 1975, 313-324.

Koenig, Esther J. : An overview of attitudes toward women in law enforcement. *Public Administration Review*, V. 39(3) May-June, 1978, 267-75.

Kohfeld, C.W. : Rational cops, rational robbers, and information. *Journal of Criminal Justice*, V. 11(5) 1983, 459-66.

Kothari, Smith : Encounters in cold blood. *Indian Express (mag.)*, 20 February, 1983, IV.

Kraus, J. and Kasleton, S.L. : Juvenile offenders: Diversion potential as a function of police perceptions. *American Journal of Community Psychology*, V. 10(2) April, 1982, 171-82.

Kripalani, J.B. : Our police during the emergency. *Indian Express*, 31 May. 1977, 4.

Krishnamurthi, K. : Police power and duties. Allahabad, Law Book, 1959.

Krishnan, R.S. : Police in a democracy. *Hindu*, 14 June, 1977.

Krishnayar, V.R. : Police in a welfare state. New Delhi, Asia Book Centre, 1959.

Ksionzky, Sheldon and Mehrabian, Albert : Temperament characteristics of successful police dispatchers : work sortings requiring continuous rapid judgements and responses to complex information. *Journal of Police Science aud Administration*, V. 14(1) March, 1986, 45-48.

Kulkarni, R.S. : Police performance in India. *Indicn Journal of Criminology*, V. 17(2) July, 1989, 104-08.

Kumar, Santh : Syndicate study on ragging in educational institutions and the role of police in combating it. *Transactions*, V. 35, 1982, 45-119.

Kuykendall, Jack : Police strategies : Executive perceptions of their relationship to crime control. *Journal of Police Science and Administration*, V. 9(4), December, 1981, 441-47.

Kuykendall, Jack L. : Styles of community policing. *Criminology : An Interdisciplinary Journal*, V. 12(2), August 1974, 229-40.

Lafave, Wayne R. : Arrest : The decision to take a suspect into custody. Boston, Little Brown and Co., 1965.

Lal, Biswanath : Judicial probe into firing demanded. *New Age*, V. 29(8) 22 February, 1981, 7.

Lambert, J. : Crime, police and race relations. London, Oxford University Press, 1970.

Lane, Roger : Policing the city, Boston, 1822-1885. Cambridge (Mass), Harvard University Press, 1967.

Langworthy, Robert H. : Police shooting and criminal homicide : Temporal relationship. *Journal of Quantitative Criminology*, V. 2(4) December, 1986, 377-388.

Laraih, K. : Garbhan firing : Part of a pattern. *Mainstream*, V. 20(52) 28 August, 1982, 26.

Larmand, Pepitone S. and Shanmugan, T.E. : Study of attitude towards rape. *Journal of Cross-cultural Psychology*, V. 12 Western, Washington University, 1981.

Larson, Lynn D. (and others) : Reduction of police vehicle accidents through mechanically aided supervision. *Journal of Applied Behaviour Analysis*, V. 13(4) Winter, 1980, 571-81.

Ledoux, John C. and Hazelwood, Robert R. : Police attitude and beliefs toward rape. *Journal of Police Science and Administration*, V. 13(3) September, 1985, 211-20.

Lee, Raymond and Malone, Michael : Multitrait-multi-method-multirater analysis of performance ratings for law enforcement personnel. *Journal of Applied Psycholagy*, V. 66(5) October, 1981, 625-32.

Leigh, L.H. : Police powers in England and Wales. London, Butterworth, 1975.

Leonard, V.A. : Police pre-disaster preparation. Springfield (Ill) Charles C. Thomas, 1973.

Leonard, V.A. : Police, the judiciary and the criminal. Springfield (Ill) Charles C. Thomas, 1969.

Lester, David : Police protection and changes in urban population. *Psychological Reports*, V. 42 (3, part 2) June, 1978, 1138.

Lester, David : Use of deadly force by police. *Police Journal*, V. 57(2) April-June, 1984, 170-71.

Lester, David (and others) : Police roles, discretion and danger. *Perceptual and Motor Skills*, V. 51(1) August 1980, 318.

Levis, Joseph H. : Evaluation of experiments in policing : What are we learning? *Evaluation Quarterly*, V. 2(2) May, 1978, 315-30.

Lewis, Roy : A force for the future : Role of the police in the next ten years. London, Temple Smith, 1976.

Lobo, John : Police role in industrial undertakings. *C.B.I. Bulletin*, V. 21(12) December, 1986, 1-2.

Loo, Robert : Policy development for psychological services in the royal Canadian mounted police. *Journal of Police Science and Administration*, V. 13(2) June 1985, 132-37.

Lubans, V.A. and Edgar, I.M. : Policing by objectives. Connecticut, Hartford, 1979.

Lundman, Richard J. (and others) : Police control of juveniles : A replication. *Journal of Research in Crime and Delinquency*, V. 15(1) January, 1978, 74-91.

Luthra, B.R. and Mohiuddin, A. : Police and labour unrest : A syndicate study. *Transactions*, V. 26, 1982, 1-49.

Lynch, William S. : Police function and organized crime. *C.B.I. Bulletin*, November, 1975, 9.

Magnus, Robert (and others) : Attitudinal testing : A tool for the effective law enforcement. *Journal of Police Science and Administration*, V. 5(1) March, 1977, 74-78.

Mahanty, A.P. : Carrier pigeon service of the Orissa police. *Indian Police Journal*, April, 1955, 39-41.

Mahmood Bin Muhammad : Policing tribal districts. *Police Research and Development*, July-September, 1975, 2-16.

Malaviya, P.D. : What is the police for? *Indian Journal of Public Administration, Quarter III*, V. 24(1) January-March, 1978, 45-48.

Malhotra, Inder : Crime in the capital : What's wrong with the police. *Times of India*, 7 September, 1978, 6.

Malhotra, Inder : Grim portents from Punjab : Police defiance and after. *Times of India*, 17 May, 1979, 6 : 3-5.

Malik, Amita : Police failures in the capital : Vip's vitiate atmosphere. *Times of India*, 12 September, 1978. 6.

Malviya, P.D. : Role of police in social defence. *Social Defence*, V. 6(19) January, 1970, 20-27.

Manning, Peter L.: Dramatic aspects of policing : Selected propositions. *Sociology and Social Research*, V. 59(1) October 1974, 21-29.

Manning, Peter K. : Police work : The social organization of policing. Cambridge, M.I.T. Press, 1977.

Manning, Peter K. and Mannen, John Van : Policing : A view from the street. California, Goodyear Publishing Co., 1978.

Manwaring, White S. : Policing revolution. Brighton, Harvester Press, 1983.

Marenin, Otwin : Policing African states : Toward a critique. *Comparative Politics*, V. 14(4), July, 1982, 379-96.

Mark, Robert : Policing a perplexed society. London, Allen & Unwin, 1977.

Marshal, G. : Police responsibility. *Public Administration (U.K.)*, Autumn 1960, 213-26.

Mathis, Rober (and others) : Police emergency operations : The management of crisis. *C.B.I. Bulletin*, V. 17(2) February, 1983, 8-11.

Mathur, Hari Mohan (ed.) : Internal security : Some current issues. Jaipur, HCM State Institute of Public Administration, 1976.

Mathur, K.M. : Internal security : Challenges and police in a developing society. Jaipur, RBSA Publishers, 1989.

Mathur, K.M. : Magnitude and dimensions of internal security problems in India. Paper presented in XIV internal security seminar, Mt. Abu, 25.

Mathur, Krishna Mohan : Problems of national integration and role of police. *Administrator*, V. 27(2) Summer, 1982, 221-30.

Maxfield, M.G. : Discretion and the delivery of police service. Ph. D. Disseration, North Western University, 1979.

Maxfield, Machael G. : Service time, dispatch time and demand for police service : Helping more serving less. *Public Administration*, V. 42(3) May-June, 1982, 252-63.

McDondald, Ian D. : Hierarchy of objectives : approach to goalsetting and evaluation in the police service. *Police Journal*, V. 61(3) July-September, 1988, 274-86.

McDougall, Allan K. : New balance in policing for Ontario, *Canadian Public Administration*, Summer, 1969, 239-60.

McPhetus, Lee R. and Strange, William B. (eds.) : Economics of crime and law enforcement. Springfield (III), Charles C. Thomas, 1975.

Mehra, Preeti : Cops can't cope with it. *Times of India (Sunday Rev.)* 26 October, 1986, 1.

Mehrajuddin, Mir : Police and correction of offenders. *Social Defence*, V. 17(65) July, 1981, 32-37.

Menon, Mukundan C. : Police, crime and punishment in Rajan case. *Economic and Political Weekly*, 30 September, 1978, 1658-59.

Mill, James : Scottish police : An outline of their powers and duties. Edinburgh, W. Green, 1994.

Mishra, B.B. : Armed police : Challenges of the change. *Indian Journal of Criminology and Criminalistics*, V. 1(2-3) June-September, 1981.

Mishra, R.B. : Police : Its present role and tasks. *Orissa Review*, V. 27(1) August, 1970, 70-71.

Misra, S.C. : Police : A force or service (Paper) in 5th Police Congress, Nainital. 1966.

Misra, S C. : Police performance : Some para meters of appraisal. *Indian Journal of Public Administration*, V. 27(2) April-June, 1981, 444-52.

Mitter, V. : Police diaries, statements, reports, investigation, prosecution, identification, interrogation, successful prosecution and convention flaws and remedies, etc. Rev. by D.D. Seth and D. Bahri. Allahabad, Law Publishers, 1970.

Modinagar firing. *Administrator*, V. 26(4) Winter, 1981, 657-59.

Mohanan, V.K. : Crime, community and police. Delhi, Gian Publishing House, 1987.

Mohanty, Govind : Orissa police running amuck against students. *New Age*, V. 27(49), 9 December, 1979, 6.

Mohanty, Manoranjan (and others) : Factors behind Inderwalli police firing. *Mainstream*, V. 19(37) 16 May, 1981, 27-31.

Momboisse, Raymond M. : Riots, revolts and insurrections. Springfield (III), Charles C. Thomas, 1970.

Moore, Mark H. and Kelling, George L. : "To serve and protect" : Learning from police history. *Public Interest*, V. 70, Winter, 1983, 49-65.

Morgenbesser, Mel : Role of a police officer in drug treatment program. *Contemporary Drug Problems*, V. 3(2) Summer, 1974, 313-20.

Morris, Narval and Hawkinds, Gordeon : Honest politician's guide to crime control. Chicago, University of Chicago Press, 1970.

Mott, Joy : Police decisions for dealing with juvenile offenders. *British Journal of Criminology*, V. 23(3) July, 1983, 249-62.

Moyer, Imogene L. : Police responses to women offenders in a southeastern city. *Journal of Police Science and Administration*, V. 10(4) December, 1982, 376-83.

Mudaliar, N. Mutugesa : Task of the police and the army. *Swarajya*, 21 June, 1975, 2-26.

Mukerjee, Mohan : Foreword to the internal security : Some current issues. (ed.) by H.M. Mathur. Jaipur, HCM Institute of Public Administration, 1976.

Mukherjee, U. : Role of police in a democracy. *Indian Police Journal*, July-September, 1968, 39-42.

Mukherji, A.P. : Changing role of the police in contemporary India. *National Police Academy Magazine*, November, 1973, 77-84.

Mullick, B.N. : Police and civil defence. *Indian Police Journal*, January, 1963, 107-12.

Mullick, B.N. : Role of police in national integration. *Indian Police Journal*, April, 1962, 1-4.

Mullick, B.N. : Role of police in national integration. *Indian Police Journal*, July, 1962, 14-21.

Murphy, Patrick V. : How the police view violence. *New York State Journal of Medicine*, V. 85(2) February, 1985, 72-73.

Muttalib, M.A. : Campus disorder vis-a-vis law and order : Theoretical perspectives. *Indian Journal of Public Administration*, V. 35(1) January-March, 1989, 92-97.

Myren, Richard A. and Swanson, Lynn D. : Police work with children : Perspectives and principles. Washington (D.C.), U.S. Department of Health, Education and Welfare, Social Security Administration, Children's Bureau, 1962.

Nabar, B.S. : A syndicate study on the problem of drug abuse : Role of police. *Transactions*, V. 24, November, 1977, 81-112.

Naik, V.V. : Police plans to serve. *National Police Academy Magazine*, November, 1970, 21-26.

Malik, B. : Criminal trails. Allahabad, Law Publishers, 1985.

Nanavatty, K.J. : Policing in India is a complex affair. *Statesman*, 15 August, 1973, 61-62.

Napier, Sam : Within a decade every police force will use hypnotism. *Police Journal*, January-March, 1980, 52-54.

Narain, Govind : A new perspective for the Indian police. *National Police Academy Magazine*, November, 1973, 39-42.

Narain, Govind : Seventh national security lecture on "Internal threats and national security". *Indian Express*, 22 January, 1986.

Narayana Rao, M.V. : Role of the police in the developing political context In G. Ram Reddy and K. Seshadri (eds.) Developing society and police. Hyderabad, Osmania University, 1972, 41-48.

Natarajan, S. : Policing in India. *Indian Journal of Criminology*, V. 17(2) July, 1989, 81-84.

Nath, D.C. : Basis of police authority cannot be mere law; It has to be public trust too. *Sardar Vallabhbhai Patel National Police Academy Magazine*, June, 1977, 83-90.

Nath, T. : Beat load (Paper). In Second All India Police Congress, Bombay, September, 1961.

Nath, T. : Enforcing social laws. *Patriot* (*Mag.*), 10 April, 1983, 1.

Nath, T. : Justice delayed : The police role. *Hindustan Times*, 5 July, 1980.

Nath, Trilok : Indian police in action. New Delhi, Super Publishing House, 1983.

National Police Academy : Expanding role of the police : Background papers and proceedings of the seminar held on 6th and 7th November, 1968, Abu, NPA, 1969.

National Police Academy : Labour unrest and the police : A syndicate study 16th Advanced Course, January-July, 1968. *Transactions of the National Police Academy*, November, 1969, 99-124.

National Police Academy : Public order : Scope and extent of effective police action. Background papers and proceedings of the seminar held on 15th and 10th November, 1971, Abu, NPA, 1972.

Nayar, Kuldip : Role of the police. *Indian Express*, 29 July, 1976, 4.

Nefarious role of police in Tripura violence. *New Age*, V. 28 (3) 28 September, 1980, 12.

New role for the police. *Link*, V. 19 (13) 7 November, 1976, 10-13.

Nigam, Sanjay : Disciplining and policing the criminals by birth : Part 2 : The development of a disciplinary system, 1871-1990. *Indian Economic and Social History Review*, V. 37 (3) July-September, 1990, 258-287.

Nolan, Seneca H. : Law enforcement officer and mentally disordered offender. In L.M. Irvine and T.B. Brelje (eds.) Law, psychiatry and the mentally disordered offender. Springfield, Charles C. Thomas, 1973.

Noorani, A.G. : Civil liberties : Accounting for encounters. *Economic and Political Weekly*, V. 16 (22) 30 May, 1981, 979-80.

Ohri, R.K. : Police in the crucible. *Indian Police Journal*, V. 25 (1) July-September, 1978, 124-36.

Ohri, R.K. : Problems of public order and policing in the third world democracies. *Indian Police Journal*, V. 31 (1) January-March, 1984, 9-18.

O'Neil, Michael J. : Calling the cops : Responses of witness to criminal incidents. *Dissertation Abstracts International*, V. 38 (9-A) 5734.

Oppenlander, Nan. : Copping or coppingout : Police service delivery in domestic disputes. *Criminology : An Interdisciplinary Journal*, V. 20 (3-4) November, 1982, 449-65.

Pagano, Mare R. and Taylor, Stourt P. : Police perceptions of alcohol intoxification. *Journal of Applied Social Psychology*, V. 10(2) March-April, 1980, 166-74.

Palenski Joseph E. : Use of mediation by police. *Mediation Quarterly*, No. 5, September, 1984, 31-38.

Palys, Ted S. (and others) : Mobile data access terminals and their implications for policing. *Journal of Social Issues*, V. 40(3) Fall, 1984, 113-27.

Pandey, D.C. : Police coercion in India. New Delhi, Service House.

Pardesi, Ghanshyam : Gua incident : Operation annihilation ? *Mainstream*, V. 19 (11) 15 November, 1980, 6-7.

Parker, K.A.L. : Police service after the war : Structure and administration. *Public Administration*, V. 68 (4) Winter, 1980, 453-475.

Patel, Chhyaya : Polic and the delinquent. *Social Welfare*, V. 36 (9) December, 1989, 4-15.

Pathi, S.S. : Crisis of "doub" in police work. *C.B.I. Bulletin*, January, 1976, 2-4.

Patterson, David M. : Police disposition of the petty offender. *Sociology and Sociology Research*, April, 1972, 320-30.

Patterson, David M. : Police officers conception of proper police work. *Police Journal*, April-June, 1974, 173-77.

Patterson, Frank M and Smith, Patrick D. : Manual of police report writing. Springfield (Ill), Charles C. Thomas, 1972.

Pearce, Jack B. and Snortum, John, R. : Police effectiveness in handling disturbance calls : An evaluation of crisis intervention training. *Criminal Justice and Behaviour*, V. 10 (1) March, 1983, 71-92.

Pillai, V. Kamnu : How to measure police productivity. *Police Research and Development, Quarter I*, January-March, 1983, 1-2.

Pillai, V.N. : Role of the police in the next decade in developing countries. *Indian Police Journal*, V. 25 (1) July-September, 1978.

Poister, Theodore H. and Mc David, James C. : Victims evaluations of police performance. *Journal of Criminal Justice*, V. 6 (2) Summer, 1978, 133-49.

Police clash with Varanasi students politically motivated. *Times of India*, 15 January, 1971, 1.

Police fails to prevent Punjab Assembly gherao : Two killed at Bhatinda. *New Age*, V. 29 (4) 25 January, 1981, 1-2.

Police firing of Bharwel : Mones in Balaghat (M.P.). *Other Side*, V. 2 (5) December, 1982, 47-55.

Police firing in the village, Kandimallaya, palli and the enquiry into it by a judicial commission. *Administrator*, V. 26 (4) Winter, 1981, 627-36.

Police firing in three Haryana towns : Dealth toll goes up to 7. *Times of India*, 1 February 1970, 1.

Police methods (Editorial). *Times of India*, 5 June, 1977, 8.

Police role in the case of the mentally retarted child. *C.B.I. Bulletin*, V. 17 (1) January, 1983, 11-12.

Policing Bihar (Editorial). *Hindustan Times*, April 25, 1990.

Policing Punjab (Editorial), *Times of India*, April 12, 1986, 8.

Policing the country. *Link*, V. 13 (46) June, 1971, 16-23.

Pontell, Henry N. (and others) : Seriousness of crimes : A survey of the nation's chiefs of police. *Journal of Criminal Justice*, V. 13(1) 1985, 1-3.

Ponting, J. Rick (and others) : Police perceptions of riot participants and dynamics. *International Journal of Group Tension*, V. 5 (3) September, 1975, 113-70.

Powell, Dennis D. : Race, rank and police discretion. *Journal of Police Science and Administration*, V. 9 (4) December, 1981, 383-89.

Prasad, K.N. : Police process : Its concept : Functions and structure. *Indian Police Journal*, V. 25 (2) October-December, 1978, 3-14.

Presis, Jack J. and Ehrlich, H. J. : An examination of role theory : The case of the state police. Lincoln, University of Nehraska Press, 1966.

Progressive role of Maharashtra police. *Lok Rajya*, V. 2 (1) May 1970, 11-15.

Prytola, Robert E. (and others): Police experience and attribution of personal responsibility. *Psychological Reports*, V. 37 (3, Part 2) December, 1975, 1346.

Quarantelli, E.L. (and others): Police department perceptions of the occurrence of civil disturbances. *Sociology and Research*, October, 1974, 30-38.

Raghu, V.: Naxalites and police in Andhra. *Mainstream*, V. 26 (42) 30 July, 1988, 25.

Raja Gopal, A.: Irrigation and equity: Behind police firing of Pullambadi. *Economic and Political Weekly*, V. 23 (41) 8 October, 1988, 291-92.

Rajgopal, P.R.: A new role of police. *Indian Express*, 18 October, 1980, 6.

Rajgopal, P.R.: Police and the challenges ahead. *Indian Express*, 9 June, 1981, 6.

Rajgopal, P.R.: Police role as an urban service. *Urban India*, V. 2 (1) March, 1982, 23-26.

Ramchandran, D. : Police service : An agenda for improvement. *Indian Journal of Public Administration*, V. 24 (1) January-March, 1978, 127-151.

Ramchandran, D.: Systems approach to organisations. *Sardar Vallabhbhai Patel National Police Academy Magazine*, November, 1977, 109-16.

Ramchandran Reddy, K.: Cyclone and the police. *Indian Police Journal*, V. 24 (3) January-March, 1978, 5 12.

Ramchandran Reddy, K.: Cyclone and the police. *Sardar Vallabhbhai Patel National Police Academy Magazine*, November, 1978, 65-73.

Ramchandran Reddy, K.: Role of police in a welfare state. *C.B I. Buletin*, V. 11(9) September, 1977, 1-3.

Ramchandran Reddy, K.: Role of police in a welfare state. *Indian Journal of Criminology*, V. 6 (2) January, 1978, 32-34.

Ramchandran Reddy, K.: Role of police in a welfare state. *Indian Police Journal*, V. 24 (2) October-December, 1977, 5-6.

Ramchandran Reddy, K. : Role of police in a welfare state. *Sardar Vallabhbhai Patel National Police Academy Magazine*, November, 1977, 27-32.

Ramlings, Frank : Policing in Scandinavia. *Indian Police Journal*, January, 1965, 50-55.

Rangnekar, Sharu S. : A challenge for the police. *Integrated Management*, March, 1973, 21-23.

Rao, M.V. Narayana : Role of police in a welfare state. *Andhra Pradesh Information*, V. 25(4) February, 1981, 23-25.

Rao, R. Prabhakar : Problem of law and order and adequate equipment for the police. In G. Ram Reddy and K. Seshadri (eds.) Developing society and police. Hyderabad, Osmania University, 1972, 99-110.

Rao, V.G. Prasad : How effective are our police : Prohibition has undermined police in Madras. *Illustrated Weekly of India*, V. 99 (45) 26 November, 1978, 5.

Reddy, C.S. and Badasiddmuni, P. : Estimation of preventive police output. *Indian Journal of Criminology*, V. 17 (1) January, 1989, 58-67.

Reddy, P. Jaganmohan : Changing society and the role of police. In M.V.K. Sivamohan : Law and society. Delhi, Ajanta Publication, 1986.

Reichman, Walter and Beidel, Bernard E. : Implementation of a state police. EAP *Journal of Drug Issues*, V. 19(3, part 1) Summer, 1989, 369-83.

Reppetto, Thomas A. : Influence of police organisational style on crime control effectiveness. *Journal of Police Science and Administration*, V. 3(3) September, 1975, 274-79.

Ries, Albert J. : Forecasting the role of the police and role of the police in social forecasting. In Rita Donelan (ed.) Maintenance of order in society. Canada, Canadian Police College, 1982.

Roche, C.J.R. : Policing by objectives from a personal appraisal to rational management : A quantum leap where ? *Police Journal*, V. 60(4) October-December, 1987, 21-36.

Roy, B K. : Emerging role of the police in social defences in India. *Resource Material Series*, No. 10, *UNAFFI*, October, 1975, 123-25.

Roy, B.K. : Police attitude in industrial strike (Papers). In Second All India Police Science Congress, Bombay, September, 1961.

Roy, Jaytilak Guha : Police role in protection of civil rights. *Indian Police Journal*, V. 36 (2) April-June, 1989, 25-28.

Roy, N.R.G. : War against crime. Calcutta, Security Publisher, 1966.

Ruchkin, Judith P. : Does school crime need the attention of policemen or educators ? *Teachers College Record*, V. 79(2) December, 1977, 225-43.

Rustamji, K.F. : Bombay police riot and after. *Hindustan Times*, 5 September, 1982, 9.

Rustamji, K.F. Internal security : Tasks—rebuilding from the bottom. *Indian Express*, November 1, 1985.

Rustamji, K.F. : Internal security tasks : Undoing the damage. *Indian Express*, October 31, 1985.

Rustamji, K.F. : Modern trends in policing. *Indian Police Journal*, January, 1970, 9-14.

Rustamji, K.F. : Policing the nation. *Indian Express*, 19 July, 1983, 6.

Rustamji, K.F. : Policing the nation. *Indian Express*, 20 July, 1983, 6.

Rustomji, K.F. : Policing the nation. *Indian Express*, 21 July, 1983, 6.

Rustamji, K.F. : Some reflections on policing. In S.K. Ghosh (ed.) Police administrators : Reminiscences. New Delhi, Ashish Publishing House, 1989, 177-183.

Rustamji, K.F. : Wrong tests of policing. *Denouement*, V. 2 (6&7) January-February, 1991, 22-24.

Rustamji, K.F. : Wrong tests of policing. *Telegraph*, August 15, 1989.

Ryan, Helen and Taylor, Max : Information usage and cue identification as a function of experience in police officers. *Journal of Police Science and Administration*, V. 16(3), September, 1988, 177-81.

S.V.P. National Police Academy, Hyderabad : National seminar on elections and role of law enforcement. *Police*

Research and Development, Quarter I, January-March 1990, 8-10.

Sabba, B.P. : Indian police : Legacy and quest for formative role. Delhi, Manas Publications, 1990.

Sadasivan, S.N. : Police firing in the village Kandimallyapalli : A case study. *Administrator,* Winter, 1977, 1185-92.

Saha, B.P. : Police on the campus : Justified when sanctity is gone. *Statesman,* 22 September, 1984, 6.

Saksena, N.S. : Can or should police abstain from enforcing the law ? *Sardar Vallabhbhai Patel National Police Academy Magazine,* July, 1976, 9-25.

Saksena, N.S. : Delhi police flying squads. *Indian Police Journal,* October, 1957, 57-60.

Saksena, N.S. : Police and mob violence : Why firmness always pays. *Times of India,* 19 October 1978, 6.

Saksena, N.S. : Police failure to protect properly. *Times of India,* 20 February, 1989, 8.

Saksena, N.S. : Rising tide of violence : Enforcing the rule of law. *Times of India,* 7 November, 1978.

Saksena, N.S. : Top men encourage third degre. *Times of India,* 18 July, 1980, 6.

Saksena, N.S. : U.P. police capable of curbing riots. *Times of India,* December, 21, 1990, 6.

Saksena, N.S. : Why the police does not serve the people of India. *Denouement,* V. 2 (6&7) January-February, 1991, 14-16.

Saldana, J.S. : A plan for national internal security. In Internal security (ed.) by H.M. Mathur. Jaipur, HCM State Institute of Public Administration, 1976, 18.

Sanwal, M. : Maintenance by public order. I. *Times of India,* 3 December, 1984, 8.

Sanwal, M. : Maintenance of public order II. *Times of India,* 4 December, 1984, 8.

Sastry, B S. : Basis of police authority cannot be mere law : It has to be public trust too. *Sardar Vallabhbhai Patel National Police Academy Magazine,* June, 1977, 70-82.

Sauders, Edward J. : Police officers attitude toward child sexual abuse : An exploratory study. *Journai of Police Science and Administration,* V. 13 (3) September, 1987, 186-91.

Saxena, N.S. : Quantum of force in suppression of riots. *Indian Journal of Criminology and Criminalistics,* V. 1 (2-3) June-September, 1981.

Scarman, Lord : Role of the police in a situation of political confronation. *Police Journal,* October-December, 1978, 317-23.

Schnelle, John F. (and others) : Patrol evaluation research : A multiple baseline analysis of saturating police patrolling day and night hours. *Journal of Applied Behaviour Analysts,* V. 10 (1) Spring, 1977, 33-40.

Schultz, Donald O. and Norton, Loran A. : Police operational intelligence. Springfield (III), Charles C. Thomas, 1971.

Scott, H. : Police problems of today. London, Stevens, 1949.

Scwartz, Louis B and Goldstein, Stephen R. : Law enforcement handbook for the police. St. Paul (Minn.) West Publishing, 1970.

Seetharam, Mukkavilli : Role of police in reducing rural tensions. *Yojana,* V. 31 (23) 16 December, 1987, 9-12.

Sen, Anikendra Nath : How effective are our police. *Illustrated Weekly of India,* V. 99 (45) 26 November, 1978, 6-10.

Sen, Astum : New police approach to crime pays. *Amrit Bazar Patrika,* 10 February, 1976.

Sen, Sankar : Controlling crime : a policeman's view. *Times of India,* 9 January, 1984, 8.

Sen, Sankar : Perspectives on use of force by the police. *Police Journal,* V. 60(1) January-March, 1987, 66-71.

Sen, Sankar : Police and the mob : Importance of infinite patience. *Statesman,* 14 April, 1984, 6.

Sen, Shankar : Role of police in industrial strikes and lockouts 13th All India police science congress, Paper, Bhopal, December, 1975.

Sen, Sankar : The cop and the crowd. *Police Research and Development, Quarter IV,* October-December, 1985, 1-2.

Shah, Giriraj : Police and its problems. *Indian Express,* 29 November, 1977, 6.

Shanti Prasad : Public order : Role of police. *Journal of the Lal Bahadur Shastri National Academy of Administration*, V. 19 (4) Winter, 1974, 719-24.

Sharma, G.C. : Police and the implementation of public law. *Canadian Public Administration*, V. 20 (2) Summer, 1977, 291-304.

Sharma, P.D. : Effectiveness of the police. *Indian Journal of Public Administration*, V. 24 (1) January-March, 1978, 96-112.

Sharma, P.D. : Indian police : A perspective. *C.B.I. Bulletin*, September, 1975, 1-3.

Sharma, P.D. : Perspectives on Indian police. *Indian Journal of Public Administration*, V. 19 (4) 1972, 525-51.

Sharma, P.D. : Maintenance of law and order : Developing some techniques. *Indian Police Journal*, V. 36(2) April-June, 1989, 29-34.

Sharma, S.K. and Sachdeva, D.R. : Municipal police : Role and responsibilities. *Indian Journal of Public Administration*, V. 24 (1) January-March, 1978, 209-216.

Sharma, Vichitra : Panel for public punishment. *Hindustan Times*, 12 March, 1987.

Shekar, Sanober : Role of the police vis-a-vis special groups. *Social Defence*, V. 19 (73) July, 1983, 12-19.

Sheopory, R.N. : Police : A social service in a welfare state. *Sardar Vallabhbhai Patel National Police Academy Magazine*, July, 1976, 38-45.

Shergil, Raghu : Police cannot go scotfree. *Sunday*, 6 November, 1977, 25-27.

Sheridan, Edward P. and Teplin, Linda A. : Police referred psychiatric emergencies : Advantages of community treatment. *Journal of Community Psychology*, V. 9 (2) April, 1981, 140-47.

Shinar, David and Sttebel, Jonathan : Effectiveness of stationary versus moving police vehicles on compliance with speed limit. *Human Factors*, V. 28(3) June 1986, 365-371.

Shukla, K.S. : Role of the police in juvenile justice. *Indian Journal of Criminology and Criminalistics*, V. 1 (2-3) June-September, 1981.

Shukla, K.S. : Thefts : A study of operational techniques. *Police Research and Development, Quarter I*, January-March, 1976, 1-10.

Shukla, R.K. : Role of police and public in the maintenance of law and order. Lawyer, V. 2 (8) August 1979, 148-55.

Singh, Bishen : Police officer and his responsibilities (Paper), In Second All India Police Science Congress. Bombay, September, 1961.

Singh, D.R. : Youth unrest : role of law, enforcement agencies. *Indian Police Journal*, V. 26 (4) April-June, 1980, 32-37.

Singh, Gurdial : Challenge of policing. *Indian Police Journal* V. 25(1) July-September, 1978, 21-36.

Singh, J.P. : Effectiveness of police performance. *Indian Police Journal*, V. 36 (1) January-March, 1989, 3-10.

Singh, L.P. : Policing India. *Denouement*, V. 2 (6&7) January-February, 1991, 8-13.

Singh, L.P. : Problem of policing India. *Fourth Sardar Vallabhbhai Patel Memorial Lecture*, 31 October, 1987, SVPNPA, Hyderabad, 16.

Singh, N.K. : Police always kill in "self defence". *Perspective*, V. 2 (2) September, 1978, 27-29.

Singh, R.R. Police and the welfare state. *Nation Police Academy Magazine*, November, 1968, 42-53.

Singh, Sudurshan : Who will police the police ? *Tribune*, 7 April, 1975, 1.

Singhvi, G.C. : Professionalism in handling unruly crowds. *C.B.I. Bulletin*, V. 9 (8), August, 1975, 1-4.

Singhvi, G.C. : Quasi-judicial functions of police and the rule of law. *Journal of National Academy of Administration*, V. 15 (4) October-December, 1970, 81-84.

Singhvi, G.C. : Separation of prosecution from police : A new dimension to rule of law. *Management in Government*, July-September, 1972, 125-38.

Sinha, B.N. : Extent of the centre's role in police functions. Souvenir, 10th symposum of All India Principals Police Training College. Dated 22.19.1981 to 24.10.1981, Patna, 7-9.

Sinha, K.C. : Police effectiveness : Some experiments. *Hindustan Times*, January, 17, 1989, 8.

Sinha, M.K. : Role of the police. *Decision*, V. 13 (3) July, 1986, 233-37.

Sinha, S. : Crisis in culture and role of police : Some broad observations. *Journal of Social Research*, V. 28-29 September, 1985, March, 1986. 105-111.

Siwik, Robert A. and Blount, William R. : Law enforcement attitudes on handgun control. *Journal of Police Science Administration*, V. 12(2) June 1984, 157-64.

Skogan, Wesley G. : Coping with crime. London, Sage Publications, 1981.

Smith, C.R. : Responsibilities of rank in the police service. *Police Journal*, October, 1970, 283-92.

Smith, David H. : Domestic crisis intervention : A comparison of observational learning models police officers. *Dissertation Abstracts International*, V. 35 (I-B) July, 1974, 524.

Smith, Dennis C. : Police attitudes and performance : The impact of residency. *Urban Affairs Quarterly*, V. 15 (3) March, 1980, 317-34.

Smith, Douglas A. : Police response to interpersonal violence : Defining the parameters of legal control. *Social Forces*, V. 65 (3) March, 1987, 767-82.

Smith, Douglas A. and Klein, Jody R. : Police control of interpersonal disputes. *Social Problems*, V. 31 (4), April, 1984, 468-81.

Smith, Douglas A. (and others): Equity and discretionary justice : The influence of race on police arrest decisions. *Journal of Criminal Law and Criminology*, V. 75 (1) Spring, 1984, 234-49.

Smith, Michael R. : Civil liability for police activities. *Poper Government*, V. 45 (3) Winter, 1980, 42-49.

Sowle, Clauede R. (ed.) : Police power and freedom : The quest for balance. Chicago, Aldine, 1962.

Spark that may turn into a fire. *Link*, V. 24 (50), 25 July, 1982, 22-24.

Sridharan, A.R. : Police transport. *Transactions of the Nation Police Academy*, November, 1969, 24-42.

Stead, Philip John : Pioneers in policing. New Jersey, Smith, 1977.

Stenross, Barbara : Police response to residential burglaries : Dusting for prints as a negative rite. *Criminology : An Interdisciplinary Journal*, V. 22 (3) August, 1984, 389-402.

Stracey, E.L. : Police and observance of law. *Crapler*, 31 December, 1977, 13.

Stratton, John, : Cops and drunk : Police attitudes and actions in dealing with Indian drunks. *International Journal of Addictions*, V. 8 (4) 1973, 613-21.

Stratton, John : Rape and the victim : A new role for law enforcement. *F.B.I. Law Enforcement Bulletin*, V. 44(11) November, 1974.

Stretcher, V C. : Environment of law enforcement. Englewood Cliffs (N.J.) Prentice-Hall, 1971.

Subrahmanyam, K.V.V. : Police and political development. In G. Ram Reddy and K. Seshadri (eds.) Developing society and police. Hydernbad, Osmania University, 1972.

Subramanian, K.S. : Administrative response to agrarian struggles in the context of Bihar : A public policy approach. New Delhi, Nehru Memorial Museum and Library, 1986.

Subramanian, P.S. : General elections and the role of the police. *Indian Police Journal*, January, 1964, 8-20.

Subramanyam, K. : Indian security perspective. New Delhi, Publishing House, 1982.

Subramanyam, K. : Threats to security-internal one more formidable. *Times of India*, 12 September, 1987.

Sulnick, Robert, H. : Civil litigation and the police : A method of communication. Sprinfield, Charles Thomas, 1976.

Summala, H. (and others) : Exceptional condition of police enforcement : Driving speeds durding the police strike. *Accident Analysis and Prevention*, V. 12 (3) September, 1980, 179-84.

Swain, N. : In the service of the demand and the destitute. In S.K. Ghosh (ed.) Police administrators : Reminiscences. New Delhi, Ashish Publishing Aouse, 1979, 202-209.

Tampi, B.J.K. : Police and power. *C.B.I. Bulletin*, September, 1974, 7-9.

Tandon, P.K. : Real face of anti goonda campaign of the police. *People's Democracy*, V. 3 (37) 16 September, 1979, 5.

Tenzel, James H. (and others) : Symbols and behaviour : An experiment in allering the police role. *Journal of Police Science and Administration*, V. 4 (1) March, 1979, 21-27.

Terris, Bruce J. : Role of the police. *Annals of the American Academy of Political and Soci.l Science*, November, 1967, 58-69.

Third degree : Routine treatment ? *Times of India* (*Magazine*), 17 April, 1977, II.

Thomas, Charles W. and Hyman, Jeffrey M. : Perceptions of crime, fear of victimization, and public perception of police performance. *Journal of Police Science and Administration*, V. 5 (3) September, 1977, 305-17.

Tiberius Syndrome : Policing of provincial campuses. *Economic and Political Weekly*, V. 19 (4) 28 January, 1984, 156-59.

Tiwari, M.M. and Hussain Ahmad : Syndicate study on "Pattern of crime and social services in major cities and steps taken by police to prevent and to detect the same". *Transactions*, V. 37, 1983, 206-258.

Toch, Hans H. : Psychological consequence of the police role. In A. Nieder hofler and Abrahams Blumberg (eds.) Ambivalent force : Perspectives on the police. U.S.A., Gunn & Co., 1970, 49-53.

Towler, Juby E. : Police role in racial conflicts. Springfield (III), Charles C. Thomas, 1964.

Trikha, M.C. : British police at work. *Police Research and Development, Quarter I*, January-June, 1974, 64-68.

Trojanowicz, Robert C. : An evaluation of a neighbourhood foot patrol program. *Journal of Police Science and Administration*, V. 11 (4) December, 1983, 409-19.

Tulivinod : Concepts of specialisation police functioning. *Indian Police Journal*, V. 29(2) October-December, 1982, 24-28.

Turcom, Ronald N. : Police shootings : Psychoanalytic view points. *International Journal of Offender Theraphy and Comparative Criminology*, V. 30 (1) 1996, 53-58.

Turk, Austin T. : Policing in political context. In Rita Denelan (ed.) Maintenance of order in society. Canada, Canadian Police College, 1972.

Ulberg, Cyrus G. : Role conception, job satisfactions and performance in a police department. *Dissertation Abstracts International*, V. 34 (8-A, Part-2) February, 1974, 6318.

Vaduchumcharry, James : Third degree method and police public relationship. *Indian Police Journal*, V. 23 (2) October-December, 1977, 23-26.

Vaidya, Chunibhai : Police repression in Assam. *Radical Humanist*, V. 47 (12) March 1984, 34-37.

Vaidanathan, S.S. : Scope for personal discretion in law enforcement. *Indian Police Journal*, V. 24 (2) October-December, 1977, 11-27.

Valecha, G.K. and Venkataraman, Subba : Improving efficiency and ensuring impartiality police force. *Vikalapa*, V. 11 (1) January-March, 1986, 55-63.

Varghese, A. : New and challenging role of the police. In G. Ram Reddy and K. Seshadri (eds,) Developing society and police. Hyderabad, Osmania University, 1972.

Varghese, A. : Practice and precepts in police work. *Transaction of the Central Police Training College*, November, 1964, 53-82.

Venugopal Rao, S. : Emerging role of the police. *Indian Police Journal*, October-December, 1975, 29-36.

Venugopal Reddy, Y. : Police as a social service. In G. Ram Redy and K. Seshadri (eds.) Developing society and police. Hyderabad, Osmania University, 1972.

Verma, S.K. : Violent agitation : Need for clear policy (Paper) In 5th Police Science, Congress, Nainital, 1966.

Verma, Upendra : SHO and the Indian police. *Indian Police Journal*, V. 22 (3) January-March, 1976, 56-61.

Vingillis, E. (and others) : Police enforcement practices and a perception of drinking drining laws. *Canadian Journal of Criminology*, V. 28(2) April, 1986, 147-56.

Visher, Christry A. : Gender, police arrest decisions, and notions of chivalry. *Criminology : An Interdisciplinary Journal*, V. 21(1) February, 1983, 5-28.

Vohra, K.B. : Dynamics of police raids. *Indian Police Journal*, V. 27(2) October-December, 1980, 4-12.

Vohra, K.B. : Protection of human rights by the police. *Indian Police Journal*, V. 26 (4) April-June, 1980, 4-13.

Wachtel, Julius : Production and craftsmanship in police narcotics enforcement. *Journal of Police Science and Administration*, 13 (4) December, 1985, 263-74.

Waegel, William B. : How police justify the use of deadly force. *Social Problems*, 32 (2) December, 1984, 144-55.

Wagle, S.N. : New role for police : Test before the Dharma Vira Panel. *Sunday*, 3 September, 1978, 57.

Wagle, S.N. : Tough lot of Maharashtra policemen. *Business Standard*, 10 June, 1979, 4.

Wall, Mary N. : Law enforcement officers and death notification : A plea for relevant education. *Journal of Police Science and Administration*, V. 10(2) June, 1982, 189-93.

Walter, James D. : Police in the middle : A study of police intervention in domestic disputes. *Dissertation Abstracts International*, 34(11-A) May, 1974, 7361.

Warier, K.U. : Opposition MLA provokes incident in Kerala. *New Age.*, 28 (32) 10 August, 1980, 14.

Was Maharashtra police action right or wrong ? *Organiser*, 34 (17) 12 September, 1982, 6.

Wenger, Dennis : Reluctant army : Functioning of police departments during civil disturbances. *American Behavioural Scientist*, V. 16 (3) January, 1973, 326-42.

Westley, William A. : Violence and the police : A sociological study of law, custom and morality. Cambridge, M.I.T. Press, 1970.

Whitaker, Ben : Police efficiency. *New Society*, 23 April, 1964, 7-9.

Wilk, Ruth J. and McCarthy, Carolyn R. : Intervention in child sexual abuse : A survey of attitudes. *Social Case Work*, V. 67 (1) January, 1986, 20-26.

William, David : Keeping the police and public order. London, Hutchinson, 1967.

Willoughby, Kenneth R. and Blount, William R. : Relationship between law enforcement officer height aggression and job performance. *Journal of Police Science and Administration*, 13(3) September, 1985, 225-29.

Yarmey, A. Doniel : Perceived exportness and credibility of police officers as eye witnesses. (French). *Canadian police College Journal*, No. 1, 1986, 36-58.

Yer, Alan : Social and demographic factors in prediction of demand for the police service. *Police Journal*, January-March, 1976, 42-49.

Younger, E.J. : Challenges to police in changing world. *Indian Express*, February 21, 1969.

Younger, Evelle J. : Challenges to police in changing world. *Indian Police Journal*, January,-March, 1970 37-40.

Yuker, Horold E. : Disability and the law : Attitudes of police, lawyers and mental health professionals. *Rehabilitation Psychology*, 31(1) Spring, 1986, 13-25.

Zander, Michael : Police powers and the citizen. *Listener*, 2 April, 1970, 446-47.

25

Police and Crime Investigation

Arora, Gurvinder K. and Singh, T.P. : Dermatoglyphic study of Indian female criminals. *Police Research and Development, Quarter I*, 1984, 18-21.

Arul, F.V. : Scientific techniques in investigation. *C.B.I. Bulletin*, V. 22 (7) July, 1988, 1-4.

Ashbaugh, D.R. : Kidgeoscopy : The time is now. *C.B.I. Bulletin*, V. 17(11) November, 1983, 5-6.

Banerjea, D. and Tiwari, M.M. : Inquire into the system of investigation and prosecution, the reasons for delay and failure, the use of improper methods and the extent of their prevalence; and suggest how the system may be modified or changed and made efficient scientific and consistent with human dignity and how the related laws may be suitably amended. *Transactions*, V. 27, 1978, 107-166.

Bani, H.I. : Modernisation of crime investigation. *Indian Police Journal*, V. 25 (2) October-December, 1988, 35-41.

Biswas, U.N. : Level of scientific attitudes of detectives in India. *Police Research and Development, Quarter II*, April-June, 1984, 1-6.

Chandra, Sahib Singh : Crime scene investigation with aid of physical clues. *C.B.I. Bulletin*, V. 19(8) August, 1985, 1-4.

Chandra, Sahib Singh : Uses of scientific aid in investigation. *C.B.I. Bulletin*, V. 18(6) Jupe, 1984, 5-8.

Chatterjee, R.K. : Concepts offen pay in crime detection. *Indian Police Journal*, V. 28 (2) October-December, 1981, 34-36.

Colaso, F.T.R. and Shukla, K.S. : Reluctance of the public aid in the detection of crime and crime reporting at police station. New Delhi, BPR&D, Ministry of Home Affairs, 1973.

Crime investigation : Probing forensically. *Link*, V. 23 (50) 26 July, 1981, 36-38.

Criminals beware ? Forensic science in crime detection. *March of Mysore*, V. 6 (3) March, 1969, 17-18.

David, L. : A syndicate study on "the process of witness examination in courts". *Transactions*, V. 29, 1979, 1-52.

Deb, R. : Principles of criminology, criminal law and investigation. Calcutta, S.C. Sarkar and Sons, 1958.

Deshpande, A.A. : Investigation to the foundation of trial. *Journal of National Police Academy of Administration*, V. 9 (1) January, 1964, 17-21.

Dhange, S. and Maheshwari, H.S. : Fractures on triolex glass sheet by the fired projectile. *Indian Journal of Criminology*, V. 17 (2) July, 1989, 125-29.

Dhange, Sunanda and Maheshwari, H.S. : Influence of shifting of striking place of impact on resultant glass fracture. *Indian Journal of Criminology*, V. 16 (1) January, 1988, 65-74.

Diaz, S.M. : Admissibility in criminal tricks of statements made to investigating police officers. *Indian Journal of Criminology*, V. 4 (2) July, 1976, 69-71.

Farah, S.A. : Utility of lie detection. *Indian Nation*, 3 September, 1987.

Farah, S.A. : Value of scientific evidence. *Indian Nation*, (*Sunday Magazine*) July, 1988, I-V.

Farah, S.A. and Prasad, Ramanand : Vaigyanik apradh anusandhan. Patna, Vijai Prakashan, 1988.

Furedy, John J. : Credulous vs. critical police use of the polygraph in criminal investigations. *Canadian Journal of Criminology*, V. 27(4) October, 1985, 491-95.

Ganguly, A.K. : Psychological basis of polygraph ; Lie detector examination and its role in crime investigation. *C.B.I. Bulletin*, Vol. 17 (12) December, 1983, 1-5.

Ganguly, A.K. : Psychological techniques in crime investigation. *C.B.I. Bulletin*, V. 21 (5) May 1987, 3-6.

Gibson, H.B. : Use of hypnosis by the police in the investigation of crime; Is guided imagery a sole substitute ? Comment. *British Journal of Experimental and Clinical Hypnosis*, V. 3 (1) October, 1985, 33-35.

Hinojosa, Antonio V. : Police questioning. *Indian Police Journal*, V. 27 (1) July-September, 1980, 33-43.

Ink analysis : Weapons against white collar crime. *Indian Police Journal*, V. 24 (2) October-December, 1977, 61-64.

Iyer, M.I.S. : An appraisal of forensic science evidence in criminal investigation and trials. *Transactions*, V. 28. 1978, 74-135.

Iyer, T.G.L. : Investigation techniques in India : Some suggestions for improvement. *C.B.I. Bulletin*, April, 1978, 1-7.

Iyer, T.G.L. : Police investigation : Difficulties and limitations. *Police Research and Development, Quarter IV*, October-December, 1979, 8-10.

Jha, M.K. and Lal, Murari : Problems of the detection of economic crimes at the police level. *C.B.I. Bulletin*, V. 20 (10) October, 1986, 1-5.

Jhala, R.M. : Crime investigation and medical science. Vora, 1976.

Kannupillai, V.: Operational research and the investigation of crimes. *Police Research and Development, Quarter I*, January-March, 1985, 11-14.

Kumar, Anoop and Chandra, S.S. : Importance of sex and age in medico legal cases. *C.B.I. Bulletin*, V. 23 (7) July, 1989, 11-24.

Lahri, S.K. and Ganguli, A.K. : Polygraph (Lie-detector) : Its application and success in criminal investigations connected with homicide. *Police Research and Development, Quarter I*, January-March, 1981, 18-21.

Lahri, S.K. (and others) : Accura of polygraphic detector examination on female Indian population. *Indian Police Journal*, V. 31 (1) January-March, 1984, 23-29.

Liebert, John A. : Contributions of psychiatric consultation in the investigation of serial murder. *International Journal of Offender Therapy and Comparative Criminology*, V. 29(3) 1985, 187-200.

Lobo, John : Complete investigator. *C.B.I. Bulletin*, V. 20 (8) August, 1986, 1-5.

Madhavan, K. : Laying of traps and investigation of trap cases. *C.B.I. Bulletin*, V. 18 (2) February, 1984, 4-11.

Madiwale, M.S. : Biological evidence in crime detection. *Lok Rajya*, V. 29 (10) September, 1973, 16-19.

Maheswari, H.S. and Ahmad, Mansoor : Influence of berrel length on dispersion in muzzle loading guns. *Indian Journal of Criminology*, V. 11 (1) January, 1983, 63-64.

Malik, M.S. : Standards of investigation improvements and innovations. *Police Research and Development, Quarter III*, July-September 1984, 1-22.

Marjit, D. : Forensic examination of paints by thermal analysis. *Indian Journal of Criminology and Criminalistics*, V. 3 (1-2) March-June, 1983, 42-49.

Matto, B.N. : Forensic science helps to detect crime. *Lok Rajya*, V. 22 (8) 16 August, 1973, 56-57.

Mir, Mehrajuddin : Criminal investigation : Its legal dimensions. *Indian Police Journal*, V. 29 (4) April-June, 1983, 46-51.

Mir, Mehrajuddin : Machinery of criminal investigation : Some ideas and reflections. *Indian Journal of Criminology*, V. 6 (1) January, 1982, 59-62.

Misra, Ghanendra and Jain, Parmeet : Metallurgy in the aid of criminal investigation. *Police Research and Development, Quarter I*, 1986, 9-12.

Nabar, B.S. : A syndicate study on the effective utilisation of forensic science in crime investigation. *Transactions*, V. 21, November, 1975, 50-70.

Nath, Surinder : Identification and analysis of physical evidence in criminal investigation. *Indian Police Journal*, V. 30 (2) October-December, 1983, 19-21.

Nath, T. : Police and the third degree. *INFA Feature*, 5 February, 1976.

Nayar, Kuldip : An inadequate police inquiry. *Indian Express*, 21 February, 1979, 6.

Nelson, John G. : Preliminary investigations and police reporting : A complete guide to police written communication. Beverly Hills, Glencoe Press, 1970.

Norayanaswami, K. (and others) : Phenolphthalein in trap cases. *Indian Police Journal*, V. 26 (2) October-December, 1979, 13-16.

Pandeya, Vijay Nand : Investigation of cases involving cheating and forgery. Souvenir, 10th Symposium of All India Principals Police Training College, Dated 22.10.1981 to 24.10.1981, Patna, 38-43.

Perry, Campbell and Nogrady, Heather : Use of hypnosis by the police in the investigation of crime : Is guided imagery a sole substitute. *British Journal of Experimental and Clinical Hypnosis*, V. 3 (1) October, 1985, 25-31.

Pitchandi, N. : Scientific methods of crime investigation. *Indian Journal of Criminology*, V. 6 (2) July, 1978, 113-14.

Raffel, Robert T. : Criminal investigation at airports : an overview. *C.B I. Bulletin*, V. 17 (8) August, 1983, 8-10.

Rajdewan, D. Subramanyam : Scene of crime never disappoints. *Indian Police Journal*, V. 24(3) January-March, 1978, 39-42.

Ramchandran, D. : Great aid to investigating officers (an interview article). *Business India*, 27 November, 1978, 64.

Ramkrishnan, J. : Exhibit P-2. *Indian Police Journal*, V. 24 (3) January-March, 1978, 13-23.

Rao, A. Narayana : Who killed the school watchman ? *Indian Police Journal*, V. 23 (4) April-June, 1977, 3-7.

Rao, K.V. Sambasiva (and others) : Role of odontology in the investigation of crime. *Indian Journal of Criminology*, V. 16 (1) January, 1988, 75-77.

Reiser, Martin (and others) : An evaluation of the use of psychics in investigation of major crimes. *Journal of Police Science and Administration*, V. 7 (1) March, 1979.

Saha, B.P. : Criminal investigation by private organisations : Its legality and locus standi. *C.B.I. Bulletin*, V. 18 (8) August, 1984, 7-10.

Saha, B.P. : Prejudice and police investigation. *C.B.I. Bulletin*, V. 22 (6) June, 1988, 1-3.

Sairam, T.V. : An approach to kinesics and proxemics in criminal interrogation. *Indian Police Journal*, V. 26(1) July-September, 1979, 32-36.

Saksena, N.S. : Public support in the investigation of crime. *Indian Police Journal*, V. 22 (1) July-September, 1975, 4-12.

Sarkar, B.R. and Subrahmanyam, B.V. : Role of forensic immunology and serology in crime investigation. *Police Research and Development*, *Quarter*, *IV*, October-December, 1980, 13-15.

Sehgal, V.N. : Evidence of tool marks in criminal cases. *C.B.I. Bulletin*, V. 22 (11) November, 1988, 12-16.

Sharma, B.R. : Firemen in criminal investigation and trials. *New Delhi*, Tripathi, 1976.

Sharma, B.R. : Forensic science in India—An appraisal. *Indian Journal of Public Administration*, V. 24 (1) January-March, 1978, 194-208.

Sharma, B.R. : Problems of proof in questioned documents investigating aspects. *C.B.I. Bulletin*, V. 17(2) February, 1983, 1-3.

Sharma, S.N. and Misra, G. : An evaluation of bullet proof jackets. *C.B.I. Bulletin*, V. 21 (12) December, 1987, 1-4.

Simpson, Keith : Police : The investigation of violence. U.K., Macdonald and Evans, 1978.

Singh, R.D. : Significance of extraneous marks in documents. *Indian Police Journal*, V. 23 (4) April-June, 1977, 43-44.

Singh, S.R. and Sehgal, V.N. : Analysis of rust by emission spectrograph using internal standard : A case report. *C.B.I. Bulletin*, V. (17) July, 1983, 4-5.

Singh, Sahib : Crime scene investigation with aid of physical clues. *C.B.I. Bulletin*, V. 19 (8) August, 1985, 1-4.

Singh, Sita Ram : Evidentiary value of identification parades. *C.B.I. Bulletin*, V. 17 (8) August, 1983, 1-4.

Singh, Sita Ram : Judicial intervention in police investigation. *C.B.I. Bulletin*, V. 22 (1) January, 1988, 6-9.

Sirohi, J.P.S. : Probation officers investigation report in the realm of criminal judicial administration. *Journal of Indian Law Institute*, V. 21(3) July-September, 1979, 313-35.

Vadackumcharry, James : Third degree method and police-public relationship. *Indian Police Journal*, October-December, 1976, 23-26.

Verma, R.S. : Investigators role in trap cases. *C.B.I. Bulletin*, V. 19 (3) March, 1985, 1-2.

Vohra, K.B. : Impact of new criminal procedure code on Police investigation. *Police Research and Development, Quarter I*, 1984, 8-13.

Waegel, William B. : Case routinization in investigation : police works. *Social Problems*, V. 28 (3) February, 1981, 263-75.

Waegel, William B. : Patterns of police investigation of urban crimes. *Journal of Police and Administration*, V. 10(4) December, 1982, 45?-65.

Wagstaff, Graham F. : Use of hypnosis by the police in the investigation of crime : Is guided imagery a sole substitute ? Comment. *British Journal of Experimental and Clinical Hypnosis*, V. 3 (1) October, 1985, 39-42.

Walker, Roy O. : Exploratory investigation of police attitudes towards violence. *Journal of Police Science and Administration*, V. 10 (1) March, 1982, 93-130.

Walsh, Cecil Heary : Indian village crimes, with an introduction on police investigation and confessions. London, E. Benn, 1929.

Whitehead, P.H. : Importance of science in crime detection. *Indian Police Journal*, V. 24 (4) April-June, 1978, 23-28.

26

Police and Crime Prevention

Agarwal, Daya : Women can train the mind of children. *Social Welfare*, V. 22 (4) July, 1985, 11-12.

Agarwal, R.S. : Prevention of crime. New Delhi, Radiant Publishers, 1977.

Agarwal, Rajendra Saran : Participation of public in prevention of crime. *Social Welfare*, V. 20 (6) September, 1973, 27-28.

Agarwal, Rajendra Saran : Public participation vital in prevention of crime. *Social Welfare*, V. 22 (4) July, 1975, 12-14.

Arul, F.V. : Crime prevention in India. *C.B.I. Bulletin*, V. 20 (2) February, 1986, 1-4.

Arul, F.V. : Some thoughts on prevention of crime. *C.B.I. Bulletin*, V. 19 (10), October, 1985, 1-2.

Balkrishnan, S. : Report of the fifth UN Congress on prevention of crime and treatment of offenders held in Geneva from September 1 to 12, 1975, *Social Defence*, V. 11 (42) October, 1975, 33-39.

Bambawale, P.A. : Problem of prevention and detection of cattle theft (Paper). In second All India Police Science Congress, Bombay, September, 1961.

Bayley, David H. : Crime, culture and change. *Indian Journal of Social Work*, V. 41 (1) April, 1980, 1-9.

Bayley, David H. (ed.) : Prevention detention in India : A case study of democratic social control. Calcutta, Firma K.L. Mukhopadhyaya, 1962.

Bhadura, Y.S. : Surveillance and crime prevention. *Social Welfare*, V. 30 (9) December, 1983, 6-7.

Chapman, Jeffrey I. (and others) : Crime prevention. *Public of Finance*, V. 30 (2) 1975, 197-215.

Chaudhary, Pawan : Social support and crime prevention. *Social Welfare*, V. 15 (6) September, 1968, 7-8

Clifford, W. : Crime prevention planning. *Indian Journal of Criminology and Criminalistics*, V. 1 (1) March, 1981, 19-21.

Clifford, William : Planning to prevent crime in India. *Indian Journal of Social Work*, V. 47 (3) October, 1986, 327-34.

David, L. : Crime prevention through community involvement : A syndicate study. *Transactions*, V. 31, 1980, 56-416.

Deb, R. : Police and crime prevention. *Indian Police Journal*, V. 14 (1) July, 1967, 38-41.

Deb, R. : Police and crime prevention. *National Police Academy Magazine*, November, 1967, 26-39.

Diaz, S.M. : Role of police in prevention of crime and treatment of offenders. *Social Defence*, V. 11 (42) October, 1975, 9-18.

Farah, S.A. : Environmental design in crime prevention. *Radiance*, 8 August, 1988.

Farah, S.A. : Tips for crime control in Patna. *Indian Nation*, 14 June, 1989, 4.

Ghosh, Hirak : Preventive detention law and its operation in India. New Delhi, Indian Institute of Public Administration, 1978.

Giri, V.V. : Prevention of crime : The role of the society. *Social Welfare*, V. 18(9) December, 1971, 1-2.

Gokhale, S.D. : Crime prevention (Paper). In second All India Police Science Congress, Bombay, September, 1971.

Heal, K. : The police, the public and the prevention of crime. *Howard Journal of Penology and Crime Prevention*, V. 22(2) 1983.

Jagannadham, V. : Prevention of crime in a welfare state. *Indian Police Journal*, V. 16(3) January, 1970, 19-23.

Jayewardhene, C.H.S. : Contextual constraints on police action. *Indian Journal of Criminology*, V. 10(2) July, 1982, 100-07.

Jayewardhene, C.H.S. : Control of crime in developing countries. *Indian Journal of Social Work*, V. 42(4) January, 1982, 381-92.

Jeyasingh, J. Visuvathas : Community participation in prevention committee and rehabilitation. *Social Defence*, V. 14 (55) January, 1979, 15-25.

Jeyasingh, J. Visuvathas : Crime prevention. *Police Research and Development, Quarter III*, July-September, 1983, 1-4.

Kanga, S.H.J. : Control of juvenile delinquency as a crime preventive measure and the political role therein (Paper). In second All India Police Congress, Bombay, September, 1961.

Kenetkar, V.G. : Checking the rising crime. *Lok Rajya*, V. 24(2) 16 May, 1968, 12-13.

Krishnamurty, S. : Syndicate study on air hijacking : Existing preventive arrangements and suggestions for improvement. *Transactions*, V. 30, 1980, 1-21.

Krishnaswamy, N. : Prevention of crime (Two papers). In second All India Police Science Congress, Bombay. September, 1961.

Kumar, Gyanendra : People have a crucial role. *Social Welfare*, V. 23(4) July, 1975, 15-16.

Kumar, Santh : Syndicate study on evaluation of the effectiveness of surveillance system over known bed characters with a view to preventing recidivism. *Transactions*, Vol. 30, 1980, 126-164.

Kumaraswamy, M. : Role of the Borstal School in prevention of crime and treatment of young offenders. *Journal of Karnataka University*, (Soc. Sc.) 15, 1979, 58-63.

Masterson, Ken W. : How can the police prevent minor incident of public disorder from developing into major riots. *Police Journal*, V. 61(3) July-September, 1988, 234-44.

Mehta, Asoka : To convert the brute in man : Symposium on social defence in New Delhi. *Social Welfare*, V. 15(3) June 1968, 3.

Menon, N.R. Madhava : Aurangabad experiment in preventive action : Prospects for a national strategy on crime prevention. *Indian Journal of Criminology*, V. 10(1) January. 1982, 12-15.

Modern methods of preventing and detecting crime. *Link*, V. 7 (31) 14 March, 1965, 43-44.

Murphy, George E. (and others) : Role of the police on suicide prevention. *Life Threatening Behaviour*, V. 1(2) Summer 1972, 96-105.

Nandy, Raj : Crime control : Need for a new outlook. *Man and Development*, V. 4 (4) December, 1982, 79-87.

Paranjape, N.V. : Role of the police in crime prevention. *Indian Police Journal*, V. 25(4) April-June, 1979, 3-9.

Patil, C.B. : Role of correctional services in prevention of crime. *Andhra Pradesh*, V. 12 (7-8) May-June, 1968, 32-34.

Rajan, V.N. : Role of voluntary organisation in community crime preventions. *Indian Journal of Criminology and Criminalistics*, V. 1(2-3) June-September, 1981.

Ramachandran, K.R. : Rate of probation and social services in the prevention of crime and treatment of youthful offenders. *Social Defence*, V. 11(42) October, 1979, 4-8.

Razdan, Usha : Community participation in crime prevention. *Indian Journal of Criminology*, V. 14(1) January, 1986, 22-28.

Reddy, C.S. and Balasiddamuni : Estimation of preventive police output. *Indian Journal of Criminology*, V. 17(1) Janaary, 1989, 58-67.

Saran, Rajendra : Participation of public in prevention of crime. *Social Welfare*, V. 20(6) September, 1973, 27-28.

Sen, Sankar : Controlling crime : A policeman's view. *Times of India*, 9 January, 1984, 8.

Shah, Hyatsna H. : Crime and development : Fourth United Nations Congress on the prevention of crime and treatment of offenders. Kyoto, Japan. *Social Welfare*, V. 17(8) November, 1970, 22-24.

Sirohi, J.S. : A strategy for crime prevention. New Delhi, University Book House, 1977.

Soman, D.S. : Organisation of crime prevention surveillance. (Paper) In second All India Police Science Congress, Bombay, September, 1961.

Srivastava, R.G. : Police-public cooperation in the context of crime prevention. *Social Defence*, V. 11(44) April, 1976, 11-15.

Talwar, H.R.K. : Crime trends and crime prevention strategies. *Indian Police Journal*, V. 28(2) October-December, 1981, 20-28.

Thiagarajan, K. : Prevention of crime : Explode into crime. *Social Welfare*, V. 20(9) December, 1973, 9.

Tiwari, K.P. : Public co-operation in crime prevention. *National Police Academy Magazine*, November, 1967, 21-25.

Trivedi, B.V. : Police and crime prevention : Problems and prospects. *C.B.I. Bulletin*, V. 21(6) June, 1987, 4-6.

United Nations General Assembly. Secratary General : Crime prevention and control. *Police Research and Development, Quarter III-IV*, July-December, 1972, 54-58.

Venugopal Rao, S. : Crime prevention in India (Paper). In Second All India Police Science Congress, Bombay, September, 1961.

27

Police Atrocities

A.P. : Police raj under Congress-I government. *New Age*, V. 27(52) 30 December, 1979, 3.

Abraham, A.S : From Bhagalpur to Belgrade : Unesco bid for global arms control. *Times of India*, 5 December, 1980, 8.

Acute and Obtuse : Eyeless in Bihar. *Times of India*, 5 December, 1980, 8.

After Baghpat Dabwali. *New Age*, V. 28(30) 27 July, 1980, 1.

Alam, M. Jabbar : Regin of police killings in Bihar flourishing. *New Age*, V. 37(5) 29 January, 1989, 3-4.

Another massacre on tribals. *Economic and Political Weekly*, V. 16(18) 2 May, 1981, 796-97.

Ashok Kumar : Sambalpur : Police repression continues. *New Age*, V. 29(14) 5 April, 1981, 11.

Assault on the blind : New record by police. *New Age*, V. 28(12) 2 March, 1980, 1.

Aulette, Judy and Aulette, Albert : Police harassment of the homeless, political purpose of the criminalization of homelessness. *Humanity and Society*, V. 11(2) May 1987, 244-56.

Baghpat—The rising menace (Editorial). *Janata*, V. 35(23) 20 July, 1980, 1-2.

Balagopal, K. : Deaths in police custody : Whom and why do the police kill? *Economic and Political Weekly*, V. 21(47) 22 November, 1986, 2028-29.

Balagopal, K. : Police repression in Warangal. *Economic and Political Weekly*, V. 16(39) 20 September, 1981, 1564-65.

Banani, Arun K. : A closed file. *Economic Times*, 6 December, 1981, 4.

Bandh paralyses life in Bhagalpur. *Times of India*, 5 December, 1980, 1.

Basu condemns Islampur incidents. *Times of India*, 12 April, 1980, 9.

Bhagalpur (Editorial). *Times of India*, 22 December, 1980, 6.

Bhagalpur (Editorial). *Times of India*, 27 December, 1980, 8.

Bhagalpur jail official suspended. *Times of India*, 2 December, 1980, 9.

Bhagalpur people have their own stories to tell. *Times of India*, 7 December, 1980, 1.

Bhalpur people begin satyagraha. *Times of India*, 9 December, 1980. 1.

Big rally by armed policemen in Bhagalpur. *Times of India*. 17 December, 1980, 1.

Bihar clampdown on data on convicts. *Times of India*, 3 December, 1980, 1.

Bihar government turned a blind eye to blindings. *Times of India*, 3 December, 1980, 9.

Bihar's Jallianwala bagh. *Indian Express* (*Mag.*), 8 June, 1986, III.

Bisi, Ashok Kumar : Sambalpur : Police repression continues. *New Age*, V. 29(14), 5 April, 1981, 11.

Blinding barbarism (Editorial). *Commerce*, V. 141(3624) 6 December, 1980, 1059-60.

Bora, Dulal : Police butcher tribal peasants in Assam. *New Age*, V. 27(49) 9 December, 1979, 5.

Brutalising the police. *Illustrated Weekly of India*, V. 104(13) 27 March, 1983, 8-9.

Chanda, Asok : Police outrage in West Bengal : Whose responsibility. *Times of India*, 11 August, 1969, 6.

Charges of police excessfully established. *New Age*, V. 21(10) 11 March 1973, 6.

Chaudhury, Dilip Ghosh : Naked police terror stalks. President ruled W. Bengal. *New Age*, V. 18(41) 11 October, 1970, 3.

Chevigny, Paul : Police power; police abuses in New York City, New York, Pantheon Books, 1969.

Children victims of police torture in Brazil. *Link*, V. 33(17) December 2, 1990, 20-23.

Chittaranjan, C.N. : Time for shock treatment. *Mainstream*, V. 18(46) 12 July, 1980, 1-3.

Costa, Benedict : Undertrials in their torture cells. *Illustrated Weekly of India*, V. 102(5) 1 February, 1981, 28-30.

Culture of torture. *Economic and Political Weekly*, V. 15(48) 20 November, 1980, 1993-94.

Daji, Homi : R.S.S Chief Minister installs police raj in M.P. *New Age*, V. 27(39), 30 September, 1979, 10.

Dang, Satyapal : Lesson of Batala police excesses. *New Age*, V. 37(13) 26 March, 1989, 1.

Dang, Vimla : November 10 : Anti-police repression day observed all over Punjab. *New Age*, V. 19(47) 21 November, 1971, 11.

Dang, Vimla : Police terror reaches new high in Punjab. *New Age*, V. 19(44) 31 October, 1971, 4.

Dang, Vimla : Students revolt against police repression. *New Age*, V. 19(37) 12 September, 1971, 5.

Das, Arvind Narayan : Murder to landlord's order. *Economic and Political Weekly*, 14 June, 1975.

Dasgupta, Rajashri : Deaths under police protection. *Economic and Political Weekly*, V. 25(5) February, 1980, 245-246.

Dave, Rohit : Bhagalpur : A throughly sick society. *Commerce*, V. 141 (3625) 13 December, 1980, 1121.

David, L. : Syndicate study on management of police misbehaviour. *Transactions*, V. 33, 1981, 51-95.

Death in encounter (Editorial). *Economic and Political Weekly*, V. 15(44) 1 November, 1980, 1869.

Death in police lockups. *Indian Express* (*Mag*.), 19 February, 1989, I.

Death in police custody. *Economic and Political Weekly*, V. 14(45) 10 November, 1979, 1831.

Devi, Mahasveta : Gua again. *Economic and Political Weekly*, V. 18(41) 8 October, 1983, 1739-40.

Devi, Mahasveta : Witch-Sabbalh at Singhbhum. *Economic and Political Weekly*, V. 16(40) 3 October, 1981, 1595-97.

Dhagamwar, Vasudha : After the silence : Social sanctions in Bhagalpur. *Mainstream*, V. 19(19) 10 January, 81-7.

Dinakar, C. : Police excesses. *Sardar Vallabhbhai Patel National Police Academy Magazine*, 1976, 87-92.

Disgraceful episode (Editorial). *Commerce*, V. 140(3587) 22 March, 1980, 469.

D'Mello, Bernard : Arwal massacre : Report of people tribunal. *Economic and Political Weekly*, V. 22(35) 29 August, 1987, 1485-87.

Dorairaj, S. : Police butchery in Tamil Nadu. *New Age*, V. 30(29) 18 July, 1982, 1-2.

Dorairaj, S. : Police-goonda attack on Tamil Nadu peasants. *New Age*, V. 30(1) 3 January, 1982, 16.

Dorairaj, S. : T.N. : C.P.I. to protest police zoolum. *New Age*, V. 30(6) 7 February, 1982, 5.

Doshi, Yashavant : Behind the police brutality. *Commerce*, V. 140 (3592) 26 April, 1980, 740.

Dravid, V.V. : Who is to be blamed for the negative outcome, *Indian Worker*, V. 26(30-31) 1 May, 1978, 9-10.

Eightyseven undertrials reportedly blinded in ten months. *Times of India*, 30 November, 1980, 9.

"Encounters" in Bihar (Editorial). *Times of India*, 5 November, 1981, 7.

Farah, S.A. : Jehanabad again. *Indian Nation*, 14 July 1988.

Farah, S.A. : Jehanabad incident. *Indian Nation*, 8 July, 1988.

Faridi, Javed : Police brutality. *Hindustan Times (Magazine)*, 21 December, 1980, 1.

Forty Bihar undertrials blinded. *Times of India*, 26 November, 1980, 11.

Ghosh, S.K. : Outcry of police brutality. New Delhi, Ashish Publishing House, 1983.

Gill, Gurbhajan Singh : Police atrocities in Punjab and other states. *Sikh Review*, V. 37(29) September, 1989, 38-43.

Gill, Y.S. : Police atrocities in Haryana : Rouse united public protest. *New Age*, V. 29(4) 25 January, 1981, 8-9.

Gill, Y.S. : Police zoolum in Ghaziabad : CPI, MP beaten up. *New Age*, V. 29(15) 12 April, 1981, 1.

Guilty men in Bihar (Editorial). *Times of India*, 4 December, 1980, 8

Gupta, Ajoy Das : Bar association enquiry into West Bengal. Police atrocities. *New Age*, V. 14(20) 15 May, 1966, 6.

Gupta, Indrajit : New technique of police killings of Bailadila. *New Age*, V. 26(26) 25 June, 1978, 5.

Hackler, James C. and Janssen, Christian, T. : Police killings in perspective. *Canadian Journal of Criminology*. V. 27(2) April, 1985, 227-32.

Heinous crime (Editorial). *Economic Times*, 4 December, 1980, 7.

Hoodlum still stalks Bhagalpur areas. *Times of India*, 8 December, 1980, 7.

How the public see Bhagalpur. *Illustrated Weekly of India,* V. 102(2) 11 January, 1981, 21-23.

If you prick them, do they not bleed? *Times of India,* 3 December, 1980, 7.

Increasing police atrocities in Punjab. *New Age,* V. 20(4) 20 January, 1972, 16.

Intimidation of witnesses to police atrocities. *Economic and Political Weekly,* V. 12(37) 10 September, 1977, 1601-03.

Islampur police violence : Serious political overtones. *Economic Times,* 16 April, 1980, 5.

Jana, Radheshyam : Victim of lathi-charge. *Popular Journal,* V. 5 (2) March-April, 1988, 24-30.

Job brutalises them. *Illustrated Weekly of India,* V. 104(13) 27 March, 1983, 10.

Joshi, G.P. : Police brutality in perspective. *Times of India,* 26 February, 1981, 6.

Judicial probe ordered into Islampur incident. *Times of India,* 17 April, 1980, 1.

Kalathil, Mathew : Police terror in a tribal village. *Economic and Political Weekly,* V. 15(48) 29 November, 1980, 2005-06.

Kalathil, Mathew : Unequal battle in valiataluka. *Economic and Political Weekly,* V. 16(41) 10 October, 1981, 1641-42.

Kalathil, Mathew : When law enforcers turn criminals? *Economic and Political Weekly,* V. 22(29) 18 July, 1987.

Kamath, M.V. : Operation gangajal. *Illustrated Weekly of India,* V. 102(2) 11 January, 1981, 6-20.

Kannabiran, K.G. : Who are the real 'extremists'. *Indian Express (Magazine),* 11 December, 1983, 111.

Killings, rape, torture in custody : Story of violence in West Bengal. *People's Democracy,* V. 6(51) 20 December, 1970, 6-8.

Kripalani alleges government cover up on blindings. *Times of India,* 17 December, 1980, 3.

Lal, Bishwanath : Bihar : Enquiry ordered into police atrocities *New Age,* V. 28(48) 30 November, 1980, 12.

Lal, Bishwanath : Police officer beats to death C.P.I. leader. *New Age,* V. 29(18) 3 May, 1981, 1-2.

Lal, Sham : National scene : The coarsening will go on. *Times of India*, 6 December, 1980, 8.

Landlord-police collusion in Lahsuna. *Economic and Political Weekly*, V. 16(48) 28 November, 1981, 1941-42.

Landlord-police conspiracy behind arrest of volunteers. *People's Democracy*, V. 6(1) 4 January, 1970, 4.

Lange, Altred and Verhallen, Wim : Similarity of attitudes and instrumentality as determinants of aggression by policemen. *European Journal of Social Psychology*, V. 8(4) October-December, 1978, 489-505.

Lester, David and Tenbrink, William : Police solidarity and tolerance for police misbehaviour. *Psychological Reports*, V. 57(1) August, 1985, 326.

Let assault on the blind open our eyes wider (Editorial). *New Age*, V. 28(12) 23 March, 1980, 2.

Life and death in Kerala's torture camps. *Economic and Political Weekly*, V. 12(19) 7 May, 1977, 747-48.

Living testimony to police barbarity. *Times of India*, 1 December, 1980, 1.

Llaiah, K. : Police terror against tobacco growers. *Mainstream*, V. 21(36) 7 May, 1983, 17-18.

Lok Sabha to debate blinded undertrials. *Times of India*, 29 November, 1980, 1.

MacDonald, V.N., Martin, M.A. and Richard son, A.J. : Physical and verbal excesses in policing. *Canadian Police College Journal*, V. 9(3) 1985, 295-341.

Madhok, Sujata : Arwal victims cry for justice. *Hindustan Times* (*Mag.*), 22 February, 1987, 5.

Malhotra, Inder : Brutalities by the police : A problem without end. *Times of India*, 21 June, 1983, 6.

Malik, Harji : Condemned to terror. *Mainstream*, V-19(14) 6 December, 1980, 31-33.

Marching through front door (Editorial). *Economic and Political Weekly*, V. 16(17) 25 April, 1981, 733-34.

Menon, Venu : Night without end. *Illustrated Weekly of India*, V. 107(47) 30 November, 1986, 20-23.

Minattur, Joseph : Victims of police criminality : Compensation and rehabilitation. *Cochin University Law Review*, V. 5(2-3) January-September, 1981, 177-83.

Misconceived drive by Uttar Pradesh police. *New Age*, V. 33(47) 24 November, 1985, 13.

Mishra, Ashutosh and Sharma, Aneeta : Killing at the wedding. *Times of India*, June 8, 1991, 8.

Mishra, Brahmanand : Cold blooded murders "encounters". *Organiser*, V. 33(21) 11 October, 1981, 8-9.

Misra, Shailendra : Police brutality : an analysis of police behaviour. Delhi, Vikas Publication, 1988.

Misra, Udayon : Remembering a police killing. *Economic and Political Weekly*, V. 19(17) 28 April, 1984, 704-05.

Mohan, Surendra : Moving forward. *Janata*, V. 35(42) 14 December, 1980, 5-6.

Mohanty, Govind : Orissa police collusion in Cong. I attacks on CPI men. *New Age*, V. 28(29) 20 July, 1980, 7.

Moses, Brindvane : Violation of human rights in Tamil Nadu. *Religion and Society*, V. 28(1) March, 1981, 25-47.

Mounting protest against Bailadila killing. *New Age*, V. 26(17) 13 April, 1978, 11.

Murder reign of police in many states. *New Age*, V. 25(37) 11 September, 1977, 1.

Nails pulled, grease put in eyes and ears : Beastly acts of Haryana police. *New Age*, 20(5') 21 December, 1980, 3.

Nair, Hema : Making of 'dirty harry.' *Economic Times*, 12 April, 1981, 5.

Nair, M.N. Govindan : Police terror, starvation market Kerala situation. *New Age*, V. 14(1) 2 January, 1966, 3.

Narayan, R. : Sad plight of Samastipur jail inmates. *Economic Time*, 21 January, 1981, 5.

Narayanaswamy, R. : Death in police custody. *Administrator*, V. 27(3) July-September, 1983, 609-18.

Nayar, B.B. : Kerala : Police goonda raj. *People's Democracy*, V. 5(46) 15 November, 1981, 1.

Nayar, Kuldip : Police turning into a mob. *Indian Nation*. April 10, 1984, 4.

Noorani, A.G. : Campaign against torture. *Indian Express*, 16 May, 1975.

Noorani, A.G. : Compensation for police outrages. *Economic and Political Weekly*, V. 17(26) 26 June, 1982, 1056-57.

Noorani, A.G. : Deaths in police custody : Encounters in India. *Economic and Political Weekly*, V. 22(41) 10 October, 1987, 1725.

Noorani, A.G. : Police excesses : Need for institutional safeguards. *Indian Express*, 9 March, 1976, 4.

Noorani, A.G. : Policemen and obscenity. *Economic and Political Weekly*, V. 16(50) 12 December, 1981, 2033.

Noorani, A.G. : Reports on police outrages. *Indian Express*, 13 September, 1978, 6.

Officials turned a blind eye to blindings. *Times of India*, 18 December, 1980, 1.

Operation cover up. *Economic and Political Weekly*, V. 15(49) 6 December, 1980, 2030.

Opolot, James S.E. : Police violence and prison suicides in South Africa. *Indian Journal of Criminology*, V. 17(1) January, 1989, 42-52.

Pal, Rup Chand : Wrath of Bihar outrage. *People's Democracy*, V. 4(50) 14 December, 1980, 5.

Pandemonium in Bihar assembly. *Times of India*, 11 December, 1980, 1.

Pandit, Kameshwar : Himachal firing probe holds police guilty. *New Age*, V. 37(14) 2 April, 1989, 6.

Parakal, Pauly V. : Sati to blindings back to primevalism? *New Age*, V. 28(50) 14 December, 1980, 5.

Pardesi, Ghanshyam : Terror stalls Bihar tribal belt. *Mainstream*, V. 19(12) 22 November, 1980, 5-7.

Pantnaik, Kiran S. : In Orissa : At the mercy of police. *New Age*, V. 29(36) 6 September, 1981, 7.

People's protest against police brutality. *Economic and Political Weekly*, V. 13(17) 29 April, 1978, 719-20.

Philip, A.J. and Banerjee, Sanjay : Will the cops go scot-free? *Hindustan Times* (*Mag*), 13 May, 1988, 1.

Police and crime. *Economic and Political Weekly*, V. 15(9) 1 March, 1980, 451-52.

Police atrocities against tribals. *New Age*, V. 27(44) 4 November, 1979, 5.

Police atrocities against rural poor (Editorial). *Commerce*, V. 136(3489) 22 April, 1978, 631-632.

Police : Baghpat outrage. *Economic and Political Weekly*, V. 15, July, 1980, 1255.

Police brutality in Haryana does not move Indira Gandhi. *New Age*, V. 28(8) 24 February, 1980, 6.

Police brutalities on Haryana students. *People's Democracy*, V. 4(49) 7 December, 1980, 3.

Police excesses. *Link*, V. 11(11) 27 October, 1968, 10.

Police excesses in Bihar. *Janata*, V. 37(4) 28 February, 1982, 7-8.

Police go berserk. *People's Democracy*, V. 5(1) 4 January, 1981, 3.

Police-goonda terror against CPI (Editorial). *New Age*, V. 32(27) 1 July, 1984, 2.

Police in U.P. becomes an organised gang of dacoits. *Organiser*, V. 22(9) 12 October, 1968, 3.

Police management attacks on workers. *People's Democracy*, V. 6 (20) 10 May, 1982, 5.

Police massacre in Faridabad : Report of the fact finding team. *Economic and Political Weekly*, V. 14(44) 3 November, 1979, 1792-94.

Police on landlords side. *Economic and Political Weekly*, V. 15(33) 16 August, 1980, 1375-76.

Police on rampage. *Economic and Political Weekly*, V. 12(49) 3 December, 1977, 2000-01.

Police orgy of Bailadilla (Editorial). *New Age*, V. 26(16) 16 April, 1978, 2.

Police raj in Chirala. *Secular Democracy*, No. 12, December, 1979, 34-37.

Police run amuck. *Economic and Political Weekly*, V. 5(49) 5 December, 1970, 1052-53.

Police terror against Bihar students. *New Age*, V. 19(32) 9 August, 1981, 13.

Police terror against Chhehar workers. *New Age*, V. 28 (19) 11 May, 1980, 11.

Police terror in Khammam. *Economic and Political Weekly*, V. 14 (17) 28 September, 1979, 768-69.

Police terror in Telengana. *Secular Democracy*, V. 13 (1) January, 1980, 26-27.

Police terror, repression hallmark of Indira rule. *New Age*, V. 28 (19) 11 May, 1980, 4.

Police terrorism in West Bengal (Editorial). *Call*, V. 22(7), December, 1970, 3-5.

Policemen's excesses (Editorial). *Times of India*, 4 March, 1973, 8.

Pramod, I.P. : Protecting people from police. *Popular Jurist*, V. 2 (6) January-February, 1986, 23-27.

Probe in Gujarat police role ordered. *Times of India*, 21 April, 1985, 1.

Probe panel for blinded Bihar undertrials. *Times of India*, 27 November, 1980, 1.

Punjab : It was murder in name of encounter. *New Age*, V. 26 (44) 29 October, 1978, 11.

Punjab police terror raised in Rajya Sabha. *New Age*, V. 29 (47) 21 November, 1971, 10.

Radha, Kumar : Evils to the force. *Seminar* (*Annual Number*), No. 257, January, 1981, 55-57.

Raghuram, M. : Carnage at the Indravelli : A report. *Economic and Political Weekly*, V. 16 (24) 13 June, 1981, 1047-50.

Ranadive, B.T. : Meeting threats to national unity. *Mainstream* (Annual Number), V. 19 (1-5) 1980, 35-40.

Ranjan, C.N. Chitta : World of the judge. *Mainstream*, V. 18 (34) 19 April, 1980, 3.

Rao, Amiya : Police : Baghpat outrage. *Economic and Political Weekly*, V. 15 (30) July 26, 1980, 1255-56.

Rao, B. Mallikarjuna : Anjayya Govt. lets loose of brute police on people. *New Age*, V. 28 (52) 28 December, 1980, 1.

Rao, B. Mallikarjuna : Chenna Reddy police gun down tribal leader. *New Age*, V. 27 (28) 15 July, 1979, 5.

Rao, B. Mallikarjuna : Landlord-Cong. I conspiracy behind Nellore firings. *New Age*, V. 27 (12) 25 March, 1979, 16.

Rao, L. Venkata : Beasts in uniform dance in Baghpat. *New Age*, V. 28 (26) 29 June, 1980, 1.

Rao, Venkata, L. : In Bhajan Lal's Haryana murder in police station, killing protestors, *New Age*, V. 28 (24) 15 June, 1980, 4.

Rao, L. Venkata : Police terror in Khetri. *New Age*, V. 29 (12) 2 March, 1981, 1.

Rao, L. Venkata : Political game over police barbarity. *New Age*, V. 28 (7) 17 February, 1980, 15.

Rao, L. Venkata : Zail's Baghpat visit turned into force. *New Age*, V. 28 (27) 6 July, 1980, 2.

Rao, S. Narsing : Police terror in Khammam. *New Age*, V. 32 (26) 24, June, 1984, 1-2.

Rau, M. Chalapathi : Dark age. *Link*, V. 23 (18) 14 December, 1980, 8.

Recompense for blindings reverberations. *Economic Times*, 6 December, 1981, 4.

Relapsing into barbarism (Editorial). *Janata*, V. 35 (48) 25 January, 1981, 1-2.

Reports of killings and police torture in Bihar. *Popular Jurist*, V. 5 (6) November-December, 1988, 31-34.

Repression in Singhbhum. *Mainstream*, V. 17 (32) 7 April, 1979, 23-32.

Repression on Chattisgarh miners. *Mainstream*, V. 19 (29) 21 March, 1981, 15-19.

Rizvi, Abbas : Police brutality of Ferozepur. *New Age*, V. 26 (39) 24 September, 1978, 6.

Rustamji, K.F. : Blind eye of justice. *Hindustan Times* (*Mag.*), 21 December, 1980, 1.

Sahay, Anand : Bailadila on April 5. *Mainstream*, V. 16(35) 29 April, 1978, 7-8.

Sahay, Bhupendra : Did Munger repeat operation Gangajal ? *Indian Nation*, November, 7, 1983, 1.

Sebastian, P.A. : Deaths in police custody. *Economic and Political Weekly*, V. 19 (11) 17 March, 1984, 447-40.

Sengupta, Uttam : Criminal cover up : Policemen go unpunished for role in Bhagalpur riots. *India Today*, V. 15 (5) March 1-15, 1990, 63.

Shah, Abid : Where cops are killers. *Hindustan Times* (*Mag.*) 20 August, 1986, VI.

Sharma, Sima : Atrocities and firings. *Illustrated Weekly of India*, V. 101 (35) 31 August, 1980, 15.

Shatrugna, M. : Police killing of political activity in Kondapur. *Economic and Political Weekly*, V. 20 (17) 27 April, 1985, 748-49.

Shocking brutality (Editorial). *Times of India*, 27 November, 1980, 8.

Shocking incident (Editorial). *Times of India*, 24 April, 1981, 8.

Shourie, Arun : Lethal custodians. *Indian Express*, 11 August, 1980.

Singh, Ashok K. : Landlord law and order in Baluaha. *Economic and Political Weekly*, V. 17 (25) 19 June, 1982, 1015-16.

Singh, Gurbir : Notes on a dead house. *Economic Times*, 12 April, 1981, 4.

Sinha, Umesh : Teaching the landless a lesson. *Economic and Political Weekly*, V. 20 (9) 2 March, 1985, 343-44.

Soman, P. : Attacks on human rights. *Mainstream*, V. 20 14 February, 1982, 27-29.

Sreekumar, R. : Police war on tribals in Andhra district. *Mainstream*, V. 19 (36) 9 May, 1981, 7-8.

Supreme Court pulls up Bihar for laxity. *Times of India*, 3 December, 1980, 1.

Supreme Court team to visit jail. *Times of India*, 2 December, 1980, 1.

Swaminandhan, Srilata : Endless night in Dabi Pada. *Indian Express* (*Mag.*), 25 January, 1987, IV.

Taban, Ghulam Rabbani : New meaning of encounter. *Secular Democracy*, V. 14(6) June, 1981, 20-21.

Tandan, P.K. : Narainpur police atrocities. *People's Democracy* V. 4 (7) February, 1980, 1.

Tarkunde, V.M. : Police violence in Punjab. *Sikh Review*, V. 37 (425) May, 1989, 54-57.

Ten Brink, William and Lester, David : Reporting fellow officers for brutality : A preliminary study. *Psychological Reports*, V. 54 (1) February, 1984, 36-44.

Thapar, Romesh : Blind, blind, blind. *Economic and Political Weekly*, V. 15 (52) 27 December, 1980, 2167.

There must be an end to police brutalities. *People's Democracy*, V. 4 (49) 7 December, 1980, 1.

Trade unionist death in police custody. *Economic and Political Weekly*, V. 14 (50) 15 December, 1979, 2037.

Tripathi, Srihivas : Another Narainpur in Uttar Pradesh. *New Age*, V. 29(7) 15 February, 1981, 1.

Tripathi, Srinivas : Can repetition of Narainpur be prevented by this government ? *New Age*, V. 28 (9) 2 March, 1980, 7.

Tripathi, Srinivas : Ghazipur maimed talks of police vengeance. *New Age*, V. 29 (7) 15 February, 1981, 16.

Tripathi, Srinivas : Many crimes of police in Uttar Pradesh. *New Age*, V. 28 (28) 13 July, 1980, 8.

Tripathi, Srinivas : Murders passed all encounter deaths. *New Age*, V. 29 (24) 14 June, 1981, 2.

Tripathi, Srinivas : Murders through "encounters" continue in U.P. *New Age*, V. 29 (29) 19 July, 1981, 5.

Tripathi, Srinivas : Police lay seize to Azamgarh. *New Age*, V. 31 (9) 27 February, 1983, 7.

Tripathi, Srinivas : Police raj in Almora to beat student stir. *New Age*, V. 27 (18) 6 May, 1979, 7.

Tripathi, Srinivas : Police vendetta on U.P. students. *New Age*, V. 28 (51) 21 December, 1980, 16.

Tripathi, Srinivas : S.P. has no comment on Ghazipur maiming. *New Age*, V. 29 (6) 8 February, 1981, 1.

Tripathi, Srinivas : U.P. police kill, claim died in encounter. *New Age*, V. 28 (40) 5 October, 1980, 4.

Tripathi, Srinivas : U.P. : Resistance grows against police zolum. *New Age*, V. 30 (34) 22 August, 1982, 3.

Tripathi, Srinivas : U.P. students want action against erring police. *New Age*, V. 28 (42) 19 October, 1980, 5.

Unending outrages. *Economic and Political Weekly*, V. 15 (27) 5 July, 1980, 1115.

U.P. police break arms and legs of undertrials. *New Age*, V. 29 (5) 1 February, 1981, 6.

U.P. Sangh probe into police atrocities. *Times of India*, 1 January, 1969, 4.

Upadhyay, Navin : An area of darkness. *Illustrated Weekly of India*, V. 110 (36) September, 3, 1989, 32-35.

Uproar over blinding of undertrials : Government assures stern action against guilty. *Times of India*, 2 December, 1980, 1.

Wanton killing in Bihar (Editorial). *Times of India*, 29 April, 1985, 8.

When police ran amuck in Kerala on December 1. *People's Democracy*, V. 5 (50) 14 December, 1969, 2.

28

Police as Victim

Baum, Lisa and Baum, Slevenna : Fear of death in Ontario police. *Ontario Psychologist*, V. 17 (5) October, 1985, 9-10.

Bixler, Terry, J. : An exploratory study of assaults on police officers. *Dissertation Abstracts International*, V. 38 (9-A) March 1978, 5733.

Chengappa, Raj : Kiran Bedi in the dock : Senior police officer indicated. *India Today*, V. 15 (1) May 1-15, 1990, 57.

Ganguly, Tarun : Why policemen require protection : Political interference has crippled force. *Telegraph*, 17 January, 1991, 6.

Handberg, Roger : Organizational and ecological explanation for violence against the police : a preliminary analysis. *International Review of History and Political Science*, V. 23 (4) November, 1986, 23-34.

Handberg, Roger (and others) : Organizations for violence against the police. *International Review of History and Political Science*, V. 24 (2), May, 1987, 67-68.

Heiman, Michael F. : Police suicide. *Journal of Police Science and Administration*, V. 3 (3) September, 1975, 267-73.

Heiman, Michael F. : Suicide among police. *American Journal of Psychology*, V. 134 (11) November, 1977, 1286-90.

Lester, David : Assaults of police officers in American cities. *Psychological Reports*, V. 42 (3, part-1) June, 1978, 946.

Lester, David : Murder followed by suicide in those who murder police officers. *Psychological Reports*, V. 60 (3, part 2) June, 1987, 1130.

Lester, David : Murder of police officers in American cities, victimization rates and public attitudes to safety. *Psychological Reports* V. 57(2) October, 1985, 534.

Lester, David : Police as victims : Role of guns in the murder of police. *Psychological Reports*, V. 60 (2) April, 1987, 366.

Lester, David : Police officers killed and the guns used by criminals. *Psychological Reports*, V. 50 (3, part 2) June, 1982, 1206.

Loo, Robert : Suicide among police in a federal force. *Suicide and Life Threatening Behavior*, V. 16 (3) Fall, 1986, 379-388.

Meyer, C. Kenneth (and others) : An analysis of actors related to robbery : Associated assaults on police officers. *Journal of Police Science and Administration*, V. 10(1) March, 1982, 1-27.

Meyer, C. Kenneth (and others) : An analysis of factors related to robbery : Associated assaults on police officers. *Journal of Police Science and Administration*, V. 10 (2) June, 1982, 127-50.

Meyer, C. Kenneth (and others) : An analysis of factors related to robbery : Associated assaults on police officers. *Journal of Police Science and Administration*, V.10(3) September, 1982, 249-72.

National Police Academy : Social security measures for the police in India. Background Papers and Proceedings of the Seminar held on 12th and 13th November, 1969, Abu, NPA, 1969.

Reiser, Mortin and Geiger, Steven P. : Police officer as victim. *Professional Psychology : Research and Practice*, V. 15 (3) June, 1984, 315-23.

Wirtz, Philip, and Harrell, Adele V. : Police and victims of physical assault. *Criminal Justice and Behaviour*, V. 14 (1) March, 1987, 81-92.

29

Police Women

Abel, Eileen M. and Suh, Edward K. : Use of police services by battered women. *Social Work*, V. 32 (6) November-December, 1987, 526-28.

Aleem, Shamim : Emerging role of women in law enforcement : A study of women police with special reference to Andhra Pradesh. *Indian Journal of Public Administration*, V. 29 (1) January-March, 1983, 85-96.

Alladin, Bilkiz : Women in the Indian police service. *Eve's Weekly*, 3 December, 1987, 13-15.

Allen, Mary Sophia : Pioneer police women. London, Chutto & Winders, 1925.

Anderson, Deborah J. : An evaluation of the methodological and police implications of the D.C. police women on patrol study. *Dissertation Abstracts International*, V. 37 (5-8) November, 1976, 2490-91.

Arun, S.R. : Women police in U.P. *Police Research and Development, Quarter I*, January-March, 1990, 11-14.

Bahi, Prabha : Police women. *Weekend Review*, V. 2 (21) 27 April, 1968, 33-34.

Barlow, V.M. : Police women : An asset to law enforcement. *Australian Police Journal*, V. 29 (4) October, 1975.

Barse, Sheela : Policing by women for women. *Indian Express (Mag.)*, 12 January, 1986, 2.

Becke, Shirley : Training of women police as specialists. *Police Journal*, April, 1963, 167-70.

Bell, Daniel J. : Police women : Myths and reality. *Journal of Police Science and Administration*, V. 10(1) March, 1982, 112-20.

Berg, Bruce L. and Budnick, Kimberly J. : Defeminization of women in law enforcement : A new twist in the traditional police personality. *Journal of Police Science and Administration*, V. 14(4) December, 1986, 314-319.

Bharadwaj, Aruna : Police modernisation in India : A study of woman police in Delhi. *Indian Journal of Social Work*, V. 37(1) April, 1976, 39-48.

Bhaskar, Danti : Women in uniform. *Hindustan Times* (*Mag.*) 13 March, 1988, 6.

Bouza, Anthony V. : Women in policing. *FBI Law Enforcement Bulletin*, V. 44 (9) September, 1975.

Charles, Michael T. : An evaluation of female recruit performance and male-female recruit perceptions of the female trooper's role in the 90th Michigan Police Training Academy. *Dissertation Abstracts International*, V. 39 (3-A) September, 1978, 1858.

Charles, Michael T. : Women in policing : The physical aspect. *Journal of Police Science and Administration*, V. 10 (2) June, 1982, 194-205.

Chopra, Ashok : Police women for better service. *Indian Express*, 13 June, 1977.

Connolly, Harriet : Police women as patrol officers : A study in role adaptation. *Dissertation Abstracts International*, V. 36 (3-B) September, 1975, 1501.

Devenport, John C. : Police women serve with success in law enforcement. *FBI Law Enforcement Bulletin*, 27 August, 1958.

Devi, Anjali and Dharmadhikari, Ashutosh : Working with the establishment : a new challenge. *Indian Journal of Social Work*, V. 48 (3) October, 1987, 315-23.

Davis, James A. : Perspectives of police women in Texas and Oklahoma. *Journal of Police Science and Administration*, V. 12(4) December, 1984, 395-403.

Davis, L.G. : Police women in American society. Monticello, Council of Planning Librarians, 1976.

Dhagamwar, Vasudha : A girl called Nandi. *Mainstream*, V. 19 (12) November, 1980, 25-30.

Fagerstrom, Dorothy : Practical handbook of police women. *Law and Order*, 12 February, 1964.

Fairchild, Erika S. : Women police in Weimar : professionalism, politics and innovation in police organisations. *Law and Society Review*, V. 21 (3) 1987, 375-402.

Farah, S.A. : Role of women police. *Indian Nation*, 26 May, 1987, 4.

Fry, Louis W. and Greenfeld, Sue : An examination of attitudinal differences between police women and policemen. *Journal of Applied Psychology*, V. 65(1) February, 1980, 123-26.

Ghosh, S.K. : Interpol : Women in policing. New Delhi, Ashish Publishing House, 1987.

Ghosh, S.K. : Police women and their role. *Illustrated Weekly of India*, V. 101 (3) 20 March, 1980, 41-43.

Ghosh, S.K. : Police woman comes in to her own. *Hindustan Times*, 25 March, 1990, 10.

Ghosh, S.K. : Woman in policing. New Delhi, Light and Life Publications, 1981.

Gibbons, Thomas J. : Police women undercover. *Law and Order*, 4 September, 1956.

Gopinath, K. : First all women police station in India. *Social Welfare*, V. 36 (6) September, 1989, 10-11.

Grant, Nancyts (and others) : Perceived utilization, job satisfaction and advancement of police women. *Public Personnel Management*, V. 19 (2) Summer, 1990, 147-154.

Growing importance of women police. *Social Welfare*, V. 28 (9) December, 1981, 18.

Higgins, Lois Lundell : Police women's manual. Springfield (III), Charles C. Thomas, 1961.

Higgins, Lois Lundell : Women in law enforcement. *Law and Order*, 10 August, 1962.

Hilton, J. : Women in police service. *Police Journal*, April-June, 1976.

Hindman, R.F. : Survey related to use of female law enforcement officers. *Police Chief*, V. 42 (4) April, 1975.

Horne, Peter : Women in law enforcemeut. Springfield (III), Charles C. Thomas, 1975.

Jacobs, Pearl : Women in police work : Whats the attraction ? *Free Inquiry in Creative Sociology*, V. 15 (2) November, 1987, 213-17.

Jadhav, Maryclubwata : Women police. *Indian Police Journal*, January, 1958, 42-47.

Helley, Geraldine A. : Police women play important role in Philadelphia and Pennsylvania. *FBI Law Enforcement Bulletin*, November, 1957.

Kerber, Kenneth W. (and others) : Citizen attitudes regarding the competence of female police officers. *Journal of Police Science and Administration*, V. 5(3) September, 1977, 337-47.

Knochuizen, R. : Women in police work in Chicago. Chicago, Law Enforcement Study Group Report, 1974.

Koenig, Esther J. and Juni, Samuel : Attitudes toward police women : A study of interrelationships and determinants. *Journal of Police Science and Administration*, V. 9 (4) December, 1981, 1463-74.

Lady cops. *Link*, V. 11 (48) 13 July, 1969, 36.

Lester, David (and others) : Personality and attitudes of female police officers : Needs androgyny and attitudes towards rape. *Journal of Police Science and Administration*, V. 10 (3), September, 1982, 357-60.

Lewis, Rodney W. : Toward an understanding of police anomie. *Journal of Police Science and Administration*, V. 1 (4) December, 1973, 484-90.

Lord, Lesti K. : Comparison of male and female peace officers' stereotypic perceptions of women and women peace officers. *Journal of Police Science and Administration*, V. 14 (2) June, 1986, 83-97.

Mahajan, Amarjit : Indian police women (a sociological study of a new role). New Delhi, Deep and Deep Publications, 1982.

Malik, K.N. : No longer the friendly bobby. *Times of India*, 16 December, 1983, 8.

Matthew, I. : Women in the police : should they be integrated or used with reservations? *Kriminalistik*, V. 29(7) July, 1975.

May, Doreen : Paying the price of equality. *Police Review*, May, 1978, 692-97.

Melchionne, T.M. : Changing role of police women. *Police Journal*, V. 47 (4) October-December, 1974, 340-58.

Melchionne, T.M. : Where police women are better than men. *American City*, March, 1960.

Milton, Catherine H. : Women in policing. Washington, D.C., Police Foundation, 1972.

Mishkin, Barry D. : Female police in the United States. *Police Journal*, V. 54 (1) January-March, 1981, 22-23.

Mogeorge, J. : Comparison of attitudes between men and women police officers. *Criminal Justice Review*, V. 1 (2) 1976.

Moghe, Varunda Dev : Women in the police force. *Eve's Weekly*, 23 September, 1978.

Morash, Merry and Greene, Jack R.: Evaluating women on patrol: A critique on contemporary wisdom. *Evaluation Review*, V. 10 (2) April 1986, 230-55.

Nair, G. Ravindran : Story of women police in India. *Social Welfare*, V. 36 (6) September, 1989, 4-9.

Opoit, James S.E. : African police women : An issue in criminal justice administration. *Indian Journal of Criminology*, V. 12 (2) July, 1904, 118-21.

Owings, Chloc : Women police. New Jersey, Patterson Smith, 1969.

Pead, David : Rise of police women on the beat. *Indian Nation*, February, 1, 1989, 4.

Pead, David : Rise of police women on the beat. *Monthly Public Opinion Survey*, V. 34(5) and (6) February-March, 1989, 47-48.

Pead, David : Rise of policemen on the beat. *Social Welfare*, V. 36 (6) September, 1989, 12-16.

Perlstein, Gray R. : Exploratory analysis of certain characteristics of police women. *Police Journal*, January, 1972.

Perlstein, Gray R.: Policewomen and policemen : A comparative look. *Police Journal*, September-October, 1970.

Pogrebin, Mark : Changing role of women : Female police officers occupational problems. *Police Journal*, V. 64 (2) April-June, 1986, 127-33.

Police women are as good as men. *Statesman*, 18 July, 1983, 5.

Police women of Kerala. *Hindu*, 24 February, 1972.

Poodhun, E.E. : Indian police women in south African police force. *Indian Journal of Criminology and Criminalistics*, V. 5(182) January-June, 1985, 1-2.

Potts, Lee W. : Equal employment opportunity and female employment in police agencies. *Journal of Criminal Justice*, V. 11(6) 1983, 505-23.

Powers, William F. : Police women in Massachusetts. *Law and Order*, 16 March, 1968.

Price, B.R. : A study of leadership strength of female police executives. In police, perspectives, problems, and prospects, by Macnamara, Domal, E.J. and Riedel, M. (eds.), New York, Praeger Publishers, 1974.

Profile of women police. *Statesman*, 22 September, 1973, 3.

Purcell, Philip : Use of police women a valuable asset to law enforcement. *FBI Law Enforcement Bulletin*, May, 1960.

Remmington, Patricia W. : Women in the police : Integration or separation? *Qualitative Sociology*, V. 6(2) Summer, 1983, 118-35.

Sandrock, Tom : Britain's 'girls in blue'. *Indian Police Journal*, October-December, 1970, 69-72.

Sarma, N.A.K. : Women in the armed forces. *Indian Express*, March 13, 1991, 8.

Saxena, Y.N. : Our mahila sahayata prakost. *Indian Police Journal*, April-June, 1989, 43-44.

Saxena, Y.N. : Policing by women. *Indian Police Journal*, V. 29(3) January-March, 1983, 30-32.

Sethi, H S. : Women in CRPF : First ever military battalion of women. *Social Welfare*, V. 36(6) September, 1989, 19-22.

Sherman, Lewis J. : A psychological view of women in policing. *Journal of Police Science and Administration*, V. 1(14) December, 1973, 383-94.

Singer, Mings, and Singer, Alan E. : Sex differences in the perception of male and female police officers in Newzealands. *Journal ofPsychology*, V. 119(1) January, 1985, 53-57.

Singh, Pratap : Women in police. *Sardar Vallabhbhai Patel National Police Academy Magazine*, November, 1978, 141-50.

Singh, R.M. : Role of women police officers. *C.B.I Bulletin*, February, 1979, 4.

Southgate, Peter : Women in the police. *Police Journal*, V. 54(2) April-June, 1981, 157-67.

Stuart, C.G. : Changing status of women in police profession. *Police Chief*, V. 42(4), April, 1975.

Sweeny, Frank A. : Police woman and crime. *Police Chief*, 26 January, 1959.

Townsey, Roi D. : Black women in American policing : An advancement display. *Journal of Criminal Justice*, V. 10(6) 1982, 455-68.

Vastola, Anthony : Women in policing. *C.B.I. Bulletin*, August, 1977, 6-7.

Venogopal Rao, S. : Women police in India. *Police Research and Development*, *Quarter I*, January-March, 1975.

Walsh, Jude T. : Some questions in police women on patrol and reply to questions by Peter B. Block. *Police Chief*, July, 1975, 20-23.

Watner, Rebecca L. and Steel, Brent S. : Affirmative action in times of fiscal stress and changing value priorities : The case of women in policing. *Public Personnel Management*, V. 18(3) Fall, 1989, 291-309.

Weisheit, Ralph A. : Women in the state police : Concerns of male and female officers. *Journal of Police Science and Administration*, V. 15(2) June, 1987, 137-44.

Weldy, William O. : Women in policing. *Police Chief*, January, 1976.

Wexler, Judie G. and Quinn, Vicki : Considerations in the training and development of women sergents. *Journal of Police Science and Administration*, V. 13(2) June, 1985, 98-105.

Where woman lay down the law. *Illustrated Weekly of India*, V. 87(17) 24 April, 1966, 44-46.

Winters, Clyde Ahmad : Affirmative section and Chicago female police. *Police Journal*, V. 42(2) April-June 1989, 136-32.

Women police in Cyprus. *Social Welfare*, V. 36(6) September, 1989, 17-18.

Women police in India. *Indian Police Journal*, V. 15(2) October-December, 1968, 64-69.

Women police in India. *Indian Police Journal*, V. 15(3) January-March, 1969, 72-76.

Women police in India. *Indian Police Journal*, V. 15(4) April-June, 1969, 80-83.

Women police in India. *Indian Police Journal*, V. 16(2) October, 1969.

Wyles, Lilian : Women and Scotland Yard. London, Faber and Faber, 1952.

30

Police Research

Arul, F.V. : Research methodology, *C.B.I. Bulletin*, V. 20(9) September, 1986, 1-2.

Currey, George H. (and others) : Police research technology; functional relations between juvenile citations and criminal offences. *Journal of Criminal Justice*, V. 11(1) 1983, 15-26.

Diaz, S.N. : Future of criminological research in India. *Indian Journal of Criminology*, V. 7(1) January, 1969, 7-12.

India. Ministry of Home Affairs. Bureau of Police Research and Development : Study reports, 1975, New Delhi, the Bureau, 1976.

Jatar, D.P. : Teaching and research in criminology in India. *Indian Journal of Criminology*, V. 7(2) July, 1979, 25-32.

Kantiswarup : Study on allocation and utilisation of police force in Delhi. New Delhi, Indian Institute of Public Administration, 1980.

Khan, M.Z. : Criminological research in India. *Social Change*, V. 12(9) September, 1982, 3-10.

Mahmood Bin Muhammad : Areas for research and further study in police administration. In G. Ram Reddy and K. Seshadri (eds.) Developing society and police. Hyderabad, Osmania University, 1982, 173-79.

Mahmood Bin Muhammad : Planning and research in crime prevention. *Sardar Vallabhbhai Patel National Police Academy Magazine*, November, 1975, 20-39.

Mahmood Bin Mahammad : Planning and research for crime prevention. *Social Defence*, V. 12(47) January, 1977, 18-32.

Menon, Bala : Criminal tribes : Condemned for generations. *Times of India*, 9 July, 1978, 11.

Menon, N.R. Madhava : Towards evolving a research agenda for criminology and related criminal sciences : A preliminary draft proposal. *Indian Journal Criminology*, V. 6(2) July, 1978, 67-76.

Pavitran, P.V. : Identification of cerain area for study, research and planning in police administration. In G. Ram Reddy and K. Seshadri (eds.) Developing society and police. Hyderabad, Osmania University, 1972, 167-172.

Punch, Maurice : Researching police deviance : A personal encounter with the limitation and liabilities of field work. *British Journal of Sociology*, V. 40(2) June, 1989, 177-204.

Qudri, Afsal S.M. and Wani, Abdul Latif : Research report on police and discretion. Sringar, Kashmir University, 1987.

Ram Reddy, G. and Seshadri, K. : Research in police administration. In G. Ram Reddy and K. Seshadri (eds.) Developing society and police. Hyderabad, Osmania University, 1972, 181-91.

Rao, K.V. : A note on the need for strengthening the bureau of police research and development. *Journal of Social Studies State Governments*, V. 5(3-4) July-December, 1972, 275-76.

Saksena : Rise in murder rate in India : Some major factors. *Times of India*, 4 September, 1978, 6.

Saxena, D.P. : Study of victim in future criminological research in India. *Indian Journal of Criminology*, V. 6(2) July, 1978, 94-96.

Saksena, N.S. : Six illusions on crime control : Radical reform needed. *Times of India*, 23 September, 1978, 6.

Sharma, K.D. : Role of the bureau of police research and development. *Police Research and Development, Quarter I*, January-March, 1979, 1-3.

Sinha, K.C. : Criminology : what contribution should be made by the police for research and study in this field? (Paper) In second All India Police Science Congress, Bombay, September, 1961.

Tandon, Shrawan : Importance of research and development in modernising police force. *Police Research and Development*, 1977, 1-13.

Venugopal Rao, S. : Police research : An overview. *Indian Journal of Criminology*, 4(2) July, 1976, 101-03.

Venugopal Rao, S. : Power and criminality : A survey of famous crimes in Indian history. New Delhi, Allied, 1978.

Venugopal Rao, S. : Role of police research. *Indian Express*, 5 February, 1979, 6.

Yuille, John C. : Research and teaching with police : A Canadian example. *International Review of Applied Psychology*, V. 33(1) January, 1984, 5-23.

31

Police and Modern Aids

Agrawal, S.C. : Relevance of computers in police : Application in criminal justice system. *Police Research and Development, Quarter II*, April-June, 1987, 1-4.

Chopra, S.C. (and others) : Electra Van : a battery powered road vehicle. *Police Research and Development, Quarter VI*, 1984, 3-6.

Colton, Kentw : Computers and police : Patterns of success and failare. *Sloon Management Review*, Winter, 1972-73, 75-98.

Dasgupta, A.K. : Indian railway dog squads. *Indian Railway*, V. 30 (2-3), May-June, 1985, 12-13.

Delhi police dogs fine show. *Times of India*, 21 Feb. 1969, 3.

Dwivedi, J.C. : Use of personal description of the accused as a parameter for retrieval of information in a computerised crime-criminal information system *Police Research and Development, Quarter II*, April-June, 1983, 7-10.

Fagin, Games A. : Effects of police interpersonal communication skills on conflict resulting. *Dissertation Abstracts International*, V. 39 (4-A) October, 1978, 1924.

Gay, William O. : Communications and crime. *Police Journal*, April-June, 1973, 109-25.

Glauser, Michel J. and Tullar, William L. : Communication style of police officers and citizen satisfation with officer citizen telephone conversations. *Journal of Police Science and Administraton*, V. 13(1) March, 1983, 70-77.

Gupta, R.G. : Effects of patrol cars and radio communication response time of police in urban areas. *Indian Police Journal*, V. 24(3) January-March, 1978, 24-28.

Hochstedler, Ellen and Dunning, Chrutine M. : Communication and motivation in a police department. *Criminal Justice and Behaviour*, V. 10(1) March, 1983, 47-69.

Hodges, F.R. : Computerized system and police efficiency. *Police Journal*, January-March, 1973, 78-95.

Iyer, T.G.L. : Computer in police research. *Police Research and Development, Quarter II*, April-June, 1972, 11-13.

Jauhari, M. and Chatterjee, S.M. : Computerised system for determining shotgun pellet shot size specifications. *Police Research and Development, Quarter I*, January-March, 1980, 16-19.

Joshi, G.P. : Vertical communications in police. *Indian Police Journal*, V. 21(2) October-December, 1947, 23-29.

Kenney, J.F. : International communications in the police : Importance, barriers and methods. *Indian Police Journal*, April, 1971, 17-20.

Kulkarni, R.S. : Communications in the police organisation. *Social Welfare*, V. 32(4) July, 1985, 17-19.

Kulkarni, R.S. : Communication in the police organisation. *Social Welfare*, V. 32(6) September, 1985, 27-32.

Leonard, V.A. : Police communication system. Springfield (III), Charles C. Thomas, 1970.

Meehan, James B. : Modernized computerized communication : An aid in crime prevention. *Police Journal*, May-June, 1971, 39-43.

Padti, N.C. : Computerised command and control system for the police in metropolitan cities. *Police Research and Development, Quarter I*, January-March, 1983, 3-5.

Rail dogs steal the show. *Indian Railway*, V. 30(2-3) May-June, 1985, 14-1[illegible].

Saikia, B.N. : Role of police tel-communications in Assam. *Assam Information*, No. 30, November, 1978, 17-18.

Sarma, A.S. : Communication and police organisation. *Police Research and Development, Quarter I*, January-March, 1980, 8-10.

Satyanarayanan, S. : Computer aided crime control and police manpower management. *Indian Police Journal*, V. 26(2) October-December, 1979, 33-44.

Singh, N.K. : Crime and the computer. *C.B.I. Bulletin*, V. 20(6) June, 1986, 1-4.

Swayambu, Shymala : Four footed custodians of the law. *Illustrated Weekly of India*, V. 90(32), 10 Aug., 1969, 40-42.

Twentyfive years of police wireless. *Lok Rajya*, V. 28(2) 16 May, 1972, 6-8.

Webb, Lee : Computerized police systems in the U.S. *Current*, September, 1971, 14-19.

Weed, Albert C. II : Police and the modernization process. Thailand, Princeton (N.S.), Princeton University Press, 1970.

Wilkenson, Tom : Use of computers in police training. *C.B.I. Bulletin*, V. 18(6) June, 1984, 9-11.

Wilkenson, Tom and Chattin-McNichols, Jatin : Effectiveness of computer assisted instructions for police officers. *Journal of Police Science and Administration*, V. 13(3) September, 1985, 230-35.

Wisenand, Paul M. and Tamaru, Tug T. : Automatic police information system. New York, John Wiley, 1970.

32

Police Acts and Criminal Law

Ahmed, Ejaz : Code of criminal procedure. Delhi, Ashok Publishing House, 1982.

Andrew, John A. (ed.) : Human rights in criminal procedure : A comparative study. London, Moardinus Nighoff, 1982.

Beotra, B.R. : Police Acts (Central and State). Allahabad, Law Book, 1970.

Bhanage, P.O. : Bombay Police Act, 1951 (Bombay Act No. XXXI of 1951) (As amended up to date with full comments, case law, rules and (Notification)—Applicable to Maharashtra and Gujarat. Bombay, N.M. Tripathi, 1974.

Bhat, V.R. : Some observation on our criminal procedure code. *Journal of Karnatak University*, V. 8(1) 1964, 201-08.

Bid for separation of Judiciary uniformly. *Times of India*, 28 December, 1970, 10.

Bihar, Laws, statutes, etc. The Police (Bihar Amendment) Act, 1954. Patna, Supdt. Govt. Print, 1955.

Chakraborti, Ashok Mohan : New criminal procedure code : Where does it lead. *Administrator*, V. 25(1) Spring, 1980, 143-86.

Chhabra, Kirpal Singh : Quantum of punishment in criminal law in India. Punjab University, 1974.

Deb, R. : Principles of criminology, criminal law and investigation. Calcutta, S.C. Sarkar and Sons, 1958.

Deb, R. : Reforms in criminal law : Some suggestions. *Indian Police Journal*, V. 24(1) July-September, 1977, 31-47.

Deb, R. : Reforms in criminal law : Some suggestions. *Journal of Indian Law Institute*, V. 17(4) October-December, 1975, 392-604.

Deb, R. (and others) : Operation of special laws relating to externment of bad characters. *Journal of Indian Law Institute*, V. 11(1) January-March, 1969, 1-20.

Diaz, S.M. : Police responsibility to the criminal trial process in India. *Journal of Criminology*, V. 4(2) July, 1976, 111-16.

Gandhi, A.P. : Criminal code "reforms". *Times of India*, 24 February, 1974, 4.

Gatrell, V.A.C. (and others) : Crime and the law : The social history of crime in western Europe since 1950. London, Europe Publications, 1980.

Gaur, K.D. : Criminal law : Cases and materials. New Delhi, Tripathi, 1975.

Gokhale, H.R. : Criminal law need for radical change. *Social Welfare*, V. 18(9) December, 1971, 3.

Gupta, Ramlal : Guide to police laws in India. Lucknow, Eastern Book, 1967.

Gurumurthi, C. : Code of criminal procedure (Act 2 of 1974) in actual practice. *Journal of Lal Bahadur Shastri National Academy of Administration*, V. 20(4) Winter, 1975, 1221-26.

Hatolkar, L.K. : Effects of changes in Cr. P.C. *Police Research and Development, Quarter I*, January-March, 1979, 4-6.

Iyer, U.R. Krishna : Law : Social engineering to achieve justice. *Social Welfare*, V. 22(4) July, 1975, 9-11.

Iyer, U.R. Krishna : Penal reforms. *Mainstream*, V. 8(39) 30 May, 1970, 21-24.

Iyer, U.R. Krishna : Penal reforms. *Mainstream*, V. 8(40) 6 June, 1970, 17-21.

Jacobs, Francis G. : Criminal responsibility. Weidenfeld, 1971.

Jagannatha Rao, V. : Handbook of criminal law in administration. Hyderabad, Asia Law House, 1987.

Jagannatha Rao, V. : Police laws in A.P. Hyderabad, Asia Law House, 1986.

Kelkar, R.N. : Outlines of criminal procedure. Calcutta, Eastern Book Co., 1977.

Kulkarni, R.S. : Criminal law in India and England : A comparative study. *Indian Police Journal*, V. 25(3) January-March, 1979, 3-23.

Leiser, Burton M. : Liberty, justice and morals : Contemporary value conflicts. Macmillan, 1973.

Menon, N.R. Madhava : Decriminalization and the need for a rational criminal policy. *Indian Journal of Criminology*, V. 8(1) January, 1980, 3-6.

Mitra, B.C. : Police and the law. *Journal of Criminology and Criminalistics*, V. 1(2-3) June-September, 1981.

Nand Lal : Commentaries on the (new) code of criminal procedure, 1973 : Edited by M.C. Desai, Allahabad, Law Publishers, 1974.

Nath, T. : New code of conduct for police. *INFA Feature*, 17 March, 1976, 1-2.

Nath, T. : Police regulations. *Patriot*, 19 October, 1980, 2.

National Police Academy, Hyderabad : Proceedings of the seminar on protection of human rights in criminal procedure, 1979.

Nigam, K.D. : Commentaries on the Bombay Police Act, 1951 (as amended upto date) with additional laws. Allahabad, Hind Publishing House, 1971.

Pillai, Atchuthen P.S. : Criminal Law. Bombay, Tripathi, 1988.

Pollard, D.W. : Police Act, 1964. *Public Law*, Spring, 1966, 35-64.

Reddy, Chinnappa O. : Criminal Law, Police and Justice. *Mainstream*, V. 19(10) November, 1980, 7-8.

Sahay, G.B. : Penal reform. *Indian Journal of Criminology*, V. 8(2) July, 1980, 110-24.

Sankaran, M.V. : Mens rea in rope : An analysis of Reg. V. Morgan and section 375 and 79 of the Indian penal code. *Journal of India Law Institute*, V. 20(3) Aug-September, 78, 438-62.

Saksena, N.S. : Police Act of 1961 and its objectives. *Indian Police Journal*, 24(4) April-June, 1978, 3-7.

Saxsena, R.N. : Commentaries on U.P. police regulation (as amended upto-date). Allahabad, Central Law Agency, 1967.

Senapati, G.C. : Reforms in police procedural law and in substantive criminal law (Paper). In Second All India Police Science Congress, Bombay, September, 1961.

Sethi, R.B. : Police Acts (Central and State). Allahabad, Law Book, 1991.

Sethna, J.M. J. : Society and the criminal. Tripathi, 1971.

Singh, D.P. (and others) : Fundamental rights and trade unions. *Mainstream*, V. 6(29) 16 March, 1968, 16-17.

Singh, D.R. : Protection of human rights in criminal procedures. *Indian Police Journal*, V. 26(2) October-December, 1979, 45-52.

Singh, Shwa Prasad : A short note on section 107 of the code of criminal procedure. *Mankind*, V. 14(5) July, 1970, 25-28.

Singhvi, G.C. : A consolidated and updated police act : A preview. *Indian Police Journal*, V. 27(2) October-December, 1980, 13-21.

Singhvi, G.C. : Indian penal code : Need for human dignity orientation. *Social Welfare*, V. 18(5) August (1971), 1-2.

Sinha, M.K. : Maharashtra Police Ordinance : A step in the wrong direction. *Indian Nation*, April 15, 1988, 4-8.

Stephen, James : History of criminal law in England. New York, Franklin, 1883, (Reprint 1973).

Surat Prasad : New prosecution set up. *Indian Police Journal*, V. 26(2) October-December, 1979, 56-65.

Through revision of the Indian Penal Code recommended by Law Commission. *Times of India*, 7 June, 1971, 11-18.

Tiwary, M.M. and Sastry, B.S. : New code of criminal procedure and its impact on the working of the police : A syndicate study. *Transactions*, V. 21, November, 1975, 33-49.

Tiwari, O.P. : Police law in India. Delhi, Seven Stars Publication, 1983.

Vohra, K.B. : Impact of new criminal procedure code on police investigation. *Police Research and Development, Quarter I*, January-March, 1974, 8-13.

Vadackumchery, James : Provisions in the Indian penal code. *Police Research and Development, Quarter III*, April-June, 1980, 1-4.

33

Police Commission and Committees

Assam. Police Commission, 1969. Report. Gauhati, 1971. (Chairman : Shanti Prasad).

Bihar. Police Commission, 1958. Report. Patna, 1961 (Chairman : B.P. Jamur).

Committee of Inquiry on the Police : Reports on negctiating machinary and pay. London, HMSO, 1978.

Great Britain. Committee on Police Extraneous Duties, 1952 : Report, London, 1953.

Great Britain. Royal Commission on Police powers and procedure, 1928 : Report, London, 1929 (Cmd. 3297-Chairman : Arthur Hamilton, Viscount Lee of Faretiam).

Great Britain. Royal Commission on the police, 1960 : Report. London, 1962 (Cmd 1728-Chairman : Henry Urmaton Willink).

Great Britain. Advisory committee on police in Northern Ireland, 1969 : Report. London, 1969. (Cmd. 535-Chairman : Baron Hunt).

Hart, Jenifer : Some reflections on the report of the Royal Commission on the police. *Public News*. Autumn, 1963, 283-304.

India. Committee on Police Training, 1971 : Report, New Delhi, Ministry of Home Affairs, 1974, (Chairman : M.S. Gore).

India. Delhi Police Commission. 1966-68 : 2 Vol. (Chairman : G.D. Khosla).

India. Ministry of Home Affairs. Administrative Reforms Commission : Report of the working group on police administration, 1967.

India. Ministry of Home Affairs. Committee on Police Training : A report of the task force, emerging social processes and patterns and its implication for police training. New Delhi, Govt. Publications, 1972.

India. Ministry of Home Affairs : Delhi Police Commission report, 1966.

India. Ministry of Home Affairs. National Police Commission : Reports : 1 to 8. Delhi, Controller of Publications.

India. Ministry of Home Affairs : Report of the committee on police training. New Delhi. Government of India Press, 1972.

India. Ministry of Home Affaries : Report of the committee on prevention of corruption (Santhanam Committee), 1964.

India. Ministry of Home Affairs : Report of the Shah commission on emergency excesses. New Delhi, Publication, 1978.

India. Ministry of Home Affairs : Report on the system of service of summons. New Delhi, Bureau of Police Research and Development, 1984.

India. Police commission : History of police organisation in India and Indian village police : Select chapters of the report of India police commission, 1902-03, Calcutta, University of Calcutta.

India. Police commission : Report of the Indian Police Commission and the resolution of the government of India. London, HMSO, 1905. (Cd. 2478-President : A.H.L. Fraser).

India. Special Police Establishment Enquiry Committee 1949-52 : Report, 1952 (Chairman : Dr. Bakshi Tek Chand).

Kerala Police reorganisation committee, 1959-60 : Report, 1960 (Chairman : N C. Chatterjee).

Luthra, B.R. : Committee on police training. *Police Research and Development*, January-June, 1974, 21-26.

Maharashtra. Police commission, 1962 : Report. Bombay, 1962. (Chairman : Y.U. Dixit).

Maharashtra. Police commission 1962 : Summary of recommendation of the Maharashtra state police commission, 1964 (Chairman : Y.D. Dixit).

Mahmood Bin Muhammad : Gap between recommendations and their implementation : A syndicate study to the police commission of Tamil Nadu, Maharashtra, Delhi, and the Kerala reorganization committee. *Transactions*, V. 22, April, 1976, 3-35.

Mishra, S.C. : All India Police and the proposed Police Commission. *Orissa Review*, August, 1977, 23-26.

Pakistan. Police commission, 1959 : Report. Karachi, 1961.

Police Panel report (Editorial). *Times of India*, 2 April, 1983, 8.

Police Commission for parity between IPS and IAS. *Indian Nation*, April 3, 1983, 4.

Police Commission Report : Revamping a limping force. *Link*, V. 23(44) 14 June, 1981, 27-28.

Prasad, K.B. : Report of the Bihar police commission, 1961. *Indian Police Journal*, April, 1962, 52-58.

Punjab. Police commission, 1960 : Report. Chandigarh, 1961 (Chairman : M.C. Mahajan).

Rajasthan. Committee on Reorganisation of Rajasthan Police, 1972.

Report of Bihar Police Commission. Patna, Secretariat Press, 1961.

Report of Madhya Pradesh police commission. Bhopal, Government Central Press, 1967.

Report of the Joint Committee of Parliament on the Indian Penal Code (Amendment) Bill (1972), (1976).

Report of the Uttar Pradesh Police Commission. Lucknow, Supdt. Printing and Stationery, 1961.

Tamil Nadu. Police Commission, 1969 : Report. Madras, 1971 (Chairman : R.A. Gopalswami).

Tandon, S. : Police commissions in India. *Indian Police Journal*, V. 25(1) July-September, 1978, 78-102.

Tarkunde Committee's focus on police atrocities. *Capital*, V. 178(449) June, 23, 1977, 900.

Uttar Pradesh. Police Commission, 1960 : Report. Allahabad, 1961 (Chairman : Ajit Prasad Jain).

Uttar Pradesh. Police Commission, 1970-71 : Report. Allahabad, 1972 (Chairman : Ganeswar Prasad).

Varma, Paripurnanand : National Police Commission : A gloomy record of 123 years. *Economic Times*, 17 April, 1984, 5.

Vera Institute of Justice, New York : Report on felony arrests : their prosecution and deposition in New York City's Courts, 1976.

West Bengal. Police Commission, 1960-61 : Report, Calcutta, 1964 (Chairman : K.C. Sen).

34

Para Police Force

Anand, V.K. : Special police force. *Hindustan Times*, 13 November, 1980.

Ansari, N.H. : P.A.C. opens fire on Basti students. *New Age*, V. 29(46), 15 November, 1981, 4.

Ashwini Kumar : B.S.F.'s gallant performance on western border. *Advance*, January-March, 1970, 10-14.

Ashwani Kumar : Border security. *Indian Police Journal*, April-June, 1975, 33-39.

Bajwa, K.S : Para-military forces : Need for clear division of duties and command. *Indian Express*, 28 August, 1980, 6.

Banerjee, S.R. and Das, K.M : Modern industrial security. Calcutta, K.L.M. Ltd., 1981.

Bennett, Stephen and Wilkie, Roy : Management of Scottish police forces : A case of research. *Police Journal*, V. 54(3) July-September, 1981, 281-89.

Bhambhari, C.P. : Public order, para-military organisations in Indian federalism. *Indian Journal of Public Administration*, V. 24(1) January-March, 1988, 31-37.

Bhandari, Arvind : B.S.F. is three years old. *Indian Express*, 1 December, 1968, 4.

B.S.F. can now tackle new problems. *Times of India*, 1 December, 1975, 1.

CRP's role. *Times of India*, 28 March, 1969, 6.

Carter, A.F. : The West German "Bundeskriminalamt." *Police Journal*, July-September, 1976, 199-209.

Chakravarty, F. : Men who guard our frontiers. *Indian Express*, 1 December, 1974, 1.

Chandran, Ramesh : Central reserve police force. *Illustrated Weekly of India*, V. 97(27) 4 July, 1976, 20-25.

Chanaire, J.S. : RPF : 25 years in the service of railways. *Indian Railway*, V. 29(6) September, 1984, 5-9.

Cook, Fred J. : The FBI : Nobody knows. London, Janadhan Cape, 1964.

Curry, J.C. : The C.I.D. in Bombay, (The mild centenary period). *National Police Academy Magazine*, October, 1961, 18-23.

Delarue, Jacques : History of the guestapo: Tr. from French by Mervyn Savill. London, Macdonald, 1964.

Dewhurst, H.S. : The railroad police. Springfield (III), Charles C. Thomas, 1955.

Doval, N.K. : Life along the line for BSF. *Indian Express*, 13 February, 1969, 4.

Doval, N.K. : Vigil on hilly homes of legend. *Indian Express*, 18 February, 1969, 4.

Fallon, Tom : River police. London, Frederick Muller, 1956.

Farah, S.A. : B.M.P. battalions. *Indian Nation*, March 4, 1989, 4.

Farah, S.A. : Bihar G.R.P., *Indian Nation*, March, 7, 1989, 4.

Genz, John L. and Lester, David : Military service, education and authoritarian attitudes of municipal police officers. *Psychological Reports*, V. 40(2) April, 1977, 402.

Hobley, L.F. : Police force. London, Allman and Son Ltd., 1969.

Igbinovia, Patrick Edobar : Interpol and international police co-operation. *Indian Journal of Criminology*, V. 15(1) January 1987, 25-36.

Iyer, T.G.L. : Private investigating agencies and security services in India. *Police Research and Development*, January-March, 1978, 1-13.

Jackson, R.L. : Interpol. *Indian Police Journal*, October, 1966, 31-37.

Joshi, B.K. : Growth of private police in U.K. : A threat to privacy. *Times of India*, 30 July, 1977, 6.

Kakalik, James S. and Wildhorn, Sorrel : Private police in United States : Findings and recommendations. Washington (D.C.), National Institute of Law Enforcement and Criminal Justice, 1972.

Kanetkar. V.G. : Licencing of private investigation. *C.B.I. Bulletin*, V. 19(4) August, 1985, 1-3.

Katoch, G.O. : Border forces : A blue print for reorganization. *Statesman*, 20 April, 1981, 6.

Katyal, K.K. : Central police forces. *Hindu*, 21 October, 1980, 8.

Katyal, K.K. : Centre's armed forces and state's autonomy. *Hindu*, 28 June, 1979, 8.

Kaul, T.N. : Wide range of the CRP's role in helping the states. *Times of India*, 31 October, 1975, 7.

Khanna, K.C. : Maintaining public peace—Abuse of para-military forces. *Times of India*, 17 August, 1984.

Khosla, Mukesh : CRPF : Strong arm of the centre. *Illustrated Weekly of India*, V. 96(43) 26 October, 1975, 47.

Lal, S. : Policing on U.K. railways. *Police Research and Development, Quarter III*, July-September, 1979, 13-15.

Mart, V C. : Private police. *Police Journal*, April-June, 1975, 122-32.

Nayak, R.K. : Central reserve police force in federal polity. *Socialist India*, V. 15(16) 8 October, 1977, 10.

Nayak, R.K. : Central reserve police force in federal polity. *Socialist India*, V. 15(17) 15 October, 1977, 6.

Noorani, A.G. : Central reserve police and the constitution. *Indian Express*, 20 May. 1970, 6.

Noorani, A.G. : Central reserve police force : Legal or illegal. *Commerce*, 29 April, 1972, 1090-91.

Palit, D.K. : Para-military forces : A specialist role. *Hindustan Times*, 9 March, 1980.

Pandalai, K.M. : Role of para-military forces. *Economic Times*, 23 November, 1980.

Pandey, S.D. : Education for BSF Jawans and their children. *Times of India*, 28 February, 1976, 5.

Pattabhir, M. : Men who defend our Pak borders. *Hindu*, 14 August, 1968, 6.

Railway protection force. *Indian Railway*, V. 23(2) May, 1978, 21-22.

Rikhye, Ravi : Towards a border range command : New Orientation of the B.S.F. *Vikrant*, March, 1974, 33-36.

Sahai, Shashi Bhushan : Constitution of a riot police in India (Paper). In 7th Police Science Congress, Jaipur, 1968.

Sahay, S. : Military and para-military force. *Statesman* 28 August, 1980, 6.

Saksena, N.S. : Militarisation of the Indian police. *Times of India*, 20 October, 1988, 6.

Sarkar, Subhash Chandra : Central police force. *Commerce*, V. 14(3621) 15 November, 1980, 933.

Sarkar, Subhash Chandra : High cost of central police force. *Janata*, V. 29(41) 17-24.

Sethi, H.S. : CRPF : Nomads in uniform. *Hindustan Times*, 4 November, 1980.

Sethi, H.S. : CRPF's record of humane service. *C.B.I. Bulletin*, V. 12(1) January, 1978, 7-8.

Sharma, Gautam : Need to reorganise the para-military forces. *Indian Express*, 15 September, 1977, 6.

Shearing, Clifford D. (and others) : Police perceptions of private security. *Canadian Police College Journal*, V. 9(2) 1985, 127-53.

Singhvi, G.C. : A case for induction of railway police in the union list. *Journal of Constitutional and Parliamentary Studies*, V. 6(4) October-December, 1972, 82-93.

Sinha, K.C. : A better image for R and F. *Indian Railway*, V. 21(2) May, 1976, 20-31.

Sinha, K.C. : Railway protection force : Tomorrow. *Sardar Vallabhbhai Patel National Police Academy Magazine*, July, 1976, 48-53.

Sinha, R.N. : Interpol : Its functions and procedures. *C.B.I Bulletin*, V. 17(10) October, 1983, 4-8.

Sinha, S.K. : Army police co-operation. *U.S.I. Journal*, V. 98(410) January-March, 1968, 23-33.

Smith, Brent L. and Ward, Richard M. : Maladaptive behaviours among military police personnel and implications for administrative policy. *Journal of Criminal Justice*, V. 14(4) 1986, 307-17.

Spitzer, Steven and Scull, Andrew T. : Privatization and capitalist development : The case of the private police. *Social Problems*, V. 26(1) October, 1977, 18-29.

Subramaniam, K. : Threats to security—Internal ones more formidable. *Times of India*, September, 12, 1987.

Vohra, Bikram : B.S.F. : They patrol our border. *Illustrated Weekly of India*, 2 July, 1972, 20-25.

Vohra, K.B. : A syndicate study on private security and detective agencies in India. *Transactions*, V. 23, November, 1976, 1-48.

Wolin, S. and Slausser, R.M. : Soviet secret police. New York, Praeger, 1957.